PRECOLONIAL AFRICA

PRECOLONIAL AFRICA

An Economic and Social History

ROBERT W. JULY

CHARLES SCRIBNER'S SONS   NEW YORK

Library of Congress Cataloging in Publication Data

July, Robert William.
  Precolonial Africa.

  Bibliography: p.
  Includes index.
  1. Ethnology—Africa. 2. Economics, Primitive.
  3. Africa—Economic conditions. I. Title.
  GN645.J84   330.9′39′7   75-6920
  ISBN 0-684-14318-6
  ISBN 0-684-14319-4 pbk.

For Catherine and Richard

PREFACE

Interest marking the study of Africa during the last two decades or more has understandably concentrated much attention on the present and the recent past. The problems of newly independent nations and the circumstances that brought them into being have been appropriate preoccupations for both the serious student and the inquiring, if more general, observer. Attention to the near past, however, has tended to conceal the important fact of Africa's long history stretching back over the millennia, a chronicle of great consequence in itself but also essential in providing an understanding of African societies as they exist today.

My own concern for earlier African history arose initially from a desire to identify those elements of age-old African civilizations still extant in the world of modern Africa. My curiosity was stimulated, therefore, not so much by the grand sweep of political and military affairs as it was by the need better to understand the more prosaic substance of everyday existence—how people earned their living, what sort of recreation they favored, which foods they fancied or crafts they practiced, why they designed their homes and villages as they did, what varieties of personal relationships they evolved—in short, how people lived and why. Such interests drew me sharply to the study of social, and particularly of economic, developments. It is this emphasis that the present volume reflects.

An economic and social survey raises difficulties in organization not encountered in more orderly political histories. Simple chronology is confounded by the need to discuss subjects often found flourishing equally in different eras as well as varying locales. The essential step from description to analysis, moreover, demands treatment which draws into synthesis materials representing diverse times and places. I have tried to meet these multidimensional difficulties by organizing my chapters roughly in chronological fashion, by providing temporal guideposts where appropriate, and by keeping the discussion of different parts of the continent as clearly defined as possible. The concluding sections of many chapters are devoted to assessments of economic or social phenomena often found widely spread through time and space— for example, environment and economic adaptation, concepts of private property, the idea of profit, the uses of surplus, or the role of the state in mercantile development. Such all-embracing themes necessarily range broadly; hopefully they do so in a fashion that illuminates and simplifies while avoiding complications of unhistorical juxtaposition.

I have indeed been fortunate that my own interest in African economies has come at a time of fast-growing activity among Africanists in the long-neglected field of economic history. I have therefore been able to draw upon a mounting body of research which has been especially helpful to an appreciation of commercial activities in earlier times. Unfortunately, this welcome interest in economic history has rarely extended beyond the study of trading systems to include the even more fundamental examination of agriculture and the technology that sustained and accompanied food production. In these realms I have found profit in the work of anthropologists and botanists whose studies of more recent traditional economies in Africa help to support and amplify the observations of early chroniclers. Perhaps most helpful of all has been the testimony of those same travelers from Herodotus onward who came to Africa with sharp eye and ready pen and recorded their observations of the many peoples who have become the subject of this book.

CONTENTS

ix

Part Three THE HERDERS

Part Four   THE TRADERS

Part Five   THE CRAFTSMEN

MAPS

Part One

BEGINNINGS

Bronze figure, Dahomey.
Photo courtesy of the author.

1

THE AFRICAN ENVIRONMENT

The Struggle for Existence

It was in Africa that life began for man, but for man in Africa life has often stinted its gifts. He has been victimized by disease, robbing him of his energy, slaughtering his children, blotting out his herds, and causing his crops to shrivel in their first bloom. He has been made sport of by a capricious climate whose smiling sun brings forth the fruits of the earth only to scorch them in its withering heat, whose life-giving rains turn destroyer in their flood or abandon the land to the dead hand of drought and famine. He has been plagued by pests—insect, virus, plant, and animal—which have obliged him from the first to struggle for survival at the level of bare subsistence, all in a land where severity of climate is unknown, where frost and snow are strangers, and where, paradoxically, life can and does multiply without apparent check.

Such from the beginning has been man's lot in Africa, and even today, in the era of modern science and technology, a stubborn environment still grants its produce but grudgingly. Take the example of cocoa, which was introduced to serious cultivation in Africa at the end of the

3

nineteenth century and which quickly became an important cash crop in West Africa, where at present is produced almost two-thirds of the world's output. In Ghana the plant was attacked during the 1940s and 1950s by the swollen shoot virus, a lethal affliction which defied cure and forced the destruction of approximately one hundred million diseased trees. Such a blow for a time threatened the survival of both the cocoa farmer and a major element in Ghana's domestic economy; but happily a more resistant stock was found, and this has proved even more productive than its predecessor. Less fortunate was the large-scale peanut project which was initiated in Tanganyika in 1947. Launched without sufficient examination of soil character, climatic conditions, and the experience of African farmers, the scheme ended in total disaster after only three years, the ultimate victim of unyielding nature, its plows shattered on the rugged land, its harvest smothered in drought.

In the Senegal and Niger valleys, to take another example, sorghum and other small grains have been found to thrive, while recent experiments in rice production have shown promise. Yet an important rice-growing program in Senegal has been seriously threatened by weaver birds and other pests, and weavers may eventually force abandonment of sorghum and millet culture in the West African savanna unless effective controls can eliminate the hundreds of millions of this ubiquitous, voracious creature which descends annually to ravage the maturing crops. Pest control has also been a chronic problem in the Kenyan highlands where, for years, wheat rust checked the efforts of Lord Delamere and others to initiate successful wheat farming under what were otherwise ideal growing conditions. Eventually, resistant strains were developed, but variants of the disease still break through periodically, requiring the introduction of new wheat varieties by watchful agriculture officers. The alternative to constant surveillance and continuing research in plant genetics, it is said, would be the total extinction of wheat production in Kenya.

Such examples merely punctuate the unexpected fact that seemingly genial Africa possesses an inhospitable and severe environment which has ever complicated man's efforts at self-improvement with flood and drought, disease and famine. The explanation for this anomaly must be sought first of all in the geology and geography of a unique continent.

The Geological Record

Many geologists have hypothesized that the earth's great continental land masses are essentially rigid blocks of ancient rock floating on a basic subcrust which heat and pressure have kept in a viscous condition. Under such circumstances the continental masses might drift laterally over long periods of time, and indeed it has been suggested that at one point Africa, Antarctica, the Indian peninsula, Australia, and most of South America were joined in an ancestral continent located near the South Pole and named Gondwanaland after the Gondwana district of central India. Though in dispute, this theory has persisted along with the contention that these southern-hemisphere continents began an outward drift from their Gondwanaland site about two hundred million years ago with Africa reaching its present location and dimension as recently as the Miocene period approximately twenty million years ago.

Throughout these times and much earlier still, the African continental block had been undergoing other geological transformations. During the long Precambrian era there was extensive activity in the form of elevation, folding, faulting, and erosion which resulted in the development of a continental shield of crystalline character in which granites were prominent, many in a metamorphic form. Subsequent to the Precambrian, activity was relatively limited, restricted primarily to uplift and erosion with little of the folding or massive intrusive thrust of igneous materials usually associated with mountain building. What evolved over time was a continental surface tilting slightly upward to the east and the south but consisting in its interior of a series of plateaus and basins of differing altitudes, generally level or undulating in aspect. At present, sea level elevations in West African coastal regions like the Niger Delta gradually rise to the high plains of eastern and southern Africa where altitudes of a mile or more are common and where the continental block terminates at its southeastern edge in the magnificent Drakensberg scarp of Natal with its ten-thousand-foot heights.

On the northern side of the continent the Atlas Mountains of Morocco appear to have been folded up along with Europe's Alpine ranges, squeezed by the northward drift of the African section of Gondwanaland. Internal ranges, however—for instance, the Tibesti and Ahaggar

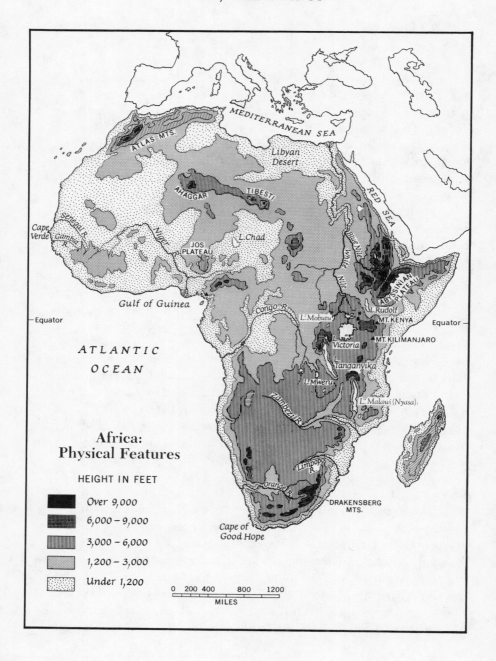

MEDITERRANEAN SEA

Libyan
Desert

ATLAS MTS.

AHAGGAR   TIBESTI

Cape
Verde   Senegal R.
Gambia
R.   Niger R.   L. Chad

JOS
PLATEAU

RED SEA

Blue Nile

White Nile

Nile

Gulf of Guinea   Congo R.   L. Mobutu   ABYSSINIAN
PLATEAU

L. Rudolf   MT. KENYA

Equator   Victoria   MT. KILIMANJARO   Equator

ATLANTIC
OCEAN   L. Tanganyika

L. Mweru

Zambezi R.   L. Malawi (Nyasa)

Africa:
Physical Features

HEIGHT IN FEET

Limpopo
R.

Orange R.   DRAKENSBERG
MTS.

Cape of
Good Hope

	Over 9,000
	6,000 – 9,000
	3,000 – 6,000
	1,200 – 3,000
	Under 1,200

0   200 400   800   1200

MILES

massifs of the Sahara, the Jos plateau in Nigeria, or the Futa Jalon upland of Guinea—are the result of complex interior warping and faulting, which also created the regional basins now occupied by important drainage systems such as the Nile, Niger, Congo, Zambezi, and Chad.

By far the most spectacular example of the faulting process is to be found in the celebrated Rift Valley system. This gigantic displacement traces a four-thousand-mile course beginning in the Middle East and ending in the vicinity of Beira in modern Mozambique. Responsible for the Dead Sea, the Gulf of Aqaba, and the Red Sea, it crosses into Africa, cutting its trench through the Ethiopian highlands, then moves south across the East African plateau to form the long line of finger lakes, Mobutu (Albert), Amin (Edward), Kivu, and Tanganyika, in its western prong, while to the east it has etched the Rift Valley of Kenya and Tanzania. The two faults join in the narrow depression of Lake Malawi, and the basin formed by their action contains the vast but shallow Lake Victoria, the world's third-largest inland sea and source of the White Nile.

Volcanic activity accompanied the formation of the Rift system, throwing up such lofty peaks as Mount Elgon and Mount Kilimanjaro, as well as Mount Kenya's three-mile-high glaciated summit which lies directly athwart the equator. Indeed, volcanic action has been widespread, being responsible for such landmarks as Mount Cameroon, the uplands of Ethiopia, and the Tibesti mountain mass, but also producing extensive, if less spectacular, lava flows to be found in various locations across the continent.

The series of interior basins formed by warping and faulting of the continental block have acted through time as catchments for sedimentary deposits, like the vast Karoo formations of southern Africa, eroded from earlier Precambrian materials. Many of these sediments have in turn been stripped away in the course of repeated cycles of uplift and erosion, but the essential pattern of basins has prevailed to the present, providing Africa with its characteristic major river systems. In each of the five main drainage complexes—Nile, Niger, Congo, Zambezi, and Orange—a young stream rising in the mountains settles down to a meandering middle course as it moves through the basin area. Thus, the Sudd and Bahr al-Ghazal region of the Nile, the Barotse floodplain of the Zambezi, or the lake district of the Niger are analogous phenomena, followed in each case by rapids and cataracts as the suddenly rejuvenated rivers spill out of their basins over the edge of the uplifted continent for their final passage to the sea. Depending on the age of the river, these fall points have worked themselves to various sites upstream, but in all cases, whether the cataracts of the Nile, the rapids of the Congo, the great Victoria Falls at Livingstone, or the Niger rapids at Jebba, they are the result of an ancient rhythm of uplift and erosion and are found characteristically in their lower courses although sometimes several hundred miles from the sea.

In times past these depressions were areas of internal drainage containing inland seas, and in some cases this is still true, for example, the Lake Chad basin. Relatively recent downward warping of the northern continental mass, however, introduced a somewhat different phenomenon, causing shallow external marine inundations from the Mediterranean area. Elsewhere the basic pattern of uplift produced, in addition to the river cataracts, an unbroken coastline raised from the sea and largely bereft of lagoons, estuaries, and other natural harbor sites. Along the eastern, Indian Ocean shore, the continental tilt has also created a region of rugged uplands and mountain scarps which effectively separates the broad sweep of the high interior plateau from the narrow coastal plain.

Africa's geological development has led to a number of important economic consequences. In the first place, her complex rock formations are the source not only of the continent's soil cover, but of Africa's many mineral assets as well. From the crystalline rocks of the continental shield come the immense deposits of copper and gold, the former today propelling the economies of Zaire and Zambia, the latter giving South Africa control over two-thirds of the free world gold supply. In earlier times West African gold was a major commodity in the trans-Saharan trade and a prime support for Europe's currency, while gold from the region between the Zambezi and Limpopo rivers once sustained mighty kingdoms and fed the trading emporiums of the East African coast. African diamonds, which have dominated the world market since their discovery on the Orange River in 1867, come from both alluvial deposits and volcanic materials and are to be found in Zaire, Tanzania, Angola, and Sierra Leone, as well as in South Africa. The coal beds of the Karoo system have helped initiate the industrialization of Zambia, Rhodesia, and South Africa, while Mediterranean marine sediments laid down in what is today the mid-Sahara have yielded the recent wealth of petroleum and natural gas which is in process of working an economic revolution for Algeria and Libya.

Most of these treasures have been difficult and expensive to extract, but without doubt the great reservoir of crystalline and sedimentary rocks will continue to yield substantial mineral resources as prospecting goes forward in response to rising demand for dwindling world supplies of iron, bauxite, and other sought-after ores. Beyond this, Africa's geological heritage has led to other quite different types of economic effect. For example, the periodic uplift of the vast continental block, producing an uninviting coastline, the difficult and sometimes mountainous terrain facing the Indian Ocean, and rivers more scenic than navigable in their lower courses, has by consequence greatly hampered both penetration from the outside and emergence from within—a major factor in the prolonged isolation of Africa from other areas of the world. Nonetheless, Africa's turbulent streams in their more sedate middle passages provide thousands of miles of serviceable waterways, and these have always been of great significance in facilitating the movements of peoples within the continent. The river systems have, in addition, brought their life-giving waters to regions deficient in natural rainfall, while their cataracts, an impediment to communication and transportation, are now in the modern era potential sites for the manufacture of great quantities of electric power.

Finally, the African geological record bears a direct if distant relationship to patterns of climate across the continent, for her present equatorial position, the key to African precipitation, is traceable to her original continental drift from Gondwanaland.

The Matter of Climate

Africa is the most tropical of the world's continents. Her great land mass stretches squarely across the equator, the northern and southern limits resting approximately at the thirty-fifth parallels, while more than three-fourths of her 11.7 million square miles are contained between the two Tropics of Cancer and Capricorn. Because of this equatorial location, much of Africa's weather is keyed to the characteristics and movements of the Intertropical Convergence Zone (I.T.C.), a band of air located in equatorial latitudes which shifts back and forth between the hemispheres with the annual rhythm of the seasons.

The Intertropical Convergence Zone is a belt of low atmospheric pressure characterized by rising currents of moist air which, cooling as they rise, condense and form rain clouds and heavy precipitation. This condition occurs in the latitudes adjacent to the equator, caused by the near-vertical rays of the sun which heat the land, thus setting in motion the convection system of ascending air with its abundant rainfall. The upward-moving equatorial air currents create a region of continued low pressure near ground level, and into this weak zone are sucked the trade winds. These prevailing northeasterlies in the northern hemisphere and southeasterlies in the southern hemisphere begin their journey at about the thirtieth parallel in the form of dry, hot winds moving close to the earth's surface, their temperature and low saturation enabling them to soak up moisture as they proceed. When the trades and other air pass into the I.T.C., they ascend to high altitudes, releasing their moisture load as they rise; then, moving back north and south, still at very high altitudes, they gradually descend, cold and dry, into a prevailing high-pressure cell in the vicinity of the thirtieth parallel. Here they are again propelled equatorward, once more hot, dry trade winds ready to renew the convection cycle.

Were the I.T.C. to remain stationary at or near the equator throughout the year, it would produce heavy rainfall in the narrow band under its influence, leaving large arid areas north and south to be constantly swept by drying winds. As the earth moves through its annual seasonal sequence, however, the I.T.C. travels back and forth across the equator, reaching the vicinity of the twentieth parallel north during the northern summer months of July and August and achieving a comparable southerly limit during the January summer of the southern hemisphere. In this way the characteristically hot, moist air in the Intertropical Zone of converging trade winds follows along behind the changing position of the sun, bringing precipitation with it in the form of summer rains to balance the winter drought. Precipitation gradually decreases as the

I.T.C. progressively invades the high-pressure system that is parent to the trade winds. In northern latitudes the heavy equatorial rainfall of sixty to one hundred inches and more is reduced to approximately ten inches a year in the neighborhood of the fifteenth parallel, which marks the beginning of the semiarid and arid conditions of the Sahara. In the subequatorial south, precipitation is more extensive, and semiarid conditions are not encountered to any appreciable degree before the twentieth parallel.

This basic pattern of African climate—heavy equatorial rain gradually diminishing to desert aridity—must be qualified in certain important respects. First and foremost is the fact that much of eastern Africa in the region of the high plains does not readily conform to the weather pattern associated with the Intertropical Convergence Zone. In parts of northern Kenya and much of Somalia, virtual desert conditions obtain in near-equatorial latitudes, and in addition there are extensive sections within Kenya and Tanzania that receive under thirty inches of rainfall a year, far less than corresponding areas to the west. The reasons for these conditions are not well understood, but drought in the Somalia region seems to be caused by the Saharan high-pressure cell which combines with a similar high covering Arabia and southwestern Asia to neutralize the effects of the Intertropical Convergence Zone on the eastern side of the continent. Beyond this, moist Indian Ocean winds, which might be expected to bathe the East African plains, appear infrequently to penetrate inland, possibly inhibited in part by the mountainous barrier of Madagascar.

Two exceptions to the east coast dry pattern should be noted, however. In summer, the Ethiopian highlands, unlike neighboring Somalia, receive heavy equatorial rains associated with I.T.C. movement, while the narrow shelf east of the Drakensberg scarp of South Africa is also well watered, particularly by Indian Ocean winds rising over the mountains during the summer season. On the western edge of the generally dry South African plateau, however, severe desert conditions are found in the Namibia coastal region as the natural aridity of the southern-hemisphere high-pressure zone is augmented through the action of a cold ocean current along the coast which cools surface air flowing over it, thereby discouraging the upward convective motion that brings precipitation.

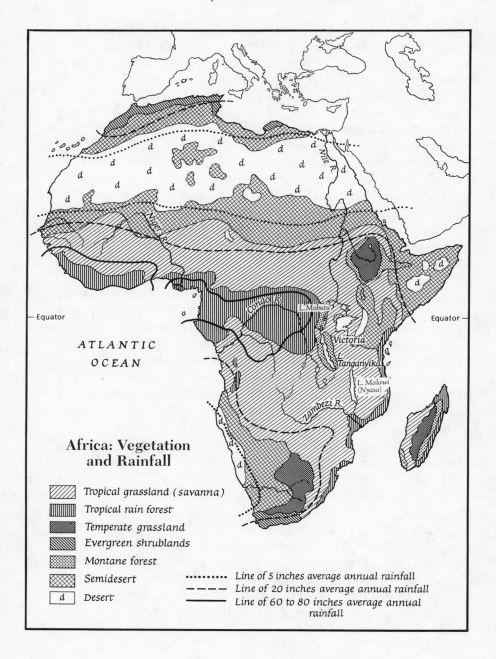

Equator

ATLANTIC
OCEAN

Nile R.

Niger R.

Congo R.

L. Mobutu

Victoria

L. Tanganyika

L. Malawi
(Nyasa)

Zambezi R.

Equator

Africa: Vegetation
and Rainfall

Tropical grassland (savanna)

Tropical rain forest

Temperate grassland

Evergreen shrublands

Montane forest

Semidesert

d | Desert

• • • • • Line of 5 inches average annual rainfall

– – – – Line of 20 inches average annual rainfall

———— Line of 60 to 80 inches average annual
rainfall

Africa's tropical location, therefore, has created a pattern of rainfall which is heavy in the equatorial latitudes but which gradually diminishes until the arid regions are reached—the vast Sahara in the north and the less extensive South African plateau and Kalahari Desert to the south. Equatorial precipitation has created a tropical rain forest in the Congo watershed and along the West African coast which covers about 8 percent of the continental land mass. Desert areas amount to 40 percent of the total, although only 8 percent can be classified as truly desiccated wasteland devoid of vegetation. Most of the remainder comprises Africa's characteristic terrain—a savanna grassland, sometimes combined with forest growth, grading off into tropical rain forest at one extreme and dwindling into desert shrub at the other.

Clearly, large sections of the African continent suffer from an inadequate water supply, a crippling impediment in an area where subsistence agriculture has long been the dominant form of economic production. Indeed, the situation is more critical than is at first apparent. One observer, for example, classifies three-fifths of Africa as arid or semiarid, another adding that almost half of the South African Republic falls within that classification. It is estimated that three-fourths of Tanzanian lands have insufficient rainfall for satisfactory agriculture, thereby causing two-thirds of the population to concentrate on one-tenth of the land area where there is enough water to support them. In Egypt, the total population is sustained by less than 5 percent of the land, all of which is watered not by rainfall but by Nile flood waters channeled and husbanded through systems of irrigation.

The example of Egypt suggests the importance of conservation and control, techniques that can help to alleviate an even more serious deficiency in Africa's water supply—the capricious irregularity of her rainfall. Not only may precipitation be deemed insufficient as averaged over a protracted period of years; it will also fluctuate enormously in total fall from year to year as well as display great diversity in the timing of onset and conclusion of the annual seasonal rains. Finally, when the rains do arrive, they characteristically appear in the form of violent storms with consequent flooding and the irretrievable loss of badly needed water through runoff.

This eccentric behavior stems from the unpredictability of the Intertropical Convergence Zone, its position frequently varying from year to year by several hundred miles as it sluggishly follows the sun, with few pronounced physical features such as mountains or valleys to impede or otherwise control and direct its flow across the broad African plateau. For agricultural communities, the consequences of this erratic pattern can quite literally swing from feast to famine. It is commonplace for weather stations to record extremes in annual precipitation of the order of two to one, and the occasion is rare when the same amount occurs two years running. This condition is especially critical in regions of lower rainfall, for it is here that the annual deviation from the mean is typically greatest. Should the I.T.C. fail to reach latitudes normally achieved, the results can be disastrous, as evidenced in the western Sudan during the extended drought that began in the late 1960s. In the savanna, precipitation is largely concentrated in a few short weeks, and when these are unproductive, respite is extremely improbable for another twelve months.

Thus it is that the perennial vagaries of rainfall traditionally have forced African societies to endure a subsistence based upon what is available to them in their worst seasons. Yet, there are still further imperfections of weather to complicate the life and livelihood of the African farmer. In the first place, the relatively short rainy season in many areas means that the annual supply is deposited too quickly, the furious bursts of rain injuring the soil through both erosion and leaching while causing runoff before the rain has had an opportunity to saturate the soil and thereby hold itself ready for later use. Moreover, the rains tend to arrive in the summer season when temperatures are highest and the degree of evaporation and transpiration most severe. African plants have learned to combat transpiration through various devices including shedding their leaves, but both transpiration and evaporation continue to cause enormous water losses throughout the continent. To take one case, virtually all the rain falling on the actual surface of Lake Victoria is consumed by evaporation, while the Nile lakes, such as Amin, Mobutu, and Kyoga, rely on tributaries for replenishment since evaporation actually exceeds the amount of rain reaching their surfaces. Again, experimenters working in South Africa arrived at the conclusion that for every inch of rainfall on a local crop only half was utilized by the plant itself, a third disappearing through evaporation and the rest lost in runoff or percolation.

One final disability must be mentioned, and ironically it stems from the apparent advantage of a prevailing tropical climate that entails none of winter's hardships and provides growing seasons far exceeding those of the so-called temperate zones. In all parts of the world farmers are familiar with the fact that crop concentrations tend to attract natural enemies which can in part be evaded by planting rotation but which are also checked by the winter freeze. In Africa, however, the problem is much more acute. In the absence of a killing frost, species thrive and multiply; but as each develops in population, it becomes prey to another which devours its victim until both have achieved an uneasy coexistence, severely limited in number and scattered in area. This dismal balance of nature has not neglected man, his crops, or his livestock, for all are targets of a wide variety of pests and diseases bred in Africa's deceptively genial environment. Large range areas have been made unfit for pasturage because of tsetse-borne trypanosomiasis, and at times epidemics of rinderpest have crippled African societies by wiping out their cattle. Crops have been raised only to be swooped upon and consumed by hordes of winged vermin, while others are blighted in their initial growth by viruses and parasites. Man himself has been a major target of diverse maladies which have, until recently, produced a staggering infant mortality, decimating and scattering populations and condemning the average survivor to a life of chronic infirmity frequently terminated by early death.

The African Land

During the nineteenth century, as Europeans began to show serious interest in the modernization of agriculture in Africa, they frequently spoke with enthusiasm about the results that were certain to follow the introduction of Western scientific farming techniques to a continent of such apparent fertility. How could they fail in a land of profuse and easy growth where a tree branch thrust into the ground would soon take root and the very fence posts sprouted twigs? Africa, at least in the regions of tropical rain forest and adjacent savanna, seemed to possess the richest of soils, and it was only after repeated failure that the realization slowly dawned of a much more difficult environment, poor in resources and grudging of its gifts.

Indeed, it is now generally understood that tropical soils are often inferior, a circumstance that may be governed in part by the type of parent rock beneath but that is also the result of climatic considerations. In Africa it is rainfall and sunshine that have largely conditioned her soil cover, determining its consistency, its mineral content, its ability to absorb and hold moisture, as well as the amount and type of organic matter contained within its structure. At the same time the nature of her underlying solid rock complex has also been important, particularly in defining the character of Africa's soils at or near the land surface.

To begin with, there is the factor of a tropical climate, its high temperatures predominating in both air and soil over much of the continent, a yearly average of about 80° F. obtaining in equatorial latitudes. Under these conditions warm water percolating through the soil tends to leach out minerals present near the surface more readily than would occur in a cooler temperate zone. Silicates, iron oxides, and other salts are thus transported in solution and deposited in the lower layers, while in the dry season the movement is reversed and, through capillary action, these compounds move upward to a position at or near the surface where they accumulate after evaporation. Over time a heavy layer of earth develops, usually reddish in color because of its rich iron content, largely impervious to water, and inhospitable to vegetation. Known as laterite, it is soft and workable when newly exposed, but on contact with the air much of it hardens to a bricklike consistency, a characteristic that makes it popular in the tropics as a material for building and road construction.

To this progressive development of lateritic soils—some authorities classify them as more rock than soil—is added the action of tropical temperatures on organic content. Clearly, soil fertility is measured in part by the amount of vegetable and animal matter present, matter that is broken down into humus by bacterial action, thereby supplying plants with an important food source. At higher temperatures, however, decomposition is accelerated to the point where plants can no longer assimilate the total supply. The excess of humus then begins to disintegrate and precious organic matter is lost, converted into gases through oxidation.

These conditions help clarify the illusion of fertility in African latitudes which deceived the early modernizers. The tropical rain forest is deep rooted, quick growing, and lush, but the amount of organic matter it produces is slight, barely enough to sustain a balance of nature. The basic soil, moreover, is poor and slowly degenerating; hence, any effort to clear the land for farming has normally had disastrous results. With tree cover gone, the hot sun speeds up the processes of soil leaching and oxidation, while plowing exposes the laterite hardpan to the crusting action of the air. Moreover, because large areas of the African continent are underlain with metamorphic formations containing numerous quartz seams, angular quartz particles have become embedded in the laterite base, giving it the consistency and impenetrability of armor plate.

Finally, there is the performance of tropical rains, their torrential force pounding the earth into hardness while their sudden superabundance promotes flooding and erosion. Where a more moderate temperate-zone rainfall might soak the earth and seasonal frost encourage a loose and broken soil, tropical rains tend to reinforce processes already under way, increasing surface imperviousness, causing water loss through runoff, and stimulating the leaching action that carries minerals deep into the earth beyond the reach of all but those plants with the deepest root systems.

Such retailing of soil imperfections within the African continent gives a somewhat misleading impression—a totally intractable land largely incapable of sustaining cultivated vegetation whether in the desert wastes or in the seeming fertility of the equatorial forest. While the conditions described have long marked wide areas, they are scarcely universal in a land where, after all, the economy has rested primarily upon agricultural production. Laterites dominate only about one-third of the continent; there are, moreover, regions of good fertility—the black earths in parts of the Transvaal, Rhodesia, and the sub-Saharan savanna; the alluvial deposits of river valleys and seacoasts, or widely scattered soils of volcanic origin. It should be added, lastly, that the African farmer has adapted to these conditions with imagination and skill, developing technologies and traditions of cultivation well designed to bring forth optimum results despite the many limitations he has encountered in his land and climate.

SUGGESTIONS FOR FURTHER READING

Both the *Oxford Regional Economic Atlas: Africa* (Oxford: Clarendon Press, 1965) and Lord Hailey, *An African Survey, Revised 1956* (London: Oxford University Press, 1957), are standard source books, but there are good geographical and geological surveys of Africa as well. See, for example, L. D. Stamp, *Africa: A Study in Tropical Development*, 2nd ed. (New York and London: John Wiley and Sons, 1964); A. B. Montjoy and Clifford Embleton, *Africa: A New Geographical Survey* (New York: Praeger, 1967), which appears in a British edition as *Africa: A Geographical Study* (London: Hutchinson Educational, 1966); and W. A. Hance, *The Geography of Modern Africa* (New York and London: Columbia University Press, 1964). Other useful general works are E. B. Worthington, *Science in the Development of Africa* (London: Commission for Technical Cooperation in Africa South of the Sahara, 1958), and G. H. T. Kimble, *Tropical Africa*, vol. 1 (New York: Twentieth Century Fund, 1960).

For more specialized studies on African climate see W. G. Kendrew, *The Climates of the Continents*, 5th ed. (London and New York: Oxford University Press, 1961), and G. T. Trewartha, *The Earth's Problem Climates* (Madison: University of Wisconsin Press, 1961).

The basic survey of African soils is H. L. Shantz and C. F. Marbut, *The Vegetation and Soils of Africa* (New York: American Geographical Society, 1923), which may be supplemented by regional studies such as J. D. Tothill, ed., *Agriculture in the Sudan* (London and New York: Oxford University Press, 1948), or the same author's *Agriculture in Uganda* (London: Oxford University Press, 1940).

2

BEFORE HISTORY

Homo sapiens

Despite its harshness, it was the African environment that first brought forth man, nurturing his early development through a progressive series of refinements that culminated in the appearance of *Homo sapiens*, modern man, approximately thirty-five thousand to fifty thousand years ago. The process began far back in geological times; how far back is as yet a matter of considerable dispute among scientists.

To the zoologist the appearance of man was an extraordinary and unique event in the evolution of species, introducing for the first time a creature capable of creating abstract ideas through conceptual thought and communicating the results of his deliberations among the members of his own group. Viewed from the perspective of economics, it was a colossal breakthrough in environmental adaptation and a major triumph in closing the gap of hunger and survival. Indeed, it was more than mere adaptation, for man slowly began consciously to change and control his environment, a process that has continued without cease ever since.

Man's initial appearance was hesitant, his physical and intellectual makeup scarcely distinguishable from that of the larger apes; hence the continuing uncertainties among paleontologists concerning the precise moment of his arrival. Only the locale seems beyond dispute, for there is general agreement that the beginnings of human evolution were centered in Africa. Nearly a century ago, Charles Darwin suggested that "it is somewhat more probable that our early progenitors lived on the African continent than elsewhere," and subsequent research seems to support this proposition. The order of primates, which has produced, among other species, man, apes, monkeys, and lemurs, had its origins sixty million years ago in Eocene times, possibly even earlier. By the Oligocene age, some thirty or forty million years ago, the primates were established in Africa, and of more particular interest, it was the higher primates, including the zoological family of pongids or great apes, who were found there. In the Fayum district of modern Egypt ape fossils have been discovered with an antiquity of forty million years, and other finds have established the fact that eastern Africa was a center of pongid activity as far back as twenty million years, although early apes were also found in Europe and Southeast Asia.

The pongids were not alone, for as the primate order evolved, the higher primates gradually divided into separate family groups—for example, gibbons and certain now-extinct forms, as well as the great apes themselves. During the Miocene period, between fifteen and thirty million years ago, there appeared to be a further bifurcation as a new family split off to form still another distinct group. These were the hominids, according to some authorities different enough from pongids in physical and functional characteristics to warrant a separate family, but still so close in resemblance to their pithecoid cousins as to invite dispute among scientists over which warranted classification as an ape and which was a genuine ancestor to man.

The foremost protagonist for this early appearance of the hominid family has been Louis S. B. Leakey, the distinguished paleontologist who, from his base in East Africa, devoted a lifetime of research to the study of human origins. In 1963 Leakey discovered a fossil which he named *Kenyapithecus wickeri* and four years later another, *Kenyapithecus africanus*, the first fourteen million years old and the second six million years older still. Both, said Leakey, were hominids and as such the earliest known specimens of the human line. Leakey's opinion was based upon anatomical considerations—a shortened face and teeth essentially human in shape and arrangement—that clearly distinguished *Kenya-*

pithecus from the great apes with their massive jaws, long, stabbing canine teeth, and heavy, chomping mastication suitable for a soft vegetational diet. Here was telltale evidence of early human activity, Leakey continued, for the altered cranial and dental structure meant a creature who had abandoned the tree habitat of the apes to live on the ground where he searched out a varied food supply of animal and vegetable matter, probably already foraging by means of an upright posture, possibly manufacturing and utilizing simple tools as well.

For those who have accepted Leakey's findings, *Kenyapithecus* is in all likelihood related to *Ramapithecus*, another hominid originally found in India with a dating of seven million years ago and perhaps earlier. In any case, if Leakey's conclusions are sustained, it follows that the break between pongid and hominid occurred at some far remote point in time, older still than the twenty-million-year age of *Kenyapithecus africanus*.

Despite growing acceptance of *Ramapithecus* and *Kenyapithecus* as early hominids, there continues to be a strong current of scientific doubt concerning a very remote division between man and the apes, doubt that has been reinforced recently by evidence far removed from the more usual archaeological sources. During the past several years, studies in the blood chemistry of animal species indicate that serum constituents like hemoglobin and albumin evolve in molecular structure at definable rates, thereby making possible computation of chronological divergence between related species. While differences between man and monkeys indicate a point of separation approximately thirty million years ago, those between man and the great apes suggest a split of no more than five million years—a far closer genetic kinship than what Leakey and others have claimed from the fossil record.

Whatever the age that marked the division between hominid and pongid, the process of human evolution has been marked by a dynamic interplay between physiological and cultural development responding to the exigencies of environment. At one time man was identified primarily by his cultural capability in designing and utilizing tools, but this easy definition is no longer considered adequate. Recent research into the habits of chimpanzees has revealed their consistent manufacture of tools for specific purposes, a circumstance that has led anthropologists to identify early man by a more complex battery of criteria stressing both genetic and acquired qualities—upright carriage, prolonged childhood, certain anatomical characteristics, and the ability to fashion cutting tools.

Such a combination of traits might have emerged as the pressures of a shifting environment brought about adaptive changes on the part of particular primate species. A reduction in forest cover, for example, might have brought certain apes out of the trees, altering their exclusive soft vegetable diet to one of roots, berries, nuts, and seeds combined with animal matter gained from scavenging and possibly from hunting. A comparable modification in feeding habits is today observable among baboons during periods of drought, and over time it could have caused the heavy jaws and strong back molars of apes to be replaced with a dental anatomy more characteristic of hominids—grinding molars, small cutting incisors, and canine teeth set in a reduced, albeit powerful, jaw.

The loss of apelike canines would have posed the problem of defense for a creature of limited natural equipment no longer able to seek safety and shelter in the forest trees. The solution might then have emerged in the form of bipedal locomotion, which offered better height for the observation of enemy or prey and freed the forelimbs for the eventual use and manufacture of tools. Tools in turn would have put still less premium on heavy dental equipment for defense and feeding, while weaker physical endowments would have forced increasing reliance on mental agility. And so the evolutionary process unfolded. Compelled by environment to transform his way of life, man gradually adjusted to changing circumstances, altering his response through cultural adaptation, a process that in turn influenced physiological development proceeding by means of natural selection. Finally, as physiology and habits changed, these modifications began to affect man's environment, hopefully, though not always successfully, to his advantage.

Of all these early changes, the one that most clearly led the first hominids to evolve toward species of increasingly manlike character was not greater brain size or even as yet the faculty for conceptual thought. Rather it was bipedalism, for once the hominids took to their hind legs great consequences ensued. First, and most obvious, the hands were freed. This meant that the apposable thumb of the primates could develop in man both in strength and facility to a degree impossible among the pongids, whose forelimbs were required for locomotion. Free hands meant freedom to move objects from place to place or to collect materials in a particular locality. Free hands also meant the dawning ability to use and to manufacture tools, clumsily at first with little precision but nevertheless with slowly growing sophistication and efficiency. Now the connection between hand and brain came into prominence, for toolmaking proficiency required an intelligence to drive it, and as the brain grew in response to the new demands placed upon it, there was a corresponding growth in perception, particularly of environment, and the birth of an articulated thought process.

At the same time bipedalism caused other important structural changes. The head held erect meant a different arrangement of supporting muscles and skeletal attachments, and the widened angle between mouth and throat offered a greater range of sound production which would eventually facilitate speech and the development of language. Constant utilization of hind limbs greatly strengthened their muscular equipment, while erect posture changed their relation to the pelvis, which also was altered in structure and size. A narrowed pelvic orifice necessitated a relatively shorter period of gestation than is characteristic of the great apes; hence, the infant at birth was not only smaller but also was immature and required a long childhood for protection and survival. It was a childhood, however, that could be devoted to extended training, advantageously conducted while the offspring was in immediate contact with its environment.

The shift to bipedalism arrived slowly, consuming the millions of years of Miocene and Pliocene times until the advent of the Pleistocene era approximately two or three million years ago. This age was marked by a number of species called collectively *Australopithecines* whose small brains and heavy jaws at first seemed to classify them as apes—hence *Australopithecine*, or "southern ape"—but whose dental structure along with limb and pelvic development strongly suggested hominids. Though clumsy, they appeared to be bipeds, and it has been argued by some that they were users and makers of tools as well. The initial finds came from southern Africa, but subsequent specimens were unearthed in East Africa and the Lake Chad region, and these latter offered fresh evidence of toolmaking.

In 1959 Leakey discovered an *Australopithecine* in Tanganyika, calling him *Zinjanthropus*, "the man of Zinj," for he was an evident hominid on anatomical grounds. Found buried in sedimentary beds rich with examples of stone and bone tools, *Zinjanthropus* was soon supplemented by additional fossils exhumed at the same site, and these, Leakey insisted, were the remains of a quite different creature which he named significantly *Homo habilis*, "the skillful man." It was *Homo habilis* and not his contemporary *Zinjanthropus* who was the toolmaker, Leakey argued, adding that the former was very likely the direct forebear of modern man to boot. While other authorities disagreed, claiming that the two were members of the same species, the fact remains that toolmaking hominids existed in East Africa almost two million years ago, using their implements to break open bones of animals captured or scavenged in the search for food.

Once again it was the exigencies of environment acting upon potential intelligence that induced adaptation and stimulated inventiveness. According to Leakey, *Zinjanthropus* was primarily herbivorous, but *Homo habilis*, with a larger brain, smaller teeth, and more developed hands, was the better equipped for accommodation to a changing ecology. Drought would have forced him to scavenge for meat to supplement failing vegetable resources, his more advanced hands and brain suggesting the use of any convenient jagged stone to cut away the flesh. From here it was a natural step to the manufacture of chipped-stone implements, just as scavenging probably led logically to hunting which in turn called for tools as weapons in addition to those used for cutting and skinning. While the less talented and adaptable *Zinjanthropus* languished and then lapsed into extinction, *Homo habilis* thrived and set the stage for still more resourceful descendants.

The controversy over *Homo habilis* and *Zinjanthropus* was still unresolved when Leakey died in 1972, only a few months before a new discovery was announced which both illustrated and complicated the incomplete record of human evolution. An expedition, of which the paleontologist's son Richard was coleader, reported the unearthing near Lake Rudolf of skull and limb remnants belonging to an early man with morphological characteristics far more modern than those of *Homo habilis* or *Zinjanthropus* but firmly linked to strata estimated to be between five hundred thousand and one million years older than the *Homo habilis* formations. The Rudolf fossils, explained Richard Leakey, gave evidence that contemporary with the *Australopithecines* there had existed another hominid with a much larger brain case of a shape very like that of modern man and with thigh and lower leg bones indicating that the *Homo* line already may have passed beyond the stooped, loping gait generally associated with the *Australopithecines*. In 1974, moreover, apparently human jawbone and tooth fossils were unearthed in Ethiopia, their age reported at three to five million years. If additional study should sustain these early tentative conclusions, creatures like the *Australopithecines* and the later-developing *Homo erectus* might have to be eliminated from human evolution, man's modernity having been established much further back in the distant past than had previously been suspected.

Along with these discoveries, Richard Leakey's team has introduced fresh complications in the form of recent fossil finds suggesting the concurrent existence at a given time of several parallel hominid lineages. Some of these remains exhibit anatomic characteristics that do not fit previous hypotheses concerning human evolution—for example, strikingly modern features combined with others distinctly primitive. Whether these types fought, interbred, or merely ignored each other is unknown; what does seem increasingly apparent is that at different moments in time there were several types of early man living together in approximately the same locations. Human evolution therefore may be regarded no longer as the uncomplicated linear descent of a particular hominid species, the aberrant strains of which simply died out. Rather it appears increasingly to be the product of interaction among many types, a complex of evolving strains working in a way that is as yet ill understood.

Throughout the course of human evolution, man's most distinguishing characteristic has been the flexibility of his behavior in the face of environmental change. Intellectual capacity, toolmaking facility, group cooperation, communication of ideas, all flow ultimately from this source. Other species that have successfully adjusted to environment have prevailed through specific adaptations to specific conditions, but once locked into a pattern of response, they are gravely threatened by subsequent environmental shifts. Man, on the contrary, developed the capability for adjustment to an expanding range of environmental variations. When the circumstances under which he lived remained static, his pattern of life was unchanging as well. When his environment shifted, so too did his behavior, a behavior that increasingly was capable of acting upon, as well as adjusting to, the world around him.

With the passage of time, moreover, man began to perceive that the idea of innovation provided its own logic. The early stone tools were crude affairs indeed—fist-sized rocks roughhewn to a point or jagged edge, generally serviceable but scarcely efficient for any particular job. Slowly the techniques of toolmaking improved. The stones were more finely shaped, their edges better chiseled, while newer, more specialized designs gradually joined the generalized tools. The movement from scavenging to hunting dictated coordinated activities in driving and stalking game, and the social organization that resulted brought with it specialization of activity, particularly between the sexes, along with a need for sophisticated communication through language, itself essentially another form of tool.

The development and transfer of ideas on which all these activities were based brought a marked increase in brain size, particularly in those centers that controlled the intellectual processes as distinguished from instinctive reflex reactions. A longer childhood effectively domesticated the mother, and this, in turn, furthered the movement toward specialization, while emphasis on the hunt necessitated extended absences in the field and probably eliminated the cycles of sexual receptivity characteristic of other species. As the brain increased in size and complexity, producing its battery of invented tools, certain physical attributes atrophied—for example, the massive jaw muscles and strong teeth no longer required for heavy-duty feeding. Mental activity also led to a new awareness, the first distinction drawn between man's self and man's surroundings. With self-consciousness came other developments such as the desire for personal adornment, an artistic expression, and religious impulses which signaled the beginning of man's preoccupation with his place in the universe.

The advent of art and religion suggest that man had succeeded in raising his economy above the level of sheer survival and now employed what was, in effect, leisure time in pursuit of something beyond the next meal. Such activity stimulated inventiveness and focused attention on ultimate objectives over immediate necessities, thereby increasing the prospects for further technological breakthroughs and the creation of new concepts.

Possibly the control of fire grew out of such circumstances, although there is much to be said for the argument that the use of fire followed basic climatic changes—in the Far East during the second glacial period about a quarter-million years ago, but in the tropical environment of Africa not until the onset of a cold, wet stage corresponding to the last glacial age between fifty and sixty thousand years ago. In any case, the domestication of fire introduced numerous changes in human ecology. It enabled man to take refuge in caves and rock shelters where he was much more secure and comfortable. It gave greater permanence to his camp sites, at the same time greatly enlarging the varieties of foods at his disposal. It increased his efficiency as a hunter and for the first time made it possible for him to invade and clear the forests of the equatorial belt.

The *Australopithecines* who flourished in the early Pleistocene gave way in time to a new species, *Homo erectus*, and it is this individual who is associated with the introduction of that all-purpose stone tool known as the hand ax. This was a cutting, chopping instrument similar in function to the primitive choppers of the *Australopithecines*, but much more finely wrought and efficient, and found in conjunction with scrapers and other instruments of a more specialized nature. Like his tools, *Homo erectus* was also the product of an evolutionary spiral. With a brain double that of his *Australopithecine* predecessor and approximately two-thirds the size of modern man's, he conducted his hunts in organized groups with imagination and foresight and was a skilled and resourceful artisan who apparently was the first man to make use of fire.

The hand ax, though a generalized implement, continued to dominate the tool kit from its initial appearance about a million years ago until the later Pleistocene of approximately sixty thousand years past. Geographically it spread along with its inventor far beyond Africa to western Europe, the Middle East, and the Indian subcontinent. While a number of different human species eventually predominated in these widely separated areas, the hand ax culture they developed showed marked similarities, a fact that suggests the slow spread of man and his institutions over hundreds of thousands of years combined with the continued serviceability of a basic tool.

In Africa, too, a variety of human species had evolved after *Homo erectus*, including, toward the end of the hand ax era, the first evidence of a new stock, *Homo sapiens*. At about the same time there was a fundamental shift in tool design as well. The generalized hand ax which had so long dominated the scene was replaced by smaller implements of specialized function, each tool fashioned for a particular purpose and thereby more efficient in its action. Chisels, gouges, knives, awls, cleavers, and various types of scrapers appeared for woodworking, digging, skinning, and other activities, while more efficient points improved weapons of war and the hunt. Stone balls proliferated, possibly for pounding roots or grinding, but they would also have served as effective missiles or bolos in hunting. The hand ax men had characteristically driven game into bogs or specially dug pitfalls where the quarry could be stoned or speared with facility. Now improved technology permitted abandonment of these tactics in favor of stone-tipped spears which drew blood easily to facilitate tracking and animal or vegetable poisons which made man formidable against the largest and most durable of game. Tools were fastened to handles with thong, sinew, or glues which, like the poisons, could now be processed through the use of fire.

It was during this era of tool specialization that man began to make use of personal ornamentation, to cover the walls of his caves and rock shelters with representational drawings, and to bury his dead, this last practice taken to indicate the beginning of a religious awareness. At the same time, in Europe, a second technological revolution occurred, producing still another new type of tool. The specialized implements introduced at the beginning of the late Pleistocene had been manufactured by chipping a diversity of stones to the desired shape and size. Now the artisan concentrated not on the stone core but on the chip or microlith which could be produced in the form of a blade of infinite variety to be attached to knife grip, spear tip, arrow shaft, or other handle for whatever use desired. Flexibility and efficiency were greatly enhanced through lightness of construction and adaptability of design. Bows also made their appearance at this time as did the barbed tip, while man exercised increased selectivity over the type of stones employed for his growing assortment of tools and weapons.

By 10,000 B.C., all human species had become extinct except *Homo sapiens.* This sole survivor thrived, adapting his ways to meet the special demands of particular environments while spreading widely cultural and genetic refinements locally developed. In the Middle East, Europe, and Mediterranean Africa, for example, man's microlith technology had become dominant by 15,000 B.C., possibly as a result of worsening climate related to the glacial period. By contrast, the earlier stone core tools continued to serve the hunting societies of tropical Africa until they were rapidly replaced by the microliths about 10,000 B.C. At one time it was thought that this abrupt shift was caused by outsiders, immigrant conquerors from Europe and Asia who introduced the new technology while dominating and intermixing with the older resident populations. Intercontinental migrations doubtless occurred, but students of African prehistory now conclude that the microliths entered tropical Africa essentially as ideas and were quickly adopted when their advantage became apparent within the context of the changing African environment. This would have followed moister conditions in the Sahara and East Africa which encouraged fishing equipment based upon the newer barbed harpoons and improved hunting efficiency through use of microlith multitanged spears and arrowheads.

Diffusion of cultural or genetic traits was balanced, however, by man's responsiveness to local environmental factors. It has been suggested that the *Homo* line, originating in tropical Africa, was initially dark skinned, a necessary protection through pigmentation against excessive ultraviolet radiation caused by the near-vertical rays of the sun at equatorial latitudes. Those who migrated toward the poles slowly lost their coloration as a result of natural selection, for at higher latitudes it was essential to absorb as much as possible of the sun's slanting rays, thereby synthesizing an adequate supply of life-giving vitamin D. Near the equator, heavy pigmentation screened out direct exposure that would have led to a lethal calcification of soft tissue.

Localized characteristics, therefore, evolved from the age-old interaction among environment, cultural adaptation, and natural selection. Early fossil remains widely distributed across the continent indicate that during the late prehistoric era, Africa was inhabited by a bushmanoid stock which provided the primary basis for the peoples of modern Africa. As climatic conditions began to dictate the distribution of forest, savanna, and desert that has characterized the Africa of recent millennia, localized environments, acting upon particular sections of the basic bushmanoid population, brought about the racial specialization that subsequently emerged.

In eastern and southern Africa a high plains savanna setting gave rise to the small, lithe San (Bushman), his slight stature, quickness, and stamina well suited to the hunting life he led. Within the thick forest growth of the Congo River watershed, another diminutive variant appeared—the pygmoid hunter-gatherer whose quasi-arborial existence favored agility and small size. In western and central Africa below the drying Sahara, the negroids emerged, whereas north of the desert were caucasoids, their strain very likely blended with that of immigrants from Europe and the Middle East.

Geneticists describe racial groupings not as populations with fixed homogeneous characteristics but as temporary concentrations of certain genetic qualities ever changing in response to hybridization—expanding, branching, or fusing in an exercise of adaptation. In view of these dynamic circumstances, regional populations in Africa, as elsewhere, have evidenced continued genetic and cultural alteration caused both by migrations and hybridization and by the natural selection of environmental factors. Thus, to take one example, over the many centuries of the Christian era, those West African negroids who formed the vast Bantu migration developed a variety of distinctive local traits despite their common origin—witness, among other instances, the pygmoid morphology of Bantu groups settled in the Congo rain forest or the bushmanoid cultural and genetic characteristics of those Bantu who eventually came to rest in South Africa.

Whatever his local variant, *Homo sapiens* supported himself essentially as he had since the days of the first hominids. He lived in small communities for mutual protection and support, his activities largely focused on the acquisition of food. Foraging continued to offer supplies of vegetable produce, but by 6000 B.C. or perhaps earlier, fishing with harpoon and hook began to appear in the Nile valley and other watered areas. More generally, hunting continued to be a major preoccupation and meat a regular and important item of the diet. In the forests the hunt may have been conducted largely in the trees if the activities of more recent pygmoid societies are any indication. Along the open grassy plains the hunter relied upon light projectiles—his spear and throwing stick as well as his bow and arrow.

The Hunters

This section reconstructs food-gathering and hunting activities of late Pleistocene hunting societies, particularly as evidenced under the stress of famine.

The stars glowed dimly against the black night sky. The air was sharp and the man pulled his cloak around him more closely as he huddled, half-waking, in the shallow depression under the crude screen shelter of branches and leaves that protected him against the wind. Mumbling, he turned over, trying to regain the thread of a dream, a fantasy of hunting and feasting; but suddenly the pangs in his belly struck, forcing him from his comfortable illusions to the reality of hunger. While his empty stomach continued its protest, he opened his eyes and without moving his head slowly took in the scene about him. His bag of arrows and fire sticks lay by his side next to his bow and spear. A few feet beyond were the remnants of the fire where his wives had prepared the poor scraps of the previous evening's meal. It showed no sign of life, neither glow nor smoke; but he knew it was still alive, for he had carefully covered it with ashes before retiring, fully aware that a fire must not be allowed to burn out but could be extinguished only on the rare occasion when bad sickness or a disastrous hunt called for the making of a new fire by the chief.

Perhaps it was time for such measures, he thought, and as Kwa, the leader of his band, it would be up to him to decide. He raised himself, leaning on one elbow. Beyond the fire were several other shelters which he could just make out in the gloom, for now the first faint traces of light were showing in the eastern sky. His two wives had separate shelters off to one side, and directly opposite was his brother-in-law, whose wife, Kwa's sister, lay nearby, curled up with her new baby. Soon they would leave to join her husband's people now that her confinement was at an end. Kwa would be sorry to see her go, but this was the proper way of doing things; and, of course, it would be one less family to burden the uncertain resources of the band's new hunting preserve.

There were still others. Near Kwa, his young brother, T'kwa, stirred, yawned, but went on sleeping. He was still a boy and had yet to endure the rigors of puberty rites, but already he was an accomplished hunter, swift and tireless afoot and a good shot with the bow. Next to Kwa's wives were the shelters of cousins, aunts, and uncles, their spouses and children. It was not a large band—just a few families related by blood, about two dozen individuals in all, united in pursuit of survival.

One person was not present. Kwa's father, for long the chief of the band, had been wounded in the foot on the day they were attacked by their neighbors and sent flying from their camp, forced to seek new hunting grounds in a grim competition for the meager resources of a stubborn land. They had managed to escape after hard fighting, although two of their women were captured; but during the swift march that carried them to safety, Kwa's father had found it impossible to keep up, and finally they were forced to abandon him. A shelter was constructed in a comfortable place under some bushes, a grass bed prepared, firewood collected, and a supply of food and water left. The old man settled himself stoically and prepared to die. There was no complaint, for all knew the harsh law of nature—one must go that the rest may survive.

The band had pressed on, now under Kwa's leadership, finally making camp at their present site on an ancient lake bed, its parched alkaline soil white and glaring under the noonday sun and in this season of no rain supporting patches of scrubby bushes and a few stunted trees. The territory seemed uninhabited, which meant momentary security; but the terrible necessity of locating food and water outweighed all other considerations, including the danger of attack. Some were counseling a return to their old range; others argued for a further move to better territory. Kwa had stopped here because there was water in the neighborhood, minimal but for the moment sufficient. He had set camp about an hour's journey away so that game would not be disturbed when they came to drink, and he had hoped for an early kill; but now after several days there had been little sign of a suitable quarry and the band, slowly starving, had been reduced to the meanest of diets.

Each day they set forth, food their total preoccupation. The women, their digging sticks tipped with antelope horn and weighted with a circular stone, went in search of roots, berries, seeds, insects, or any other edible matter. Some distance from camp they had found a few tubers, but these were tough and dried out from the prolonged drought, and the hard ground had cost them two broken horns, a serious loss to a group already in such extremity. The men had been no more fortunate. One day, after a morning of careful stalking, Kwa's cousin had managed a shot at an eland buck, but as he took aim his bow snapped and the game bounded away unharmed. Others had brought in a few birds, a hyrax or two, and a small cobra, the last of which, though considered tasty, was hardly enough to assuage the corporate appetite. Shortly after they made camp, the women discovered a termite nest which provided excellent, albeit insufficient, nourishment, the tiny insects baked in hot ashes and sifted through a sieve of reeds. For the most part, however, they had been obliged to rely upon the carcass of a small antelope that had apparently died of natural causes, the remains of which were rescued from an assembly of vultures before too much damage had been done. In the process three of the birds had been caught and devoured, for there was no disposition to pass up nourishment of any sort save baboons and hyenas, which were taboo.

That incident had taken place several days earlier and nothing had since been added. The evening meal the day before had consisted only of some tough, emaciated tubers, a handful of scorpions, and two small lizards. Time was beginning to run out. The children were listless, their eyes dull, their bellies distended. Adult energies were also flagging. Two of the men had been unable to hunt the day before, and the older women could no longer make the daily trip for food which on each occasion required an ever longer journey.

Kwa was on his feet now, his mind still dwelling on the difficulties of his people. The dim light of the growing dawn revealed the small, slender stature of the hunter. Kwa's legs were slim and wiry, well designed to carry him through the rigors of the long chase, but his belly was bloated like those of the children, distended from a life of alternating feast and famine. His stub-toed feet were small and calloused as were his hands, roughened from years of making and using the stone tools that sustained life. His head was small, too, his face broad and square with wide-set eyes that squinted from long habit. He had cast aside his cloak which also served as a blanket, and he wore only a scrap of animal hide around his loins. These and his weapons were his only possessions. The successful hunter traveled light; moreover, Kwa had no taste for the ostrich egg beads and other decorations fancied by many, and his only ornaments were the small black scars between his eyes—good luck marks for hunting received long ago at the time of his initiation into manhood.

There was no time for reflection on the woes of the past, however, and Kwa's thoughts quickly shifted to more constructive channels. On his return late in the afternoon the day before he had spied the faint trace of giraffe tracks on the other side of the water hole. It appeared to be a small herd, but the marks were reasonably fresh and there was a good chance the beasts might not be too far away. Kwa had a feeling that the luck was about to change—despite the long drought, despite the continued adversity. After coming across the spoor, he had paused to sketch out in the dusty ground a crude picture of the hunter tracking and finally killing an enormous giraffe. He was no artist like those whose work adorned the walls of caves, but his control of magical properties was as sure as any man's. He was certain the magic would work for him today.

There would be no meal this morning, Kwa knew that, so he contented himself with a bit of water from the ostrich egg container, removing the wad of dry grass from the hole, then carefully tilting the container to avoid spilling any of the precious liquid. Next, he moved quietly over to wake young T'kwa. The boy would accompany him today, for, despite his youth, he was the one member of the band whose assistance Kwa most desired, his speed and stamina an ideal complement to the experience and judgment of the older man. Together they sat preparing their weapons, working silently at the familiar but crucial tasks. Kwa checked his bow, then turned attention to his arrows. He would take the usual handful, but today he decided on several jointed specimens, hollow reed shanks into which were fastened slender points made of sharpened ostrich bone. Kwa liked the design, for it enabled him to reverse the bone tips, slipping the sharpened points with their smear of poison into the shank where they would remain out of harm's way until needed. It was a wise precaution, for the poison was a deadly concoction, as deadly to the hunter as to his quarry.

Kwa also carried some arrows with barbed stone tips and these, too, would be smeared with poison which the two hunters now proceeded to prepare. More dangerous to handle, the barbed weapons had the advantage of holding in the wound, thereby giving the poison more effective action. From his kit Kwa took a handful of cocoons and, placing them one by one on a small flat stone, he carefully stripped the covering away until there remained the larval form of a small beetle common in the area. Next, the larvae were rubbed into a powder which was deposited in an empty tortoise shell, and then he and the boy chewed pieces of bark from a species of thorn tree, spitting the juice into the poison dish. Soon they had a clear, sticky fluid which they daubed onto their arrow heads. The mixture thickened as it dried and when all the arrows had been treated, Kwa wound the remainder of the poison like string around a small stick which he placed in his weapons bag along with his arrows. By now the rest of the camp was awake, but there was little to say for everyone knew his job without the need for lengthy explanation. Soon the men were moving off for the day's hunt, the women preparing themselves for their forage, while the older people settled down in camp with the smaller children.

Carrying only their small skin bags and bows slung over their left shoulders, Kwa and his brother walked quickly and silently across the flat, dusty land in the direction of the rising sun. The terrain sloped gradually down to a broad, level plain; far beyond and to the south a line of hills, blue and still in shadow, marked the way from which the band had come in its flight from near disaster. There was no thought of such things now, however—only total concentration on the hunt, sharpened by the nausea and pains of hunger. Suddenly there was movement in the brush ahead. The hunters froze, peering into the brightness of the growing light. They could see nothing. Then there was a loud rustling, and with the disdain of his kind, a porcupine sauntered nonchalantly across their path. Using the heavier stone-tipped arrows, the hunters hit him three times, but the light shafts could not kill at once and the wounded animal scuttled off into some nearby cover. Despite the excitement of an impending meal, pursuit had to be most careful to avoid a volley of quills, and Kwa inched forward, restraining his more impetuous companion. It was a good quarter of an hour of slow and delicate maneuver before they discovered their quarry nestled under a bush, mercifully dead from his wounds.

Quickly, T'kwa gathered firewood while Kwa brought forth his fire sticks. Holding one firmly on the ground with his foot, he twirled the other rapidly between his palms, its point fixed in a notch that had been cut to receive it. Presently there were sparks with which he was able to ignite some dried grass, and soon a small fire was going. This was used not so much to roast their catch as to burn off the hair and quills, however; and once this task had been accomplished, the two famished hunters fell to work, consuming all that the beast had to offer. A short time later, when they had finished, there was little remaining but the charred hide and a greasy skeleton.

Such unexpected good fortune gave them a much needed lift and confirmed Kwa's conviction that their luck had indeed changed. The hunters now continued at a steady pace until they came to the place where Kwa had located the trail the day before. Through the rising heat of the forenoon they tracked their quarry, stopping only once for a brief detour to the water hole. At last, unexpectedly, they came upon the herd, but since they were downwind, it was necessary to make a wide circle in order to escape detection while maneuvering into close range. The circling tactic consumed precious time but the herd remained unaware of danger and at last the hunters began to close in, moving from bush to bush until they were about a hundred paces distant. There were three animals, a big male and two cows, all prime specimens.

One of the females was browsing in some trees slightly apart from the others and it was she that they chose for a target. The hunters separated, making their way closer from two different quarters so that each might have the opportunity for an effective shot. Their plan was executed to perfection. When Kwa was about thirty paces distant, he quietly raised from his crouch and sped an arrow true to the target, striking the huge beast in the flank. The giraffe, turning suddenly, almost ran directly over T'kwa, who was able to score with a shot high up on the shoulder as the stampeding animal rushed past.

This was luck indeed, for two shots would take effect much more quickly than one. Kwa at once sent his brother back to tell the others, then set out in a steady trot to follow the wounded prey. There was no question but that the giraffe was doomed; the poison would see to that. It was merely a matter of how long it would take—how far could she run, would she move into the preserve of another hunting band, or might she be devoured by hyenas before he could locate her? At first she far outdistanced him, but gradually she slowed her pace, winded from her run and forgetful of the cause of her initial fright. Bit by bit, too, the poison began to take its effect, hampering her movement and clouding her senses. She began to move in erratic patterns, running in circles and doubling back on her track. Kwa was able quickly to close the gap and keep the animal under direct observation. She was big and powerful, however, and as the late afternoon deepened into evening it appeared that she was still far from finished.

The darkness and cold of night posed new problems for the naked hunter. Without his cloak he would be most uncomfortable; yet he dared not abandon the chase and risk permanent loss to scavengers. In the dark it would be hard to know where the giraffe was, but he was reasonably certain she would not go too far at night. In this he was mistaken. While Kwa spent the night crouched miserably over a tiny fire, his prey, crazed by the poison, kept moving and with dawn was far away from the hunter. Fortunately, however, she had doubled back toward the base camp, thus bringing her within range of his people. Doggedly he resumed the chase, making only a brief detour for more water. When the sun was at its height, he found her again, the telltale vultures circling overhead greatly easing his task. She stood there, front legs splayed out, head sagging, looking at once formidable and pathetic. Kwa waited, fearing a charge, but the beast was in fact played out. Suddenly she toppled, finally rolling over on her side where she lay quietly awaiting her fate. She would soon have died in any event, but Kwa hastened the end with his spear and at once built a fire to signal his people.

They were not long in coming. Alerted by T'kwa's news, they were ready to break camp at dawn, and gathering their few possessions, they were soon on the march. By the time the smoke from Kwa's fire curled up into the noonday sky, they were only a few miles away, and it was not long thereafter that the first of the men, hurrying ahead, came upon the kill. Others had also been attracted. Wheeling overhead or perched impassively on boulders and branches well out of reach, the vultures waited, while jackals moved about in the bushes, also biding their time. There were no hyenas as yet; they would arrive with the night.

The men ignored these spectators as they fell on their prize with a combination of well-learned discipline and hunger-maddened violence. Several hacked at the hide, slicing it quickly away from the carcass, carving huge chunks of suet as they proceeded and stuffing these into their bulging mouths. Others busied themselves with slitting open the huge belly and bringing forth mounds of reeking entrails, the contents of which were reserved for the women by custom but some of which the butchers consumed as they proceeded. Two men were preoccupied with hacking off the limbs which they attacked with hammers and powerful stone chisels, shattering the bones and causing the much desired marrow to spurt over the workers. Kwa, as the successful hunter and leader of the band, was entitled by custom to a rib on each side and certain sections of the rump. These he had already secured, occasionally tearing at the flesh with his teeth in the process, and his princely share was now spread across several low bushes while his wives finished trimming wooden spits on which to roast the meat. Several fires were now in operation, all surrounded by enthusiastic participants. Every man was turned butcher and each butcher was his own cook, each cook his own diner. Feeding was continuous and gluttonous, meat consumed indiscriminately, some cooked, some raw. Blood and marrow was taken in great draughts to wash down huge chunks of steak or sweetbreads, suet or smoking entrails.

Yet, despite the apparent hysteria of an unrestrained orgy, there was a pattern discernible. The hide was carefully detached and laid aside for later disposition, for this would provide new cloaks, carrying bags, and other utensils. The bladder and stomach were emptied, cleaned, and then filled with blood which was drawn with something like surgical precision. The marrow was collected for cooking, and sinews were detached, later to be used for bowstrings and to bind up hafted tools in need of repair. Those sections of the carcass that went to the women were set aside, while each family proceeded systematically with the business of cutting away its appropriate share, taking care to lay the strips on bushes or hang them in trees where they would be reasonably safe from the growing audience of scavengers. Such precautions were much in order, for the air of excitement seemed to infect the watchers who attempted a number of raids. These, however, were beaten off without difficulty. The insect population could not be dealt with so easily, and the carcass was soon clouded with flies and other species successfully contesting the meal with the members of the band.

Among the hunters the consuming passion was to eat, to fill those tortured, long-denied stomachs until they ached from excess, then to fill them further, as if this were the last meal they would ever know. Arms dripping with gore, bodies covered with grease, sweat, and blood, bellies more bloated than ever, faces shining with a kind of ecstasy, they moved through their exertions relentlessly, almost insectlike, only gradually slowing their pace as the limits of human endurance were approached. One by one they began to drop out. Some lay gasping from sheer exhaustion; others fell asleep in midpassage, their hands and mouths still filled. Still others picked daintily or absently at tidbits, while some turned to the hide to cut a new cloak or weapons bag. The orgy appeared to be burning itself out, but in fact it proved to be but a temporary lull and before long the hardier spirits were demonstrating that the party had just begun. At one side a group of girls began a song, tentatively at first, then louder and with stronger rhythm. Some of the men began to dance, and soon much of the group was engaged in this new revelry.

At first it was a dance of sheer animal satisfaction, but this was a day of epic dimension and the dance now turned to the story of the hunt. Kwa came forward, acting out his role, then his brother followed, while the rest, singing and dancing, lauded the courage and skill of the hunters and the judgment of their leader. As darkness fell the dance continued and the feasting was renewed. It would probably last through the night, here at this new and more fortunate camp site. No doubt in time they would endure the pains of hunger again, but for the moment, at least, all they knew was the joy of being alive.

SUGGESTIONS FOR FURTHER READING

There are ample materials covering early man and his origins in Africa. Among generalized accounts are H. Alimen, *The Prehistory of Africa* (New York: Humanities Press, 1957); C. B. M. McBurney, *The Stone Age of Northern Africa* (Baltimore: Penguin, 1960); Sonia Cole, *The Prehistory of East Africa*, rev. ed. (New York: Mentor, 1965); and two works by J. D. Clark, *The Prehistory of*

Southern Africa (Baltimore: Penguin, 1959) and *The Prehistory of Africa* (New York: Praeger, 1970). See also G. P. Murdock, *Africa: Its Peoples and Their Culture History* (New York: McGraw-Hill, 1959); an article in the *Journal of African History*, vol. 5, no. 2 (1964), by J. D. Clark entitled "The Prehistoric Origins of African Culture"; and a series of articles by L. S. B. Leakey and others in *Tarikh*, vol. 1, no. 3 (1966). More technical materials are available in W. W. Bishop and J. D. Clark, eds., *Background to Evolution in Africa* (Chicago: University of Chicago Press, 1967), along with Professor Clark's *Atlas of African Prehistory* (Chicago: University of Chicago Press, 1967). A stimulating assessment of racial origins in Africa is contained in W. MacGaffey, "Concepts of Race in the Historiography of Northeast Africa," *Journal of African History*, vol. 7, No. 1 (1966).

For human anatomy and evolution there are numerous sources available: for example, B. G. Campbell, *Human Evolution* (Chicago: Aldine, 1966), or Ashley Montagu, *The Human Revolution* (Cleveland: World, 1965). An interesting hypothesis concerning adaptation and skin pigmentation is found in W. F. Loomis, "Skin Pigment Regulation of Vitamin-D Biosynthesis in Man," *Science* (August 4, 1967). Reconstruction of life among the late Pleistocene hunters was drawn from various sources but see particularly I. Schapera, *The Khoisan People of South Africa* (London: George Routledge and Sons, 1930).

Part Two

THE FARMERS

Bronze figure, Dahomey.
Photo courtesy of the author.

3

THE AGRICULTURAL REVOLUTION

The Beginnings of Cultivation

The origin of plant and animal husbandry, perhaps the most portentous step taken by man in the long march of civilization—this epic event is lost in time. Tantalizing bits of evidence survive to sharpen the search and quicken the debate. Here is revealed a potsherd pitted with marks that could have been caused by ancient seeds, or possibly by nothing more than normal weathering. There a stone turns up that might have once pounded grain but might also have been employed merely in the preparation of paints and cosmetics. Again, the past yields a pile of animal bones, tempting one archaeologist to argue the breeding and the slaughter of domesticated stock, another to suggest only a meal taken long ago at the end of a day's hunt. Some students go further, postulating ingenious hypotheses to compensate for deficiencies in material verification. Why, it is asked, could not primitive hunters have gained mastery over wild animals, offering in exchange for servitude a share in the evening supper and the shelter of man's encampment? Might not early man have long ago noted the reproductive qualities of the roots he foraged, the unconsumed remnants, once discarded yet observed to reproduce themselves, now placed in the ground to grow by design? And if language be any criterion, is it not reasonable to infer that this or that people have long since practiced cultivation, proof secure in the existence of agricultural words and phrases traceable to sources many thousands of years old?

Unsupported by tangible evidence, such theories claim an ancient beginning for agriculture, yet archaeology itself has recently extended previous estimates by several thousand years and now suggests that the cultivation of plants and the domestication of animals was first practiced by villagers in the Middle East as long ago as ten thousand years before Christ. For some historical botanists, however, the archaeological evidence, though incontrovertible, is insufficient, and they propose a much more remote antiquity during the later Pleistocene, an era that had previously been established as the exclusive preserve of the hunter-gatherer. The earliest gardens, it is reasoned, originated in a region where a mild climate and adequate rainfall combined to produce a genial environment—a wooded area of lakes and streams producing adequate supplies of fish and game along with freshwater plants suitable for inclusion as forage in a diet that balanced proteins from animal sources with vegetable carbohydrates. When cultivation began, continues the argument, it started not with the seed culture of Middle East cereals, but with wild root and stem sections consciously placed in the ground in the hope they might grow as they had frequently been observed to do when tossed aside as refuse. Such innovators were probably not confirmed hunters, nor were they people whose inventiveness was a desperate response to famine and disease. More likely they were fisherfolk whose basic economy permitted relatively permanent camp sites at which plantings could be supervised, husbanded, and harvested, whose reasonably affluent existence provided leisure time for experimentation— among other things, in agricultural production.

Circumstantial evidence tends to support such a bold hypothesis. Fruit and tuber plant cuttings placed in the ground produce exact replicas of the parent plant rather than offspring governed by genetic variation. Nevertheless, choice of individual plants with desirable characteristics would over time have created favored strains while discouraging others, in the process rendering the chosen specimens dependent upon human cultivation for their continued existence. When it is understood that as far back as 3000 B.C. most modern plant species had already been domesticated, some at levels of refinement far removed from their original form, it is clear that they must have been preceded by a long-lived period of anterior evolutionary development.

Concurrently the taming of beasts might have emerged from the same extended process. The first domestic animals probably were captured when young, possibly from species already living in symbiosis with man as scavengers. If taken sufficiently young, perhaps even suckled with human infants, they could have been tempted to abandon their wild state, a tendency reinforced first by isolation in captivity and then by selective breeding. Used initially as pets, as with the dog, early domesticates were ultimately to be augmented by new types as their utility became apparent in connection with farming. Goats, sheep, pigs, and cattle provided meat, milk, wool, and other products and were grazed in fallow fields or otherwise sustained through the byproducts of an agricultural society.

As their numbers increased, these animals eventually took on religious as well as economic significance—prized for their ceremonial value, slaughtered or milked ritually, and worshiped for their magical, life-giving powers. Like crops, most of the important domestic animal types were already in evidence five thousand years ago, their small number then and since presumptive of an extended period of antecedent trial and error which eliminated undesirables and concluded with a satisfactory and serviceable range of species. Although some experimentation continued into early historical times—witness the domesticated gazelles, monkeys, and hyenas of Old Kingdom Egypt—it seems clear that most of the problems of species selection had already been solved, subsequent efforts being directed toward refinements in breeding within the types already domesticated.

The moist and mild climatic conditions necessary to convert fishermen into farmers existed in Saharan Africa during pluvial periods of the middle and later Pleistocene, making today's forbidding, desiccated wastes a land of meadows interlaced with streams and dotted with lakes. Human habitation did in fact exist near present-day Khartoum at the confluence of the White and Blue Nile and at encampments roughly along the same latitude at Asselar in the full desert of modern Mali and in the Darfur region of the eastern Sudan. Substantial archaeological evidence has established that these sites were occupied by fishing communities approximately six thousand years ago, but no hint of animal or vegetable domestication has yet been uncovered. The people at Khartoum, for example, who have been described as negroid, possessed grinding stones capable of processing grain; yet it would appear that these artifacts were employed only to pulverize red ocher as a paint base. Similarly, the Khartoum pottery, one of the earliest examples to be found in Africa, offers no hint of use for grain storage or other agricultural activity. By 3000 B.C. the Khartoum community had been replaced by newer settlers who kept domestic animals including a dwarf goat; however, at this late stage agricultural production had already manifested itself at a number of locations the world over.

In fact, ethnobotanists have tentatively chosen Southeast Asia as the point of origin for the earliest experiments with plant and animal domestication, and their claims to antiquity exceed by manyfold the relatively recent appearance of the Khartoum fishermen. In like manner, these observers dismiss the earliest farmers of the Middle East as relative latecomers to cultivation, indeed so far removed in time and place from the origins of agriculture as to be grouped more readily with the modern agricultural communities of their own region in terms of crops, animals, and even styles of domestic architecture. Nevertheless, it is at Jericho in ancient Judea, at Jarmo in the hills of Iraq, and at other Middle Eastern sites that the first certain evidence of agricultural activity has been unearthed, with dating that suggests an antiquity of approximately twelve thousand years.

On the flanks of Mount Carmel and at other locations in the hills of Palestine, a people called Natufian inhabited caverns from which they sallied forth to hunt with microlith weapons, using bone hooks and harpoons to take fish from nearby streams. They buried their dead and bedecked themselves with ornaments; more than that, some of them left their caves to gather at the site of Jericho, and there they formed a community, built dwellings made of brick, and surrounded their encampment with massive fortifications that included a stone tower thirty feet high. This architectural prodigy, the earliest known example of its kind and originating as far back as the early tenth millennium before

Christ, extended over an area of approximately ten acres and probably sheltered a population approaching two thousand individuals. The cave-dwelling Natufians were basically a hunter-gatherer people, but they possessed stone sickles and grinders suggestive of agricultural pursuits, although it has been argued that these implements may have been designed for harvesting wild grains rather than the cultivation of domesticated crops.

The settlement at Jericho was something else, however. It is difficult to imagine that a community of such size could have been sustained by hunting and foraging alone; nor would its citizens have been likely to so limit themselves when they already possessed tools for the husbandry and processing of cereals. The level of architecture, moreover, argues an advanced technical sophistication while a population of such density strongly suggests a governmental organization of considerable complexity. The town was located near a permanent spring, and it does not stretch the imagination too much to infer that the site was chosen because of its reliable supply of water, available not only for human consumption but also for support of an established food-producing economy through a system of community-controlled irrigation.

Recent evidence has amply supported these inferences of agricultural activity. Examples of emmer wheat and barley excavated in the earliest archaeological levels at Jericho have been unequivocally identified as cultivated plants—mutants of wild ancestors previously developed elsewhere. It seems highly probable, therefore, that the first experiments in agriculture were made by the Natufians of Mount Carmel and other cave sites and were later brought to the Jordan valley where domesticated grains could have been cultivated more effectively.

While archaeological research has yielded further manifestations of early agricultural enterprise in the Middle East, no comparable material evidence has come out of Africa; yet there are arguments for an ancient, and possibly independent, African agriculture as well. Leaving aside the case of prehistoric Egypt with its probable Middle Eastern connections, Africa offers several regions where cultivated crops appear to have been developed from indigenous wild ancestors. Perhaps foremost among these is the highland area of Ethiopia where soil varieties and climatic conditions have always been auspicious for the development of seed crops, especially the small-seeded cereal grasses known as millets.

In Ethiopia, it is said, was first domesticated an indigenous cereal called teff and, according to some authorities, eleusine, pearl millet, and parent strains of sorghum, many of these grains subsequently spreading eastward to India and northern China. The Abyssinian plateau may also have been the birthplace of certain peas, beans, and lentils and varieties of tea, coffee, cress, and mustard. Certainly it is the point of origin for the bananalike ensete plant which flourished in the highland environment and has never been utilized elsewhere as a food crop. Ethiopia, moreover, was once thought to have been a center of domestication for barley and particular species of wheat; recent estimates, however, have assigned the highland plateau the role of an early point of dispersion, the species of wheat and barley presumably introduced from their Middle Eastern sources via Egypt and the Red Sea.

A less important place of early cultivation is the high plains region of East Africa, credited with producing only a small number of indigenous millets. Far more interesting is the claim of the West African savanna as one of the world's major cradles of agricultural activity, a center of considerable antiquity and perhaps of independent development as well. Here was the birthplace of several millets, notably fonio, an important grain in the western Sudan from Cape Verde to Lake Chad but elsewhere unknown, and here was developed a native rice, *Oryza glaberrima,* which later was abandoned in favor of an Asian strain introduced by European mariners in the fifteenth and sixteenth centuries A.D. Here, too, is the home of a number of sorghums as well as the Guinea yam, a plant of long-lived cultivation still widely in use today.

Precisely when these plants were domesticated is still a matter of dispute. It is claimed, for example, that the Guinea yam came south from the savanna to the West African forest about four thousand years ago along with peoples fleeing before the growing desiccation of the Saharan regions. These groups were still basically hunters, fishermen, and foragers, but they possessed heavy stone picks which may have been developed initially for digging wild tubers but which would have been excellent tools for yam culture. When they moved into the moist and fertile rain forest, they could have been stimulated to begin genuine cultivation of the semidomesticated yam, thereby producing an early and independent agricultural economy for West Africa.

The West African rice *Oryza glaberrima* also appears to have originated in the savanna—in Senegambia and the lake country of the upper Niger River valley—but the dating of approximately 1500 B.C. shows it as a late development, a good thousand years after rice culture had started in China and India and far later than the 5000 B.C. which has sometimes been claimed as the beginning date for independent agriculture in West Africa. For this last date the argument is essentially circumstantial. Along with rice, a number of millets—fonio in particular —seem to have originated in the Niger and Senegal watersheds, some of these later spreading eastward in a thinning wave along the southern edge of the desert. Such a distribution has suggested for some observers a movement of agricultural practice from west to east rather than the reverse and, by the end of the fourth millennium before Christ, the establishment across the savanna of a cereal cultivation dominated by millets. Since Egyptian barley and wheat are scarcely to be found within the Sudanic belt, the conclusion has been that this agricultural development took place independently of Egypt and probably in the western savanna, dating from approximately the early sixth millennium B.C.

Arrayed against this hypothesis are the views of most archaeologists to the effect that agriculture came to Africa from the Middle East, moving across Sinai and establishing itself in the delta region of Lower Egypt by the late sixth or early fifth millennium of the pre-Christian era. It then presumably made its way up the fertile Nile valley to the eastern Sudan whence it was diffused across the savanna to West Africa. This theory is based largely on the tangible evidence provided by archaeological excavations. Material indication of agriculture is available for the lower reaches of the Nile by the middle of the fifth millennium and for the upper Nile at the site of Khartoum by the late fourth millennium. Direct evidence for West Africa is lacking before the early first-millennium sites of the Nok culture located near the Jos plateau of northern Nigeria; but diggings in that area have not been extensive in the past, and earlier datings may eventually come to light. In view of the information presently available, there is some consensus among archaeologists and historical botanists in favor of agricultural beginnings along the West African savanna during the third millennium B.C.

Despite the qualifications put forward by archaeological research, there still remains the suspicion of an independent, and much earlier, beginning for agriculture in Africa. In the first place, the variety of domesticated crops that seem to have originated in Africa and the degree of evolution that many of these show imply a long period of indigenous development, much longer than archaeological evidence alone has thus far been able to sustain. Furthermore, the knowledge within Africa of certain agricultural techniques does not readily fit the hypothesis that agriculture arrived first from an outside, presumably Middle Eastern, source. It is easy to understand that the concept of crop cultivation might have entered the Sudan unaccompanied by the examples of Egyptian wheat and barley since these cereals were not suited to the Sudanic climate; at the same time, wheat-farming methods clearly could have been borrowed and applied to the cultivation of savanna millets. Much more difficult to explain is the case of West African rice, an admittedly indigenous plant first domesticated through wet cultivation, a technique so unlike wheat culture that it must be regarded as a local invention.

The complexities inherent in establishing origins for plant domestication are well illustrated by the example of cotton. The oldest surviving specimen of cultivated cotton consists of a few fragments of cloth manufactured at Mohenjo-Daro in the Indus River valley approximately five thousand years ago. These remnants resemble present-day coarse versions of the species *Gossypium arboreum* which is the basic strain for most cottons now being grown in Africa, India, China, and the Middle East. At the same time, it is generally agreed that the ancestor of all cultivated cottons is *Gossypium anomalum*, a plant native to Africa and still to be found in its wild state along the edges of the Sahara and Kalahari deserts of northern and southern Africa. Clearly, therefore, although the cotton plant originated in Africa, there remain the formidable questions of how it spread to the Indus River region of modern West Pakistan, where it was first domesticated, and when.

It appears that *Gossypium arboreum* was not the first cultivated cotton since it is itself a derivative of an older domesticate, *Gossypium herbaceum*, now to be found widely scattered across the African savanna, southern Arabia, the Middle East, and western India. Many botanists believe that cultivated *Gossypium herbaceum* was first derived solely from the wild *Gossypium anomalum* of southern Africa, but the considerable genetic and morphological differences between the wild and the cultivated plant required an intermediate stage to secure a plausible evolutionary development from *anomalum* to *herbaceum*. Such a link has been suggested—*Gossypium herbaceum africanum*, a crude lint-bearing plant growing wild from Ngamiland in Botswana to southern Mozambique and bearing the necessary family resemblances to its parent, *Gossypium anomalum*, and its derivative, *Gossypium herbaceum*. Since *africanum* never seems to have spread naturally from its limited range in southern Africa, and since the *herbaceums* have existed only as cultivated plants in their present locations, it follows that *Gossypium herbaceum africanum* must have migrated northward, either under cultivation or as a seed transported by human carrier, subsequently to give rise to the various *herbaceum* variations now extant.

For *africanum* to have migrated northward under cultivation would require the existence of agriculture in southern Africa of very ancient derivation—considerably earlier than the 3000 B.C. date of the Mohenjo-Daro specimens. Presently available archaeological evidence, however, does not sustain the existence of agriculture in the southern reaches of the continent before the early centuries of the Christian era, nor does the fact that the area had long been the exclusive habitat of later Pleistocene hunting peoples, the most recent representative of which is the San (Bushman) of historical times. Equally difficult to envision is the alternative theory that seeds were transported northward either by indigenous hunters who would have had no apparent interest in them or by outsiders. It has been suggested that in fact traders from the Middle East and India came to the East African coast seeking gold and brought the seeds home with them. Such a proposition appears unlikely. Ancient as the Indian Ocean trade surely was, there is no direct evidence of its existence before the early Christian era, and an antiquity extending beyond the early third millennium before Christ seems highly problematical.

The difficulties presented by southern Africa as a source for domesticated cotton have led to another, quite different, hypothesis supporting the Abyssinian plateau as the point of origin for cotton cultivation. An indigenous Ethiopian cotton, *Gossypium herbaceum* variation *acerfolium* has now been put forward in its ancestral form as the parent of both southern Africa's *Gossypium herbaceum africanum* and the *Gossypium herbaceum* varieties from which later developed the *Gossypium arboreum* of Mohenjo-Daro. The argument suggests that the favorable conditions of the Ethiopian highlands attracted numerous wild cotton species including *Gossypium anomalum* which eventually served as the basis of domestication. In time the domesticated plant evolved and migrated, one strain making its way to southern Africa where it reverted to a wild state as *Gossypium herbaceum africanum*, another becoming the local domesticate, *Gossypium herbaceum acerfolium*, while still others evolved into the *herbaceums* which are today spread from the West African savanna to India. The Mohenjo-Daro cotton could have been a consequence of this migration, for both genetically and morphologically it closely resembles the *Gossypium herbaceum acerfolium* of Ethiopia. Such a theory, of course, requires a very ancient beginning for agriculture in Africa. At present it totally lacks support from archaeological sources; yet while those sources may be nonexistent or irretrievably buried, their absence apparently cannot stifle the recurrent conjecture concerning the antiquity of Africa's agricultural beginnings.

Similar uncertainties surround the question of animal domestication. At one time it was thought that the pastoralist occupied a transitional position between the hunter and the husbandman, but more recent hypotheses now favor the priority of the latter. The first taming of herd animals apparently was effected by sedentary cultivators, particularly grain farmers who possessed the necessary feed. Cattle-keeping nomads then emerged somewhat later, living on the margins of agricultural areas and developing their well-known symbiotic relationship. Authorities differ over the location of initial domestication of livestock, but many favor Middle East locations such as Jarmo and Jericho which have provided the earliest archaeologically demonstrable evidence of crop cultivation. As a region of agricultural origins, the Middle East is frequently defined to include the Egyptian Nile valley, considered by many to be approximately contemporary with Palestinian sites, but the remainder of the African continent is generally regarded as having achieved the domestication of livestock at a later time, the idea presumably having reached out through diffusion from Egypt.

Unlike plant cultivation, the domestication of animals in Africa has always been severely circumscribed by disease, particularly varieties of trypanosomiasis, or sleeping sickness, carried by the tsetse fly. Today sleeping sickness is endemic in large areas of the equatorial rain forest and adjacent savanna country, although elevated regions like the high plains of East Africa or the Abyssinian plateau are largely spared. The disease does not thrive in arid latitudes and is consequently absent from southern Africa as well as the territories above the fifteenth parallel north. In times past, particularly during the so-called Makalian wet phase which held sway from approximately 5500 B.C. to 2500 B.C., parts of the Sahara were moister and it is estimated that the tsetse fly was able to range at that time as far as 18°N and to engulf most of the Ethiopian plateau, thereby ruling out cattle herding throughout much of the continent lying below what is today the central Sahara.

These circumstances lend force to the contention that the concept of animals tamed for domestic purposes came from outside Africa, introduced initially via Egypt. Of the tsetse-free regions, North Africa shows no evidence of having preceded Egypt in this respect, while sites in the full interior of the Sahara with their rock painting representations of large herds of cattle have not yet yielded dates by carbon 14 techniques earlier than the mid-fourth millennium B.C. At various locations in the Sahara and North Africa, rock drawings indicate an early presence of domestic goats, sheep, cattle, swine, and dogs, but all these species had already been flourishing in Egypt or the Middle East from considerably earlier times. It is reasonable to conclude, therefore, that these creatures, along with the concept of animal husbandry, must have entered Africa by way of Sinai to begin a continental diffusion from the valley of the Nile.

The Valley of the Nile

The Nile begins in two great lakes. The parent White Nile commences its 3,500-mile journey as it leaves the vast but shallow Lake Victoria, its early course marked by a series of falls, its middle passage a slow drift toward the sea across the sun-parched plains of the southern Sudan. Six thousand feet up on the Ethiopian plateau the Blue Nile slips unobtrusively out of Lake Tana, then descends in a sudden rush as the hurtling waters rip a great gash across the ancient plateau, gouging a wide loop along a deepening trench 450 miles long to spill out on the Sudanese plains. Farther on, at the site of Khartoum, the Blue Nile joins

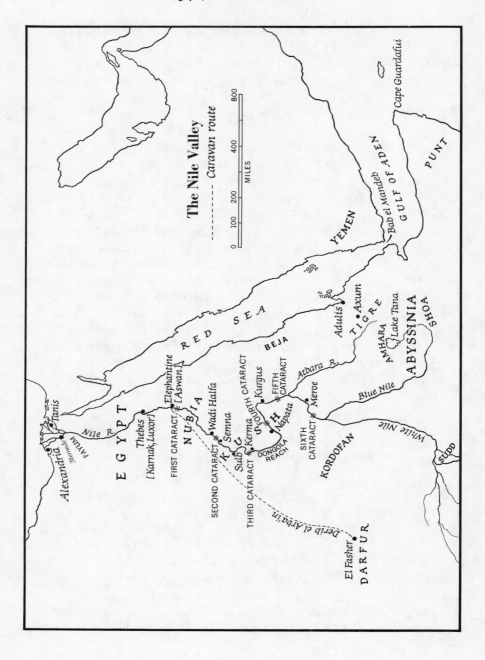

The Nile Valley

--------- *Caravan route*

800

400

200

100

0

MILES

its more sedate companion, the waters at first flowing side by side, then commingling in their journey northward to the Mediterranean Sea more than 1,700 miles away.

Climate and topography have determined the vastly different character of these two streams. It is only during the dry months of winter and early spring that the waters merge quietly at Khartoum, for in June the monsoon season arrives in Ethiopia, quickly converting the Blue Nile into a rushing torrent which rudely jostles the White Nile at the confluence, backing up her waters and thrusting forward with its hundred-thousands of tons of earth and stone ground out of the Ethiopian highland mass. It is the Blue Nile that, before the construction of the high dam, provided over two-thirds of the approximately seven hundred million cubic meters of water that each day moved past Aswan at the height of the seasonal flood, the White Nile contributing only 10 or 12 percent and the Atbara tributary which joins the Nile above Khartoum accounting for the rest. During the dry months the proportions are reversed. The Atbara shrinks to a dry bed dotted with occasional pools, the Blue Nile furnishes but 17 percent of the flow, and the White Nile comes into its own with 83 percent; but now the total at Aswan dwindles to a daily discharge of only forty-five million cubic meters. Fed by the year-round equatorial rains descending upon the Lake Victoria watershed, the White Nile maintains a steady annual flow, but it is the turbulent Blue Nile and the Atbara, both rising in the Abyssinian plateau, that have so profoundly shaped the geography and the economy of the Nile valley and thereby the history of its people.

In their approach to Khartoum, the two river branches converge across a basin floored by ancient metamorphic rock, moving northward through a region of steadily increasing aridity and mind-blurring heat. Beyond the confluence the waters enter the fullness of the desert, tracing a tortuous course between occasional hills and over granite outcrops which six times cause cataracts to interrupt the smooth passage of the river. At Aswan the last of these rocky barriers is now flooded by damming; to the north the Nile proceeds through the desert of historic Egypt, finally spilling into the Mediterranean Sea across the broad triangle of heavy black silt which the Greeks called the Delta.

In this final Egyptian passage the river has cut a channel into the soft limestone beds that lie beyond Aswan, and over time this passage has been covered by a thickening carpet of alluvial deposits brought by flood waters spreading over the valley floor and dropping their heavy load of silt carried two thousand miles from the hills of Abyssinia. The valley varies in width, usually between ten and fifteen miles but occasionally as much as thirty. On either side is a low line of cliffs a few hundred feet high which marks the desert's edge. Beyond lies the waterless desolation of rock and sand, of blinding heat by day and biting nighttime cold, which has defied human habitation for almost five millennia. From the First Cataract at Aswan to the Delta the river valley winds thinly across some seven hundred miles of wasteland, its narrow course comprising less than 4 percent of the total land mass of modern Egypt. Here is crowded 99 percent of the population, sustained by a soil of unparalleled richness, which in its time served as the basis for one of the world's great civilizations and, according to many observers, the very source of agriculture in Africa.

As a product of the late Pleistocene, the Nile in its present form is no older than *Homo sapiens*; yet its course below the First Cataract was well established by the time man in any numbers began to frequent the Nile valley. The first visitors would have found it difficult terrain—a heavy jungle of tangled reeds and brush fanning out along each side of the river in lowland swamps that supported a heavy population of faunae featuring aquatic birds, amphibious reptiles, and tropical insects. Such forbidding territory held no charms for hunters, who were content to remain on the plateau beyond the cliffs. There, during the millennia of the Sahara's wet phases, lakes and streams provided the enterprising fisherman with an ample catch and the patient bowman with many a kill from the plentiful herds that came to drink.

As the Sahara approached its most recent level of desiccation by the mid-third millennium before Christ, there was a shrinkage of the shallow basin lakes and the streams that crossed the plateau to cut through the Nile's cliffs on their way to the great river. Slowly but inexorably, grassy valleys frequented by antelope, wild sheep, and their predators degenerated into stony ravines, or wadis, that were watered only seasonally and then not at all, while the florae and faunae that had favored these places abandoned the lifeless desert and crowded into the valley floor. Man, too, came with the rest, this one-time Saharan fisherman, hunter, and forager, now at the time of the encroaching drought becoming a cultivator as well.

There is more than coincidence to account for such a momentous development. In the first place, it was during these same times that the Natufians were growing crops and building cities in Judea. The record of their attempts at cultivation as early as the tenth millennium B.C. precedes by several thousand years the first known agricultural settlements in the Nile region, an interval that easily accommodates the diffusion of the idea of cultivation across the few hundred miles separating the Nile Delta from the shores of Palestine. Moreover, domestication of plants and animals could have occurred independently along the Nile, once the incentive took hold. The wadis leading into the river valley had long supported wild grasses, and these might have included the ancestors of what were to become the domestic cereals of ancient Egypt.

The earliest evidence of agricultural activity in the Nile region comes from the Fayum, a shallow depression in the desert on the western side of the river valley just south of the Delta. There, by the mid-fifth millennium before Christ, on the shore of an ancient lake and along the wadis, small settlements of people had gathered, presumably part of an accelerating flight from the encroaching desert. While they were basically hunters and fishermen, they also raised barley and emmer wheat, crops already under cultivation in the Middle East; but in the Fayum these cereals mutated rapidly, indicating perhaps that they had been introduced from elsewhere. Logic suggests that there were possibly earlier farming settlements in the area, corresponding more closely in time to the Natufians of Palestine, but any that might have existed, especially on the more accessible Delta, are now irretrievably buried beneath heavy accumulations of silt, and in any case their remains could scarcely have survived decomposition in such a moist environment. At the same time logic compels the thought that successful hunters would not have abandoned the Sahara zone until driven by the onset of desiccation which developed after the beginning of the fifth millennium B.C. It seems probable, therefore, that the excavated Fayum communities are indeed among the earliest examples in Africa of man's response to that particular force of necessity which compelled the invention or adoption of food-producing techniques in support of gradually failing supplies provided by hunting and foraging.

In any event, these first farmers did cultivate cereals which they reaped with serrated stone sickles fixed in straight wooden shafts. They raised flax which was used for the manufacture of linen and probably kept goats, sheep, and cattle, although the evidence in this instance is equivocal. Grain was stored in underground silos lined with matting, and flour was prepared by stone grinders and cooked in clay pots which also served for storage and dishware. Very fine baskets were woven, and there is evidence that skins were used for clothing, although the coarse linen produced may also have answered this purpose. Though still firmly fixed in a hunting and fishing economy, these early Egyptians had taken the first tentative step toward agriculture, a step that was destined to produce first an economic and then a cultural revolution for the ancient Nile valley.

Other settlements followed, hesitant yet portentous. Hundreds of years passed, and then at Merimde on the southwest edge of the Delta a small village appeared and flourished. It covered only five or six acres and consisted initially of flimsy shelters later replaced by crude oval mud huts probably roofed with reed mats and arranged in rows as if to suggest some sort of street system. Arrowheads and fishhooks bear witness to the nature of the basic economy, but from the first these people raised barley and emmer, grew flax for textile manufacture, and kept domestic pigs, cattle, and sheep or goats. The cultivated plots were probably tiny, for there is no evidence that drainage or irrigation was practiced, and clearing land on any scale would surely have presented technical problems beyond the material equipment of this civilization.

During much these same times other villages came into existence at sites along the edge of the Nile valley from the Delta region of Lower Egypt as far as Upper Egypt and Nubia in the south. These may be compared with each other in several respects. First, their inhabitants showed physical characteristics that probably reflected a mix of Middle Eastern, Mediterranean, and African populations; yet their development during these early times appears to have been little affected by outside influences. Second, these cultures succeeded or overlapped one another throughout the centuries with a steadily rising sophistication in the techniques and the arts of civilization, thereby clearly preparing the way for the entrance of dynastic Egypt at the close of the fourth millennium. Finally, as the phenomenal food-producing capability of the Nile floodplain began to assert itself, the appearance of these communities was accompanied by a dramatic rise in population, its density now manifest "in terms of men to the square mile rather than square miles to the man," to borrow a felicitous phrase.*

From modern excavated type-sites comes a series of names to identify these village cultures—Tasian, Badarian, Amratian (Naqada I), and Gerzean (Naqada II). The Tasians were probably the earliest, appearing, as with Merimde, during the early fourth millennium and like the latter supplementing their hunting and fishing economy with a primitive agriculture. In time, the Tasians were succeeded by the Badarians who built upon the culture their predecessors had inaugurated in Middle Egypt. Their pottery was much more skillfully crafted, and they manufactured flasks, vases, ladles, and jewelry of finely carved ivory. More than this, they imported woods, shells, and minerals such as turquoise and malachite, this early evidence of trade and economic specialization emphasized by a corresponding interest in boat design.

The Badarians had begun to use copper, chiefly for simple ornaments, and this early knowledge of metallurgy was picked up and improved upon by the Amratian culture which followed in Middle and Upper Egypt. The Amratians produced small copper tools, cut and hammered into shape, for casting was as yet unknown; and they designed papyrus boats, intensifying the trade begun by the Badarians, in this connection possibly domesticating the donkey for overland travel. Judging from imports such as juniper berries and certain types of timber, there were Amratian contacts with the Middle East, and it was during the Amratian era that the Nile population began to expand precipitously, numerous permanent communities appearing up and down the river valley, although none has yet been found in the Delta region of Lower Egypt.

Eventually the Amratians gave way to a Gerzean culture which accelerated activities already under way, introduced refinements of its own, and brought the Nile valley to the point of recorded history which begins with the unification of Egypt under the pharaohs of the Old Kingdom. It was the Gerzeans who finally abandoned combined hunting

* R. Oliver and J. D. Fage, *A Short History of Africa*, 3rd ed., p. 23.

and farming in favor of an economy based essentially on agriculture. It was in Gerzean times that techniques of metallurgy were fully mastered with the development of cast copper implements such as adzes, axes, needles, fishhooks, and knives. The Gerzeans, moreover, greatly expanded previous commercial contacts with the outside world as numerous foreign materials came into local demand, for example, copper from Sinai and the eastern desert or lapis lazuli, the Asian source of which suggests ever closer contacts with the Middle East. The Gerzean settlements were larger and more populous than their predecessors, the architecture more splendid, boasting houses made of brick and embellished with wooden door and window frames. Grave sites indicate that these were times of a growing class system in which wealth and position set apart an incipient aristocracy from the peasant farmer. Finally, two major developments appear to have emerged during these final prehistoric years. One was the inauguration of irrigation practices with their implication of political control and coordination on behalf of economic objectives. The other was the appearance of writing, its source and moment of origin still a mystery, for it was already developed well beyond the stage of primitive beginnings by the onset of historical times.

Indeed, the genesis and makeup of the very people who lived in these early Nile valley communities remains conjectural. On the site of Khartoum at the confluence of the White and Blue Nile, a village culture existed in the late fourth millennium that utilized a type of stone bead quarried far to the west in the Saharan mountains of Tibesti and also found in the Fayum settlements of the early fourth millennium. This Khartoum culture was preceded on the same site by the earlier fishing communities dating from the beginning of the fourth millennium which produced pots of a design found two thousand miles to the west in the full Sahara of southern Algeria. Some have argued that various early Egyptians like the Badarians probably migrated northward from Nubia, while others see a wide-ranging movement of peoples across the breadth of the Sahara before the onset of desiccation. Whatever may be the origins of any particular people or civilization, however, it seems reasonably certain that the predynastic communities of the Nile valley were essentially indigenous in culture, drawing little inspiration from sources outside the continent during the several centuries directly preceding the onset of historical times.

Middle Eastern influences nevertheless seem to have found their way to Egypt at the end of the predynastic era, very probably brought in along the increasingly active trade routes. On linguistic evidence, the concept of writing appears to be possibly of Semitic origin, while certain architectural and artistic motifs argue a derivation from the civilization of Mesopotamia in the Tigris-Euphrates valley. It seems unlikely, however, that external factors produced the sudden emergence of Egyptian civilization at the end of the fourth millennium before Christ. Much more probable is the image of a long, slow buildup during predynastic times, reaching a critical point in development in the Gerzean era, then swiftly accelerating its accomplishments along with its appetite for new ideas, domestic and foreign. In any event, the arrival of outside influences coincided with the cultural flowering, political organization, and economic progress that characterized the unification of Upper and Lower Egypt and the inauguration of the great civilization of pharaonic times. For two thousand years this civilization brightened the ancient world with its artistic and scientific successes, but always its wealth of power and achievement was rooted securely in the rich silt of the Nile valley, the source of all life in an otherwise dead land.

In pharaonic Egypt the narrow green ribbon of fertility twisting across the desert supported not a mere minimum of human subsistence, but many times the demands of bare necessity, the surplus siphoned away in taxation to be converted into military might, artistic creation, or personal wealth by an aristocracy that provided the peasant in return with the security and stability he needed to tend his fields. It was an exchange, perhaps, of doubtful equity, but withal it has undergirded the civilization and guided the history of Egypt from that day to this.

Until very recently, moreover, the techniques of cultivation had not greatly changed from those employed by the peasants who worked the fields during the six dynasties of the Old Kingdom. The Egyptian calendar, probably invented in early dynastic times, started the year in mid-July, but it was late May or early June that really initiated the working cycle of the Nile valley with the first rise of the waters at Aswan. By September the monsoon rains of Ethiopia had brought a twenty-five-foot crest to the cataract at Aswan; thereafter the river receded quickly then fell gradually to its seasonal low directly before the onset of the ensuing annual flood.

It was of utmost importance that the proper level be achieved, for an eccentric flood meant disaster. Only three feet above average brought a 20 percent increase in the volume of flow with consequent destruction of dikes and systems of catchment and drainage. Thirty inches below normal brought hardship, but not catastrophe; sixty inches, however, cut the harvest by a fifth and meant famine. At the First Cataract near Aswan a king of the Third Dynasty has left an inscription recording the agony of the river's failure:

> Grain is very scarce, vegetables are lacking altogether, everything that men eat for food has come to an end, and now every man attacks his neighbour. The men who want to walk cannot move, the child wails, the young man drags his body about, and the hearts of the older men are crushed with despair. Their legs give way under them, they sink down on the ground, and they clutch their bodies with their hands. The nobles have no counsel to give, and there is nothing to be obtained from the storehouses but wind. Everything is in a state of ruin.

In normal times, however, the rising tide, heavy with its burden of silt, was permitted to overflow the river banks, spreading broadly across the valley floor to form a huge but shallow lake. At ground level a distant figure appeared to walk across the waters and villages seemed like isolated islands, but in fact the inundation was regulated by dikes and canals. The waters were guided into great catchment basins where they were held for distribution among surrounding plots. As they rested, their moisture refreshed and regenerated the parched earth and their suspended silt slowly settled to renew the fertility of the fields. Elevated ground was serviced mechanically, two men with a shallow reed basket rhythmically swinging water from one channel to a higher; or the shadoof—a leather bucket on the end of a long, counterweighted pole swiveling between two posts—could and did lift hundreds of tons of water to inaccessible terraces. Finally, the waters were permitted to drain back to the river, washing away accumulations of salt as they did, and the farmer now waited for his fields to dry out so that planting might begin.

By early November, as soon as the moist soil could bear the weight of man and animal, the sowing commenced. It was rudimentary but effective. The farmers moved forward about four yards apart spreading the seed by broadcast, then raking it into the soil by dragging branches across the wet mud. The fields were also trampled by small herds of pigs or sheep and sometimes subjected to shallow plowing with wooden hoes pulled by cattle, later models being provided with low handles to assist the farmer in controlling the instrument. During this growing season the men lived in the fields in crude reed huts, tending their livestock along with their crops. Though there may have been some quick-maturing crops, the main harvest took place in the spring, reaping done with serrated flint sickles, the ears of grain cut off and placed in bags, the straw rooted up for fodder. Threshing was accomplished through oxen and donkeys trampling the grain which was then stored in brick silos floored with lime to guard against rats. After harvest, the earth lay black and bare, hard, dry mud flats cracking under a blazing sun. This was the house season when it was too hot to be outdoors; but with the inundation life stirred again, the rats were seen running along the dikes, and all prepared for the coming season.

The slack months were the time for repairs to the system of canals and dikes, as well as for a forced stint on the construction sites of the great royal tombs. There was other work to be done as well—house building and renovation, domestic crafts, truck gardening and care of orchards, and of course the tending of livestock. These domestic animals represented an important element of farm life. There were cattle, both short- and longhorn, the oxen used for draft power, the cows for meat and dairy products. Sheep and goats were common, and donkeys had become a regular means of transport by the First Dynasty. Dogs were part of every farm, but pigs apparently were restricted to the Delta region and were generally taboo elsewhere. Hens, geese, ducks, and peacocks were bred for flesh and eggs, and these enterprising Old Kingdom farmers conducted a number of exotic experiments in domestication—for example, the forced fattening of hyenas like Strasbourg geese. Camels appear to have been known from early times but never came into general use until the era of the Arab invasions during the seventh century after Christ. Horses arrived from the East, also through invasion, introduced by the Hyksos midway in the second millennium B.C., their initial duties limited to drawing war chariots. The extent of cattle culture is attested to by many statistics, of which one may suffice as illustration. During the Fifth Dynasty, an important royal official controlled 834 oxen, 220 cows and calves, 760 donkeys, 674 sheep, and 2,234 goats.

The African Harvest

The dramatic outburst of agricultural production in the Nile valley of Egypt was far from characteristic of Africa, taken as a whole. The fertile alluvial deposits of the Nile floodplain were scarcely typical of soil quality across the continent, indigenous crops were not prepossessing in number and variety, while several of the most successfully domesticated plants appear to have originated in other parts of the world. Although it is possible that emmer wheat derived from a wild variety growing on the edge of the Nile valley, more likely it came from the Middle East. Barley conceivably could have reached Egypt from Abyssinia, but it now appears, like wheat, to have a Middle Eastern source. Cotton was an indigenous African plant, to be sure, but may not in fact have been cultivated in Africa until late in the pre-Christian era when it was introduced to Axum and Meroe through the Indian Ocean trade. West Africa possessed the oil palm, an indigenous rice, and its local species of yam, while various millets originated in the sub-Saharan savanna and along the high plains of East Africa. Ethiopia is the acknowledged birthplace only of ensete and the cereal known as teff. A few additional plants round out this slender battery which clearly required support from outside sources, but support was slow in coming to a continent largely isolated from the rest of the world after the decline of the ancient Egyptian and Mediterranean civilizations.

Very probably the first imports appeared along the East African coast as a result of Indian Ocean commerce. Cotton cloth from India had arrived by the first century after Christ and presumably gave rise to the cultivation in East Africa of the cotton plant *Gossypium arboreum indicum* which had been developed in western India. Cotton was accompanied by certain beans and peas, cucumber, ginger, hemp, and mangoes, while at the same time these very trade routes were the means by which the African millets found their way eastward to the Indian peninsula and beyond.

The Indian Ocean was also the avenue along which important plants from Southeast Asia traveled to Africa, carried presumably by Indonesian islanders during the early centuries of the Christian era. These intrepid mariners appear to have made the ocean passage to East Africa via India and southern Arabia, eventually ranging as far south as Madagascar which they colonized permanently. Merging with the local population, they contributed elements of their language and the design of their outrigger canoes to the subsequent Malagasy civilization, but there is no similar genetic or cultural evidence of their arrival on mainland East Africa. Nevertheless, that they passed along the coast is virtually without dispute for they left behind cultivated Malaysian plants of signal importance to the subsequent development of African agricultural societies. The closely related banana and plantain, along with the taro, or cocoyam, were brought from the East, and soon after their arrival these crops began a wide-ranging spread across tropical Africa where they became established dietary staples, particularly in the equatorial forest regions.

After these introductions along the East African coast, there was a lull of a thousand years and more until the era of European exploration brought new imports from the Americas and from the East. Initially, the chief agents were Portuguese naval squadrons whose early coastal reconnaissance and colonizing efforts offered splendid opportunities for the introduction of new plants. From the East Indies they brought Asian varieties of rice and yams, both of which gained popularity in West Africa, particularly the rice *Oryza sativa* which replaced the less widely adaptable indigenous West African strain *Oryza glaberrima.*

It was the western regions, however, chiefly tropical America, that contributed the most impressive additions to the African food complex. Sugarcane, although Asian in origin, nevertheless entered West Africa from Madeira and was responsible for creating the plantation economy of São Tomé island. The Portuguese planted citrus groves at a number of coastal points although lemons, limes, and oranges were already prevalent in the savanna, probably brought initially by Arab traders. Pineapple, papaya, guava, and avocado were introduced from the equatorial latitudes of the New World, arriving via the burgeoning trade that involved West Africa, the Americas, and Europe. The Portuguese were concerned with the development of fresh foods for their new settlements in West Africa as well as provisions for the long sea voyages east and west. Not surprisingly, the crops they introduced soon took hold among the indigenous populations and became part of the basic local diet. This was especially true of maize, which developed into a staple across tropical Africa, of the sweet potato which quickly moved inland from its points of entry along the West African coast, of peanuts which spread throughout the dry savanna from Cape Verde to Lake Chad, and of cassava, or manioc, which made its greatest inroads within the Congo watershed.

The history of manioc in Africa is particularly instructive of the manner in which African societies absorbed and utilized new crops to support or to replace the basic diet. By the sixteenth century, Portuguese slavers were using manioc meal obtained in the New World to feed their cargoes and crews headed for the Americas, any surplus being sold in Angola where it had a developing popularity. Within a hundred years, manioc had come under cultivation in northern Angola and the western Congo, supplementing millet, bananas, and yams, its attractiveness resting in part on its resistance to attack by locusts. Indeed, its growing demand was linked not so much to its nutritional assets, which were minimal, as to its convenience in cultivation. Through parts of the Katanga it was prized as a hedge against famine since it could be harvested at the end of the dry season. The Bisa nation east of Lake Bangweulu favored manioc because it sustained population expansion, although the neighboring Bemba found the crop insubstantial and continued to rely upon their basic millets.

In Barotseland, manioc became a staple; by contrast, the peoples of the Rift Valley gave it scant attention, preferring maize, or, in the case of the Baganda and others living north of Lake Victoria, the banana and plantain. Manioc was early introduced into West Africa but made little headway in the face of competition with yams, maize, and sweet potatoes until the onset of colonialism in the nineteenth century. By mid-century, Yoruba returning to the west coast from Brazil helped stimulate interest in manioc, but a more important factor was the pressure placed upon traditional agricultural production by the increase in trade and the rise in population that accompanied colonial administrative control. Overworked soils could no longer sustain the older crops, particularly yams, and manioc proved to be a convenient substitute. With the rise of cities, moreover, and their growing populations of men working and living away from home and family, manioc meal grew in popularity as a cheap and easily prepared food. But these are changes more keyed to the recent revolution of modernization in Africa than to the long-lived rhythm of traditional African economies.

SUGGESTIONS FOR FURTHER READING

The origin of agriculture has been the subject of much speculation and spirited debate. For a general introduction to the subject, see Carl O. Sauer, *Agricultural Origins and Dispersals*, 2nd ed. (Cambridge, Mass.: M.I.T. Press, 1969), and F. E. Zeuner, *A History of Domesticated Animals* (New York: Harper and Row, 1963). For Africa, J. D. Clark, *The Prehistory of Africa* (New York: Praeger, 1970), sums up the most recent scholarly estimates, but this may be supplemented by a number of sources: for example, G. P. Murdock, *Africa: Its Peoples and Their Culture History* (New York: McGraw-Hill, 1959); the papers and proceedings of the Third Conference on African History and Archaeology, 1961, contained in the *Journal of African History*, vol. 3, no. 2 (1962); "Speculations on the Economic Prehistory of Africa" by Christopher Wrigley in the *Journal of African History*, vol. 1, no. 2 (1960); R. Mauny, "L'Afrique et les origines de la domestication," in W. W. Bishop and J. D. Clark, eds., *Background to Evolution in Africa* (Chicago: University of Chicago Press, 1967); Roland Portères, "Vieilles agricultures de l'Afrique intertropicale: centres d'origine et de diversification variétale primaire et berceaux d'agriculture antérieurs au XVI siècle," in *L'Agronomie Tropicale*, nos. 9–10 (September–October 1950); and N. I. Vavilov, "The Origin, Variation, Immunity, and Breeding of Cultivated Plants," in *Chronica Botanica*, vol. 13 (1949–50). The question of cotton cultivation is dealt with in J. B. Hutchinson, "New Evidence on the Origin of the Old World Cottons," in *Heredity*, vol. 8, pt. 2 (1954); and G. E. Nicholson, "The Production, History, Uses and Relationships of Cotton in Ethiopia," in *Economic Botany*, vol. 14 (1960).

For agriculture in the Middle East, see V. G. Childe, *New Light on the Most Ancient East* (New York: Norton, 1953); *Digging up Jericho* (New York: Praeger, 1957); and *Archeology in the Holy Land*, 3rd ed. (New York: Praeger, 1970), both these last by Kathleen Kenyon.

The subject of cultivation in the ancient Nile valley is dealt with in a variety of sources. See, for example, Clark, Mauny, Childe, Murdock, and others cited above. Also to be consulted are W. B. Emery, *Archaic Egypt* (Baltimore: Penguin, 1961), and A. J. Arkell, *A History of the Sudan from Earliest Times to 1821*, 2nd ed. (London: Athlone Press, 1961). Numerous social histories of early Egypt provide details of Nile valley agriculture: for instance, W. M. Flinders Petrie, *Social Life in Ancient Egypt* (London: Constable and Co., 1924), and the same author's *Wisdom of the Egyptians* (London: British School of Archeology in Egypt, 1940); E. A. Wallis Budge, *The Dwellers of the Nile* (London: Religious Tract Society, 1926); Herman Kees, *Ancient Egypt* (Chicago: University of Chicago Press, 1961); and J. A. Wilson, *The Culture of Ancient Egypt* (Chicago: University of Chicago Press, 1956).

For studies of particular crops, in addition to sources cited above, see D. G. Coursey, *Yams* (London: Longmans, 1967), and W. O. Jones, *Manioc in Africa* (Stanford, Calif.: Stanford University Press, 1959).

4

THE SAVANNA FARMER

Empires in the Sudan

The brilliant civilization of pharaonic Egypt has survived in history, portrayed through her monuments which provide an incomplete yet vivid picture of daily life during the last three millennia preceding the birth of Christ. In like fashion it has been possible to trace the influence of Egypt southward along the Nile into the Sudan where ancient Kush held sway, even for a time controlling Egypt herself, and where the river city of Meroe arose as a center of trade and iron manufacturing. Egypt's impact on Kush and Meroe was pervasive and long-lived, affecting such fundamental bases of culture as language, religion, politics, and art—indeed, the whole fabric of society—but the idiomatic character of Kushitic and Meroitic civilization is also discernible, left for future generations to scrutinize in the ruins of her cities and the tombs of her kings.

No similar archaeological record awaits the historian of Africa's western and central savanna. Artifacts exhumed at widely scattered sites tell of an age-old residence by peoples who probably began retreating

69

before the growing desiccation of the Sahara approximately five thousand years ago, but it is now known that still others had long since made their home in the southern forests below the Sudan. Their presence is traceable as far back as ten thousand years, making them contemporaries of the early Natufian farmers of Palestine. There is no evidence of agriculture in West Africa at this early date, however; neither is the record clear as to when and from what direction cultivation and animal domestication first began to replace hunting and foraging as a means of livelihood. The use of iron was understood by the third century B.C. and possibly earlier, making it roughly contemporaneous with the development of an iron industry at Meroe and raising interesting and difficult questions as to the origin and diffusion of this skill. Here and there tomb sites and stone monuments of uncertain origin and antiquity attest to settlements about which little else is known but the bare fact of their existence.

Thus it is that the history of West Africa has remained a virtual blank almost until the close of the first millennium after Christ; yet at that time, when news of the western Sudan first began to trickle across the Sahara, it described the existence of wealthy and powerful Sudanic states, their prosperity based on their control of seemingly vast supplies of gold, their civilization presumably the result of long anterior development. The first tentative reports, dating from the eighth century A.D., came via trade routes established by North African merchants and spoke at once of Ghana, "the land of gold." Succeeding accounts amplified this bare statement until by the eleventh century Ghana took clear shape as a large and powerful Soninke kingdom, dominating many lesser principalities, its glittering palace substantiating the persistent legends of great wealth.

At the height of its power during the early eleventh century, Ghana controlled a territory that abutted the desert in the north and reached the Niger bend to the east while occupying the watersheds of the upper Niger and Senegal rivers to the south and west. This proud hegemony was shattered in 1076, however, when the Almoravids, a puritanical and militant group of Muslim Berbers, captured and destroyed the capital city at Kumbi. Mortally hurt, Ghana was finally overrun by former vassals, her preeminent position eventually falling to the kingdom of Mali, another vast savanna state which absorbed much of its predeces-

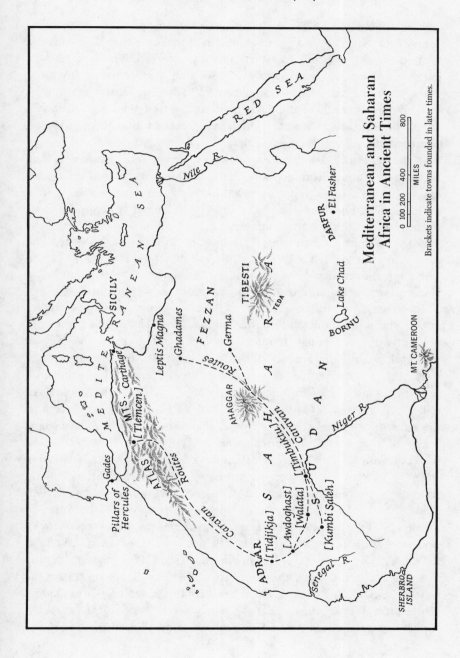

Mediterranean and Saharan
Africa in Ancient Times

Brackets indicate towns founded in later times.

sor's territory, adding further acquisitions to the east along the great bend of the Niger. Mali's greatness endured from the early thirteenth to the mid-fifteenth century, by which time it was forced to cede primacy in the western Sudan to the rising state of Songhai. For almost two hundred years this new giant bestrode the Niger and adjacent territories until the end of the sixteenth century when its armies fell before the surprise attack of a Moroccan force which had reached the Niger after an unprecedented march across the desert.

In the central Sudan another great power early took shape and long survived as Kanem-Bornu, whose territories centered around the inland sea of Lake Chad. Relying upon military prowess and administrative sophistication, her rulers founded a successful dynasty contemporaneous with Ghana's golden era, maintaining it in unbroken line until the middle of the nineteenth century. While the fortunes of this long-lived monarchy rose and fell over the centuries, it managed at various times to gain control over neighbors like Wadai and Bagirmi to the east and such Hausa states as Kano, Zaria, and Katsina on her western frontiers.

These major kingdoms aside, most other savanna states were smaller in size and more modest in political pretensions. The Hausa principalities, for example, though frequently independent, were rarely large or powerful, mainly because of the self-inflicted attrition of intramural wars. Kano experienced expansions in the fifteenth and sixteenth centuries while Zaria traditions speak of a fifteenth-century upsurge under Queen Amina. On the western flank of Hausaland, however, was the kingdom of Kebbi, able during the sixteenth century to turn back armies of both Bornu and Songhai and to extend its sway over several of the Hausa states. The Mossi principalities of the upper Volta basin were strongly entrenched in their own region during the fifteenth and sixteenth centuries and were capable raiders northward into the strongholds of Mali when the opportunity presented itself. A few others may be mentioned to illustrate the variety of peoples in the West African savanna—the Tukolor state of Tekrur which lay to the west of Ghana in the Senegal River valley; Macina in the Niger lake region, gaining independence only when the authority of Mali or Songhai was on the wane; the powerful seventeenth-century Jukun kingdom of the middle Benue; the Nupe, who established themselves during the sixteenth century along the Niger and Kaduna rivers; or Kaarta and Segu, two

Bambara powers that dominated the western Sudan during the eighteenth century.

At first view, the prosperity of the savanna peoples and the quality of their civilization seems to have been linked primarily to external factors. It was, after all, the trans-Saharan trade that introduced the much prized horses of North Africa, the life-giving salt from the desert mines of Taghaza, and the multiplicity of foodstuffs and handicraft articles fancied by king and courtier. It was the gold exported to the north that enabled savanna monarchs to equip the armies that extended and established their expanding power. It was this same international exchange that built the great cities, Timbuktu, Gao, Jenne, Kano, and others, where the marketplace of ideas competed with that of commerce, where learning flourished and books and scholars were commonplace. It was the Saharan trade that first exposed the Sudan to the influence of Islam, thereby insuring an ultimate sea change in the way of life of a whole series of peoples.

Such appearances are deceiving. Despite the glitter of court life, the influence of Muslim scribe and royal adviser, or the ubiquitous Arab and Berber merchant in the savanna cities, the pulse of life lay elsewhere—in the rolling countryside of woodlands and fields where the occasional village betrayed the presence of peasant farmers concerned mainly with drawing a livelihood from the land.

The Daily Fare

In 1352 the renowned Berber traveler Ibn Battuta, journeying between Walata and the capital of Mali, paused to remark upon the produce of the countryside. There is no need, he pointed out, to carry provisions or even money in this part of the world. Much better would be a supply of rock salt, glass ornaments, or perfume. "When the traveler arrives at a village," he went on, "the women appear at once, offering millet, sour milk, chickens . . . , rice, fonio . . . , and bean flour." The fonio was the base both for a local steamed cereal, couscous, and for a thick porridge, and Ibn Battuta pronounced it far preferable to the rice which appeared to make strangers sick. In any event, all these foodstuffs were readily available to passing caravans transporting goods for which roadside villagers were eager to make an exchange.

Ibn Battuta's report covered a substantial proportion of basic savanna cereals available in his day, but he could have mentioned others and might have been somewhat more precise in his terminology. When he spoke of millet, presumably he meant the small-seeded grains and forage grasses known as *Pennisetum*, but fonio *(Digitaria exilis)* is also classed as a millet though inferior in quality to the *Pennisetum*s. What he failed to mention at all were the varieties of large-grained sorghums prevalent throughout the savanna from Ghana to Kanem and used as stock feed as well as a staple for human consumption. Wheat, too, was grown, although more typically in oases or near the desert's edge at sites like Awdaghost, where it thrived with the help of hand-administered irrigation.

Such urban centers contained gardens where numerous vegetables and fruits were raised. At Awdaghost could be found melons, figs, and grapes, while the royal gardens of Kanem produced pomegranates, peaches, and grapes. Citrus fruit was widespread and even grew wild in the vicinity of Kano where the lemons and oranges were reported to be scarcely distinguishable in quality from the cultivated varieties. These last delicacies may have been brought to West Africa by the Arabs, who seem also to have been responsible for the introduction of cotton into that region—not one of the original African varieties but *Gossypium arboreum,* cultivated in India, which had eventually made its way back to East Africa via the Indian Ocean trade. By the early sixteenth century cotton was established as an important crop in the western savanna, supporting a cloth-manufacturing industry well designed to accommodate the dry heat of the Sudan.

In the Sudan the millets and sorghums were the staple foods simply because they best suited the local conditions of climate and soil—brief seasonal rains, intense dry heat, and extensive regions of low fertility. What was required was a crop that would balance high nourishment against a short growing season, that thrived on minimal moisture and survived in soils of indifferent quality. More than that, circumstances called for crops substantial in caloric content yet capable of providing proteins, minerals, and vitamins essential to health, since animal nutriments were not widely available to the peasantry and the cattle of pastoral peoples, though numerous, were not normally consumed for food.

Within limits, the sorghums and the small-seed millets ideally fitted these specifications. Both tolerate soils of mediocre quality; while they naturally thrive in areas rich with humus, they will endure in poorer regions provided the clay content does not make for impermeability. Both require little moisture and hold up well under extended drought conditions, resuming growth when water is once more available. Moreover, they readily withstand the dry heat that is characteristic of the Sudan. Of the two, sorghums demand the greater moisture and therefore have predominated typically in the lower latitudes nearer the forest where the average annual rainfall ranges between twenty-five and fifty inches. With precipitation under twenty-five inches the millets fare better, and since they subsist on as little as ten inches annually, they have spread themselves broadly as far north as the borders of the Saharan region. Over the centuries, however, the most noteworthy marginal crop has been fonio. Not only does it require little moisture, it also matures after a very short growing season on soils so poor as to deny other crops or in plots where fertility has already been badly depleted by previous plantings.

This tough quality earned fonio the reputation as a hunger breaker; thus it was and is frequently planted earliest, maturing before the regular harvest and providing sustenance during the lean weeks when one season's supplies are low and those of the next are yet to be gathered. Of course, there is always a price for these advantages. Fonio is a poor-quality millet of very low yield, and, indeed, this criticism of low yield may be applied more generally to all the millets and sorghums. Sorghum requires a growing season averaging five months although some varieties will mature in as few as ninety days. Millets show an even quicker growth with a typical season of only three months; yet this advantage is offset in both crops by characteristically low production as compared with other grains, a deficiency that has been especially pronounced in the case of the millets.

The only other savanna cereal of consequence was rice, which was usually sown broadcast on the wet bottom land of the Niger and other river valleys at the end of the flood season and which therefore was found in quantity in the great markets near the river courses. Beans of various sorts were also widely grown, and a few other crops deserve mention—for example, onions, sesame, cucumbers, squash, and watermelons. These were essentially auxiliaries, however; the basic foods were the sorghums and millets, their importance in local eyes exemplified by the choice of fonio seeds presented as a gift for Ibn Battuta to honor his passage through Mali.

Despite the assortment of cultivated crops available in Ibn Battuta's day, the search for serviceable wild plants was not neglected. These could range from highly palatable truffles, which sprang up near the desert's edge directly after the rains, to more pedestrian roots, seeds, stems, or leaves pressed into service chiefly in times of famine. Many of the foraged species served purposes other than nourishment. Although timber was scarce, it could be found in the form of structural beams for buildings, as furniture, tools, or weapons, as canoe and paddle for river transport, even in more exotic form as musical instrument or dancing mask. Most dishware was made from gourds, and clothing, particularly before the advent of cotton, was manufactured from bark cloth, the only other alternative to total nudity being clusters of leaves tied about the waist. Palm products were common in the forest regions along the West African coast, but in the savanna where the useful fronds were scarce, some houses were made entirely of woven straw and grass, most others equipped with straw roofs topping walls of mud construction. Woven straw served a variety of other purposes and was the basis for an important craft industry and wide-ranging commerce in matting and basketwork, the products of which were to be found equally in the simplest peasant hut and the king's own palace.

The Cultivators

In the savanna, the farms were small. Family size determined their extent; despite the widespread practice of community labor, the basic work unit was the farmer himself and those few additional hands regularly available—usually sons, sometimes a younger unmarried brother or wives, according to the custom that prevailed locally. Allowing for differences in terrain and type of crop, one man could manage about two acres. If a farmer had two or three able-bodied helpers, his tract would probably not exceed eight acres. If he were prosperous enough to have two wives and a full complement of adolescent and unmarried sons, his farm would increase accordingly, and necessarily so since there were more mouths to feed. If he were a young man newly married and established, he might make do with two acres or less.

The hands were few, the work often taxing, but in a society where four of every five villagers were full-time farmers, the whole population was necessarily preoccupied with the fruits of the land. The calendar year, for example, was keyed to the climatic rather than the astronomical seasons, beginning always with the month that brought the first rains, not the preliminary showers but the first heavy fall that continued long enough to give the ground a thorough soaking. Depending on latitude and uncertainties of climate, in the West African savanna this important event came sometime in April, May, or June, quite possibly in the form of a nighttime downpour, in which event the next morning found the village early stirring, the men quickly scattering to their fields for the important work ahead.

The farm workers proceeded singly or in small groups, a light hoe hooked over the shoulder, several gourds strung together containing food, water, and seeds, and a bow and arrow in hand for protection. Dress was minimal—a loincloth, perhaps another cloth to wrap around the shoulders against the morning chill, and a great bowl-shaped straw hat to provide shade from the sun which would later fill the day with its heat. The first crop would very likely be a quick-growing grain; in any event the fields lay waiting, those of the more enterprising farmers already prepared in long rows of earthen mounds, neatly patterned in ornamental symmetry. Leaving his supplies under one of the several shade trees purposely left standing in the field, each farmer proceeded systematically along the rows of mounds. With his hoe he scratched the soft earth, tossed in seed, covered the hole with the butt of his hoe, and stepped one stride to the next mound. Some worked with their hands alone, smoothing out each hole with a heel as they passed along the row.

The workers moved steadily forward, compelled by the rhythm of their activity. Hoe in right hand, seeds in left, each man pressed on hour upon hour almost without pause, his purposeful movement occasionally thrown into relief by the random barking of dogs and shouting of children engaged in nearby games. Within a day an acre would be complete, and the following morning the process would be repeated with variations, the sowing devoted perhaps to a slower-maturing millet or to one of the sorghums.

By the end of the first week the early planting had been completed. Later crops would go in at intervals, most often directly after further heavy rains. Techniques varied from place to place; some peoples planted their millet by broadcast, turning and working the soil to bury the seed. Others preferred ridges of earth to mound cultivation, while still others tended to postpone the preparation of their fields until immediately before the sowing was about to begin. During the planting season there were necessary waiting periods between seedings, and these were utilized for various chores such as the repair of tools or the acquisition of a new hoe for the youngest son about to join his father on the family plots. Hunting could also fill up the time usefully as well as pleasantly, and while they were in the fields, the men would also gather herbs for medicinal purposes, broad-faced leaves for wrapping food, or aromatic plants fancied by their wives at the bath.

With the sowing completed, the work slackened briefly only to pick up again at the time of weeding and transplanting, arduous and delicate operations that overlapped with the first phases of the harvest. When initially cleared, the fields had been only partially turned, while numerous trees or their stumps were left in the earth along with the root systems of burned-out brush. This incomplete clearing was important both to hold the soil against water and wind erosion and to maintain organic matter for quicker regeneration during fallow periods. Now, with a new planting in process, however, further clearing and cultivation were needed to ensure that the young crop would prosper. Weeding began usually about three weeks after the first planting and continued at intervals until the early millet was ready for harvest. First, previous undergrowth was cleared away, then new grass and weeds pulled, and finally the maturing crops were transplanted by moving the plants, mound and all, to the adjacent furrow. At the same time, the young shoots were separated and replanted in vacant areas between the mounds or sometimes in new ground specially prepared for the purpose.

These long and taxing labors were accomplished in the main through use of the classic short-handled hoe. Savanna farmers also employed long-handled hoes, the worker pushing the instrument in front of him, the purpose to break the surface crust or to chip out unwanted grasses. The short-handled variety, however, was the essential cultivating implement in all parts of tropical Africa, for plows were not used in sub-Saharan latitudes where a thin soil cover might suffer damage through deep tillage. The short-hafted hoe was found in many versions and sizes, but the essential design was a flat iron blade fixed at an acute angle to a short wooden handle. Hoeing was necessarily performed in a fatiguing stooped position, the advantage of which was greater force and precision in stroke. The larger instruments carried shovel-like blades six or eight inches wide and were used for breaking ground, turning soil, building mounds, and other heavy work. Smaller blades were sufficient for such activities as weeding or sowing.

Like the hoes, methods of cultivation varied in detail from place to place. Some peoples built their mounds by hoeing down between their widespread legs, digging up the earth and throwing it back behind them to a mound, all in a single motion. Others used a twisting stroke that tossed the earth off to one side so that a ridge was built up from earth dug out of an adjacent furrow. Those who worked with long-handled hoes developed their rows by throwing the earth ahead as they proceeded. The cultivation of sandy savanna soil was typically shallow, in some places only a few inches was deemed sufficient for the needs of the West African cereals. Concurrent with the sorghum and millet, subsidiary crops were introduced—varieties of melons, gourds, or beans occupying the same ground as the basic grains. In nearby fields cotton was planted along with rice where moisture conditions permitted or yams in the regions of greater precipitation nearer the rain forest belt.

The early millets were usually arm high at the end of two months and ready for harvest after approximately ninety days. During this busy period, the men were in the fields for long stretches, their work now complicated by the necessity of keeping animal pests such as monkeys and weaver birds at bay. This was a serious business, the danger combated in various ways, not only with scarecrows, but also through the exertions of young boys who shouted, threw stones, and brandished long sticks. At times the farmers were forced to guard their fields throughout the night, these additional activities especially taxing, for this was the hungry season when stocks from the previous year were near exhaustion and the new harvest not yet in.

The harvesting was done by cutting the stalks close to the ground and placing the sheaves in bundles along the furrows where they were allowed to dry over a period of several days. This accomplished, the grain heads were cut off and removed for storage, the stalks remaining in the fields, later to be retrieved for matting or permitted to rot where they were as fertilizer. Eventually the remains would be burned, usually during the dry season at the same time that new land was being cleared for future use.

In the West African savanna with its limited precipitation, the rains were over early, probably by September or early October. The completion of the late harvest and the onset of a long dry period was no signal for rest, however, for this was the time that new land was cleared while present fields were readied for the next planting season. The work could be done at the end of the harvest or postponed until just before the beginning of the next planting, the former being favored by those energetic farmers who wished to take advantage of the still moist, more easily worked earth, the latter the resort of the less provident who wished to rest after the harvest. In any case, it was arduous labor involving clearing bush, turning sod, and felling trees. Finally, when the dead vegetation had thoroughly dried out, the fields were fired, the resultant ash left in place to enrich the soil when washed in by the first rains.

As with the major community tasks such as road repair or bridge building, the clearing of new land was often undertaken by groups—the men of a village compound or members of an age grade association made up of individuals who had achieved manhood through commonly shared puberty rites. Such labor, performed in a gamelike manner and accompanied by spirited feasting and dancing, enabled a team of workers quickly to convert an unused area of grass and bush to the familiar pattern of mounds and rows, each hillock usually capped with a tuft of grass to discourage erosion, all ready for the coming season. The process of land clearing was a regular annual event, partly because there were always new young couples needing their own plots, but primarily because the growing cycle for any one field did not exceed a few seasons even with crop rotation, whereas the fallow period was normally two or three times as long. Conditions varied greatly from locality to locality, based upon soil fertility, water supply, and types of plant under cultivation. Where fields were fertilized by animal droppings, as they were if pastoral herds frequented the neighborhood, the growing period was greatly extended. Many people, however, relied only on the natural regeneration of fallow periods, possibly because of the easy availability of new unoccupied lands.

The harvest was the natural climax to a season of labor and, if all had gone well—adequate rainfall, healthy seed and fertile soil, careful cultivation, and a merciful deliverance from predatory pests—there was the prospect of a good crop yield and the heady anticipation of a year without hunger. Yet farm tasks scarcely ended with gathering the grain. It had to be stored, and properly so to avoid deterioration. It had to be processed through threshing, winnowing, and grinding. And finally there was the not inconsiderable effort of preparing the daily meals. It has been estimated for some locales that sorghums and millets necessitate more man-hours to prepare a unit of flour for cooking than the total time devoted to all the clearing, cultivating, sowing, and harvesting needed to produce the same quantity. For rice, the postharvest labor was less time consuming, but this reflects the uniquely heavy burden of rice harvesting which alone amounts to approximately one-third of the overall labor expenditure.

In the savanna the grain was typically stored unthreshed, for it was felt that the whole heads permitted better ventilation, thereby minimizing spoilage through mold. Granaries were large and urn-shaped, like the houses, made of mud and located within the compound near the living quarters. Constructed with thick, sturdy walls extending well above a man's height, they were propped up on stones to protect against termites and covered with a grass roofing to ward off birds and the severities of sun and rain. Each of these enclosures had a small, covered opening about halfway up one side from which the grain could be drawn, and each crop was segregated in its own granary, the beans and other legumes as well as the cereals. In the southern savanna, where yams were grown, these were stored either at home or in the fields in well-ventilated wood racks. In some areas grain was stored in large pits which, when lined with woven grass matting backed with millet chaff, offered admirable accommodation over several years with minimal danger of deterioration.

Millet and sorghum were always thoroughly dried before storage, if not through the sun's action in the fields then in special clay ovens. When grain was taken from storage for threshing, it was spread on the ground and beaten with sticks or alternatively pounded in a large wooden mortar. Winnowing was performed by slowly shifting the grain from one shallow basketry platter to another, the chaff blowing away with the wind in the process. Empty grain heads and chaff were not wasted, however; carefully gathered they served as livestock fodder, while the winnowed grain was converted to flour, either crushed in a mortar or processed on grinding stones. These latter, large-surfaced, slightly concave stones on which the kernels were milled by hand with a small circular stone grinder, gave the finer flour, but the wooden mortar was said to be quicker, albeit heavier, work.

The cuisine would scarcely have roused the enthusiasm of an epicure. Ingenious and varied it may have been within necessary limitations, but its essential purpose was survival, and only the limited numbers of nobility could habitually afford the embellishments that elevated meals from eating to dining. The basic staple was a sticky porridge made of millet or sorghum flour. Stirred into boiling water and served hot or cold, the cereals were brought to differing consistencies ranging from a soupy gruel to a thick, doughy paste, while diverse methods for preparing dishes added some further relief from monotony. Served as a cereal mush at breakfast, it might reappear at noon in the form of breadlike balls, fried in shea butter and flavored with spices. For the evening meal a stew was popular, a dumpling of heavy dough in a highly seasoned sauce containing various greens, melon seeds, and possibly some fish, meat, or chicken. Another version was couscous—small grains made of millet flour, steamed to form the base of a stew to which a vegetable sauce was added and, if available, some meat. Along with these foods was a beer brewed from millet, combining considerable nutritional value with its perennial capacity for blunting the edge of life's sharper tribulations.

The Economic Imperatives

The essential concern was indeed survival where the tenders of fire-blackened cooking pots in every dusty, sun-baked compound were necessarily preoccupied with meeting the recurring demands of daily hunger. To be sure, in a prescientific age they knew nothing of nutritional requirements—calories and proteins, mineral salts and vitamin content—yet at first sight their narrow fare appeared to add dietary imperfections to its monotony. Compared with the yams and plantains of the forest dweller, their grains were inadequate as energy-producing foods, the former providing between two and three times the calories per acre, while other crops like rice or cocoyams registered about 20 or 25 percent higher in this respect. Furthermore, while sorghum and millet demanded far fewer man-days of labor compared to yams, the return in both weight and calories per acre for yams was many times greater, thereby condemning the savanna cereals as crops requiring a high investment of production proportionate to energy yield.

Yet there were important compensations. Sorghum and millet were ideally suited to the savanna's brief cycle of rains. Moreover, although they monopolized the diet, contributing some 85 percent of the total caloric intake, they far outstripped forest crops in protein yield as well as in their content of mineral salts and vitamins. For example, the proportion of protein in millet and sorghum flour averages between 10 and 12 percent by weight whereas for yams it is 2 percent, for cocoyams 1.5 percent, and for plantains less than 1 percent. When reckoned in relation to calories, the advantage is still pronounced, though less so. Millets and sorghum provide approximately 30 grams of protein for every 1,000 calories compared with 11 grams for plantains, 17 for cocoyams, and 23 for yams. A similar advantage appears with reference to mineral and vitamin properties. Sorghum contains twice the calcium of yams, four times the iron of cocoyams, and ten times the vitamin B_1 of plantains. Millet possesses half again as much calcium as cocoyams, five times the vitamin B_2 of yams, and over five times the niacin of plantains. Both grains display similar superiorities in nutritional composition over rice.

Since the savanna cereals represented such a high proportion of the total diet, their ability to supply protein tended to offset the problem of low caloric production; in the Sudan, therefore, subsistence living was defined more in terms of undernutrition than malnutrition. Granting the special needs of pregnant mothers and growing children, the bulk of the adult population was able to sustain itself in satisfactory fashion much as vegetarians do in any society. The rub came not so much in a general debility arising from protein deficiency, which tended to encourage disease and complicated efforts at cultural and economic development. Rather, the difficulty was to secure enough food over the full yearly cycle to ensure a vigorous population capable of constructive labor, thereby preventing the downward spiral of an inadequate food supply, leading to low individual energy, limitation of physical effort, submarginal farm practice, and a further deterioration of food stocks.

The problem was particularly acute during the growing season when supplies were low or completely exhausted and the new crop not yet ready for harvest. At that time, in perhaps two years of every five, a combination of insufficient or badly distributed rainfall and seemingly improvident husbandry brought acute shortages in food. Climatic vagaries were the chief source of difficulty but were compounded by agricultural practices which, despite long experience, appeared to ignore long-range needs in favor of immediate gratification. First, there was the understandable tendency to overeat at the beginning of the harvest, daily caloric consumption soaring to over three thousand for adult farm laborers. Next was the utilization of millet for making beer, a conversion that involved some loss of energy although this may have been compensated at least in part by the production of vitamins and related proteins through the brewing process. Further, there was the bias toward committing acreage to fast-maturing grains like fonio which would be quickly available during the hunger months of July and August but which were poor in quality and forced the reduction of land and labor available to better-yielding strains. Finally, it was customary when a good season produced bumper harvests to barter away surpluses or divert them to religious ceremonies, wedding feasts, and lavish funerals instead of storing them for the lean days that would surely come again. Over all these factors there lay a mood of fatalism and apathy which appeared to paralyze efforts toward planning for the future and which has been ascribed to the overwhelming uncertainties of an existence that rendered futile any concern beyond the immediate present.

The indictment of apathetic improvidence, however, neglects a number of important qualifications. For one thing, climate was the factor least subject to control or compensation by preindustrial societies. What is more, the heavy incidence of parasitic infection among African communities led to anemia and other disabling maladies largely beyond the control of traditional medicine, afflictions that were especially debilitating during the hungry season when loss of nutritional elements to parasites could not be replaced by an insufficient and dwindling diet.

Most important, however, is the evidence that the savanna farmers did not in fact passively accept their lot, permitting themselves to be buffeted by an indifferent environment. To begin with, there was a whole range of compensatory famine practices—gathering insects such as termites, locusts, caterpillars, or crickets; trapping small rodents, birds, and reptiles; rationing grains through careful winnowing; and foraging for wild plants. Such activities had their limitations—for example, overzealous winnowing could reduce a meal to pure bran while unrecognized wild roots might prove to be dangerously toxic—but these eventualities were bearable alternatives to outright starvation.

Furthermore, savanna societies engaged in a good deal of agricultural experimentation as a means of increasing productivity. While it appears that the *foggaras* of North Africa, those underground drainage tunnels dug to tap ground water, never existed farther south than the west-central Sahara, wells equipped with seesaw lifts were widely used in the savanna, and irrigation was the basis for much agricultural activity, particularly in the districts lying close to the desert. At the caravan terminus of Awdaghost in the western Sudan, the gardens were hand watered, while in Kumbi Saleh, the chief center of the kingdom of Ghana, truck farms were successfully maintained during the dry season by locating them close to the city's wells. On the banks of the Senegal River, two seasonal crops could be raised, the first directly after the annual flooding and the second later while the alluvial soil was still moist. In Kanem the royal gardens were specifically designed for agricultural experiment, strains of wheat, sugarcane, and grapevines being attempted, though apparently without great success. Perhaps the most ambitious irrigation system was that of Timbuktu, where canals brought the Niger flood waters to the city, a dozen miles away, although there was already a plentiful supply of well water available.

This taste for experimentation and desire to reach well beyond the circumscribed counsels of peasant lore and tribal ritual was manifest as well in the general standards of husbandry and the existence of theoretical farming knowledge possessed by the more progressive communities. To take one example, the Nupe people of modern Nigeria practice a system of agriculture that argues a long-lived familiarity with farming principles approaching, within limits, the authority of scientific knowledge. There are fixed rules regarding crop rotation and lying fallow, the practice of thinning out the maturing plants, or the utilization of fertilizers. These rules make scant appeal to magic or religious sanction for they are firmly based upon experiment and experience, producing thereby a body of authority that offers stability without rigidity and the opportunity for change tempered by the wisdom of practical knowledge.

What emerged among the Nupe, as it did among others of like experience in the western Sudan and elsewhere, was a complex, delicately articulated farming routine with a sophisticated schedule of crop rotation and an intricate system of labor specialization—one, however, that was ever sensitive to the possibility of change resulting from experiment with new species and techniques. The guiding principle was efficiency, the most apparent manifestation of which was an intricate schedule of planting, cultivating, and harvesting.

Thus, the typical farming operation entailed not only successive planting of crops on particular plots during a single growing season, but also a judicious overlapping of different crops in successive years including a period for lying fallow. One plot might have begun with millets and sorghum of different rates of maturity which, after harvest, were replaced with beans. A second plot, devoted to yams, might also have sustained okra, while a third given over to cotton, groundnuts, or maize would probably have been interplanted with melons. The following season could have seen the first plot fallow, the second shifted to sorghum, and the third devoted to yams and ground beans. The choice of exact rotation on any particular farm rested upon acreage and land fertility, labor supply and market demands. For example, cotton might have been temporarily abandoned if the care required for sowing interfered with weeding late millet or if tending a cotton crop complicated the all-important yam harvest of southern savanna dwellers near the forest edge. Again, extraordinary demand at a given moment could have induced a farmer to sell his seed along with the rest of his harvest, thus eliminating that crop from the plantings of the immediate future. Conversely, a sharp drop in demand for a particular crop might have caused him to abandon the long and expensive operation of harvest and with it a whole season's yield.

Such activities suggest that a continuing process was under way in which societies probed their environment, searching for its livable limits and devising techniques designed to exploit those limits as fully as possible. Lack of a sophisticated technology and modern scientific knowledge necessarily complicated this search, forcing some to subsist without livestock because of endemic tsetse infestation, others to abandon potentially fertile lands for lack of usable surface or ground water during the dry season, and still others to eke out an uncertain existence because their soil was poor and the rains capricious. Nonetheless, some peoples were always more successful in their ability to sustain themselves under given restraints. Such success was manifest variously— it might be a vigorous trade that supplied necessary goods unobtainable locally, or yet the ability to avoid the destructiveness of warfare and political instability; it might rest upon superior farm management or the flexibility to adapt custom to the utilization of more productive crops.

Allowing for differences among people, then, there was ample receptivity to innovation provided it met certain conditions, partly social but largely economic in definition. What any potential innovation had to demonstrate was a clear superiority over an accepted practice already embedded in daily routines or tribal mores. Could some new task be fitted into a crowded schedule, competing as it must with other work priorities or with precious leisure time? Would the proposed innovation upset the delicate balance of specialization and interdependence within a particular economy? Was the change in fact clearly advantageous or did it introduce hidden complications disruptive to the fine workings of a time-tested system? What unknown risks and uncertainties had to be faced with what consequences? Clearly, here was an exercise in free economic choice.

Despite this apparent pragmatism, African agricultural communities, in the aggregate, changed but slowly over the centuries, showing their greatest adaptability in making use of new crops—manioc and maize, for example—but appearing more conservative with regard to farming techniques. Such conservatism has variously been ascribed by outsiders to indolence or improvidence, to a childish view of life which ignores thrift and remains indifferent to the notion of ultimate accountability. It might more reasonably be charged to the very process of free economic choice operating within the context of traditional African farming society.

In other words, it was not indolence and improvidence that limited the development of traditional agriculture in Africa; it was the ultimate balance between environment and preindustrial farming techniques beyond which further investment in labor and capital brought such slender returns as to make that investment unworthy of the effort. To put more land under cultivation in a community living under subsistence conditions would have helped alleviate hunger during the lean months, but it would also have strained the available labor supply, risked inattention at key moments, and thereby introduced the possibility of poor harvests. To increase the battery of tools, to invest more time and energy in cultivation and irrigation, to add seed or quantities of crude fertilizer would have raised production only minimally, not enough to warrant the added expense, however slight, of these efforts. To subdivide land for a larger variety of crops had evident limitations of time and manpower.

Long trial and error had brought these farming communities to a maximum point of efficiency, given the conditions of soil and weather and the state of technological advance. Under such circumstances the improvident and shortsighted procedure would surely have been the investment of capital and labor in activities of vanishing utility. More rational was preoccupation with the rewards of leisure-time pursuits or indulgence in so-called wasteful consumption connected with ceremonies that helped men to endure the drab and harsh realities of their daily existence.

It was not until the modern period that a fundamental change was forthcoming in African agricultural activities. Only then did the introduction of revolutionary new factors such as high-energy fertilizers, cheap transport, and the demands of a world market upset the ancient equilibrium, replacing it with a new dynamic of peasant productivity that would become a major base for the economic development of independent Africa.

The Disposition of Land

During the period of European colonial control in Africa, ownership and utilization of land everywhere was one of the most abrasive issues between the rulers and the ruled. In West Africa it was a continuing source of misunderstanding and dispute; in King Leopold's Congo it produced an infamous regime of exploitation and atrocity; in South Africa it was at the root of the struggle between Boer and Bantu; and in East Africa it led straight to the spasm of Mau Mau that shook the Kikuyu nation after the Second World War.

As with all farming societies, land was the foundation of the economy in traditional Africa, and as such it became a major element in African religious beliefs, social relationships, and political configurations. Allowing for certain differences in emphasis among African peoples, the land was variously regarded as a preserve of major deities, the sacred soil of the ancestors, an object of the most important rituals, the origin of royal power, the basis for health and prosperity; indeed, it was widely looked upon as the source of life itself. Such a central position gave land a significance in African eyes far removed from the concepts of the West. Its importance placed it above value; like the air that men breathe or the rains from heaven, it was a priceless possession that no one individual could conceive of owning in the Western sense, making that ownership a basis for personal profit. Land was something to be occupied corporately—by a nation, a clan, a lineage, or a family; it belonged to the tribal group, to the ancestors, or sometimes to the king acting as custodian for his people.

At the same time, in most areas land was readily available as needed. Being plentiful like the air, it had no owner; in economic terms, land had no scarcity value as a factor of production. Each community occupied and controlled a vaguely defined territory within which individuals and families simply cultivated whatever fields they required for their daily support.

If land was seldom owned individually, it could be so occupied. As members of the group, individuals were free to make use of as much land as they could conveniently farm, and in some societies even strangers were welcome to settle in the village, cultivating their allocated plots along with the rest. For practical purposes, therefore, each family worked its parcel of land until it was abandoned or, more rarely, given over to others for their use. In this way land became a kind of tangible census—a convenient means for identifying individuals and families, defining their social or political importance and relating them to each other and to the whole society. There were many variations of this pattern, the essential feature of which was land occupation as the palpable, most readily apparent manifestation of social organization.

With variations, these principles were observed everywhere through-out the continent. Among the Kikuyu of East Africa, to take one example, land was owned by small lineage groups, each member of which controlled his designated parcel. As the nation grew and the landholdings of its lineages diffused and interspersed, a continued sense of individual identity and family solidarity was to a notable degree dependent upon the viability of this landholding system. With the Ngoni of southern Africa, whose vast migration covered a thousand miles during the first half of the nineteenth century, there was no such well-developed system of landholding; nevertheless, the political struc-ture of Ngoni society was graphically portrayed and maintained by the relative position of individual dwellings in every residential settlement, this same pattern being repeated without variation each time the Ngoni paused to form new villages during their long migration.

In West Africa there were many similar concepts of land tenure employed to illustrate and strengthen social organization. Among the Tiv in the Benue River country, every individual had a claim to adequate farmland by right of his membership in the clan structure. Individual holdings were not defined geographically, however, since the system of shifting cultivation resulted in periodic removes to new areas. Moreover, land occupation was a direct reflection of social relationships wherein descent and genealogy provided geographical as well as lineage group-ings. Thus a man might occupy different land tracts at different times, his rights to them transitory and entirely related to his genealogical connections. In whatever region of Tiv country his family section was located at any particular moment, there he would be entitled to appropriate farmland. In time he and his lineage would occupy many different areas, while land once held by them would become in turn the temporary residence of another lineage grouping.

The Tiv allocated land for individual use in terms of need—a pregnant wife might now require more yam rows than formerly; a man whose married daughter had recently joined her husband would wish to reduce his acreage accordingly. Among other peoples, the customs varied. The Susu of the Futa Jalon plateau recognized no individual ownership of land, but the Tallensi along the upper reaches of the White Volta River held their lands in outright ownership by virtue of inheritance, and under this arrangement some farms were usually larger and wealthier than others. Perhaps this system resulted from the fact that the Tallensi practiced permanent cultivation; in any event, despite the concept of privately owned holdings, custom imposed important qualifications on the utilization and disposal of all land.

Most particularly, larger holdings sooner or later resulted in more wives and a greater drain on the resources followed by eventual redistribution of land through a wider inheritance. Furthermore, convention strongly forbade the sale of land and rental was not practiced, although a holder was free to lend his land as he wished. Tallensi land could not be taxed or commandeered by chiefly authority, while abandoned or borrowed tracts remained forever the possession of the original owner who could recover his ancestral plots at any time without fear of contention.

The Tallensi also permitted the acquisition of small personal farms brought under cultivation in virgin territory, a practice that varied from the system of the Nupe whose individual plots were normally part of a particular family holding. With the Nupe, family land was worked both singly and jointly, its disposition controlled by the family head, whereas communal land was held by the chief in the name of the village and apportioned by him according to need and demand. Thus the Nupe chief exercised a form of political control over unapportioned land, although in no sense could he claim ownership. When in the case of succession family land changed hands, the chief's sanction was always obtained, even though recognized as a formality, and he typically received a gift to seal the pact. The chief was entitled to other perquisites—for example, a form of land tax on all holdings, as well as control of the products of so-called chief's trees, economically valuable fruit-bearing species that grew on both communal and family lands.

Such multiple claims to the treasures of the land reflect the African emphasis on utility rather than ownership. While the Nupe recognized certain chiefly rights to family lands, the whole population was entitled to the uncultivated produce of virgin territories, as well as the use of common facilities such as clay pits, iron ore deposits, or town street corners devoted to modest marketing enterprises. Among the Tiv, every tract of land supported a multiplicity of individual rights. A field might belong to a particular woman who controlled most of its produce but who in return was obliged to feed her husband and children therefrom. Her husband, having helped prepare the field, was entitled to eat from it and to collect the millet grown there in normal rotation. Finally, the compound head, who had originally allotted the farm, also received a small portion of the crop which was utilized for purposes of hospitality or ritual as needed.

The delicately interconnecting web of utility and obligation regarding land frequently extended to the treatment of strangers. Some peoples did not encourage outsiders, but others looked on them as productive additions to the community. The Nupe welcomed members from other tribal groups for their skills and supplied them with farms from the common land when they chose to settle permanently. The Tiv were also hospitable to the stranger—to Hausa traders, for example, who might be given valuable farmland in order to establish a permanent colony near an important market. Such land was requisitioned without protest from particular individual farms, for these were subsequently compensated through a general readjustment of family plots ultimately involving the whole larger neighborhood that surrounded the market and gained from its presence.

Of course this openhandedness, particularly in the case of strangers, was based in the last analysis on the ready availability of land to most traditional African societies. The Nupe did not suffer shortages until the Fulani conquest in the early nineteenth century, nor the Tiv until colonial rule substituted land titles and fixed boundaries for the age-old concept of landholding by lineage relationships. In either event, outside controls forced a new ecology in which empty lands were no longer free for the taking, thereby necessitating new forms of landholding and utilization. More than that, the colonial period introduced revolutionary changes that greatly increased the size and extent of the market for Africa's agricultural production, a development that created for the first time pressures toward the private acquisition and improvement of land.

The Hedge against Disaster

Within the limitations of his experience and technology, the African farmer demonstrated an energetic resourcefulness in meeting the environmental pressures that threatened his security and at times his very survival. Basically, there were two types of risks to be endured. The first was adventitious—those discrete catastrophes such as war, slave raids, or unexpected political tyranny. The second was the normal risk of everyday existence, involving illness or accident and, more usually, the recurrent calamity of crop failure, to be anticipated in all respects save its exact timing.

Not surprisingly, the means for meeting the adventitious hazard were less successful since they lacked this very advantage of anticipation. Generally speaking, however, they involved the concept of clientship, particularly in savanna societies, like the Hausa, that harbored a definite class hierarchy. Among the Nupe, the client-patron relationship was highly developed, ranging from low-level retainers of loose allegiance to important members of the lesser nobility, all attached with varying degrees of closeness to a powerful patron who returned their loyalty with political protection and economic support. This exchange of fealty for security, so reminiscent of the feudal linkages of medieval Europe, worked with varying success, for protection was often uncertain and the development of rival factions which the system engendered was as likely to lead to the uncertainties of civil war as to the establishment of peace and security.

More effective, then, was the insurance that traditional societies developed against life's more predictable calamities. In this instance the techniques employed, though various, all rested on the actuarial principle of diluting the impact of disaster by spreading its liabilities among a widening number of individuals. Put otherwise, the process involved pooling community resources in order that they might be brought to bear on the center of difficulty.

The most evident manifestation of this principle was the concept of the close-knit family. Family solidarity through clan and lineage offered the efficiencies of division of labor. The larger the family, the easier it was to take up the slack caused by illness, accident, or old age. The bigger the work force, the greater was the possibility for effective crop rotation, a widening variety of plants under cultivation, and the allocation of domestic chores among many available wives. The more complex the organization of labor, the larger the opportunity for farsighted economic and social planning such as the arrangement of advantageous marriages. The more individuals, the bigger the farm; the bigger the farm and family, the greater the prestige and influence. Yet, although a man's influence was often expressed in terms of family size and the extent of his dependents, the suspicion remains that it was the economic efficiency of large-scale organization of labor that caused family cohesion, not some mystical African devotion to kinship. The extended family, it would appear, was economic in origin.

Much the same could be said for community cooperation through age grades which customarily assisted individual compounds when faced with unusually heavy tasks such as house building or clearing new land. Whatever the social sanctions, ultimately it was economic benefit that prevailed, and the institution of the age grade work force thrived thereby. To be sure, the moment of crisis subjected community cooperation to its greatest strains, a condition that also demonstrated its essential value. In times of famine, for example, the principle of community sharing came under heavy pressure, and substantial differences in nutritional intake were apparent between villages or households. Nevertheless, food was typically sent from the more fortunate districts; among the Tiv the process was institutionalized to the extent of having a name, "sending hunger," although the relief was always dispatched along recognized kinship lines, not in the form of a more random humanitarianism.

Kinship cooperation, with its supplies of food, clothing, and shelter, with its contribution toward obligations such as bride-price payments, and with its organization of labor, was supplemented by other forms of disaster insurance. Typical of many African societies was the system of pawning, both of goods and people, in which a loan was secured with the pawn as security, redeemable upon repayment. Such a system enabled an individual faced with a monetary crisis to obtain immediate resources, while the lender had the services of the pawn as long as the debt remained unpaid.

Another institution, found chiefly among pastoral societies, was the exchange of livestock among individual herd owners. This custom knit societies together in mutual obligation while scattering the stock of each household as insurance against drought or plague.

One final form of disaster insurance was what the Hausa called *adashi,* a free association of individuals who paid into a mutual fund on a regular basis, each member entitled to draw on the principal when needed. Like pawning, this device enabled the needy individual to gain access to a large source of wealth normally beyond his means in order to deal with some extraordinary expense—an illness, a costly funeral, or food supplies to see his family through the time of hunger.

SUGGESTIONS FOR FURTHER READING

There are two types of sources on which one may draw for information dealing with the farming societies of the West African savanna. First, there are early eyewitness accounts and studies based upon the testimony of travelers. These begin with a number of works written in Arabic, starting as early as the ninth century A.D. with the historian Ibn Abd Hakam and continuing into the era of European exploration which carries well into the nineteenth century. Among the several important sources in Arabic, particular mention should be made of the eleventh-century Arab geographer al-Bakri, the fourteenth-century Berber explorer Ibn Battuta, his contemporary from North Africa Ibn Khaldoun, and the seventeenth-century Sudanese from Timbuktu, as-Sadi. See al-Bakri, *Description de l'Afrique septentrionale*, translated by de Slane (Algiers: A. Jourdan, 1913); Ibn Khaldoun, *Histoire des Berbères*, 3 vols., translated by de Slane (Paris: P. Guenther, 1925); and as-Sadi, *Tarikh es-Soudan*, translated by O. Houdas (Paris: Adrien-Maisonneuve, 1964). For Ibn Battuta, the best edition is the translation into French, *Voyages d'Ibn Batoutah*, by C. Defrémery and B. R. Sanguinetti, 4 vols. (Paris: Imprimerie Nationale, 1926); but see also H. A. R. Gibb, tr. and ed., *Ibn Battuta: Travels in Asia and Africa* (London: G. Routledge, 1929).

Traveler accounts in European languages should begin with that of the sixteenth-century Moorish explorer Leo Africanus, the most up-to-date edition being the *Description de l'Afrique*, translated by A. Epaulard (Paris: Adrien-Maisonneuve, 1956), but which is also available in English as *The History and Description of Africa* (London: Hakluyt Society, 1896). Of the many other accounts, see especially Heinrich Barth, *Travels and Discoveries in North and Central Africa*, 3 vols. (London: Frank Cass, 1965); René Caillié, *Journal d'un voyage à Timbouctou et à Jenné*, 3 vols. (Paris: Editions Anthropos, 1965); Mungo Park, *Travels in the Interior Districts of Africa*, 2nd ed. (London: Bulmer and Nicol, 1799); Hugh Clapperton, *Journal of a Second Expedition into the Interior of Africa* (London: J. Murray, 1829); and Richard and John Lander, *Journal of an Expedition to Explore the Course and Termination of the Niger*, 3 vols. (London: J. Murray, 1832). For an indispensable guide to these and many other similar materials, see Raymond Mauny's splendid *Tableau géographique de l'ouest Africain au moyen âge* (Dakar: Institut Français d'Afrique Noire, 1961; Amsterdam: Swets and Zeitlinger, 1967).

The second major source consists of modern studies, usually by anthropologists, of traditional African societies, in which social, economic, and other institutions are examined in detail. See, for example, S. F. Nadel, *A Black Byzantium* (London: Oxford University Press, 1942); Paul and Laura Bohannan, *Tiv Economy* (Evanston, Ill.: Northwestern University Press, 1968); J. Richard-Molard, *L'Afrique occidentale française* (Paris: Berger-Levrault, 1949); or M. Delafosse, *Haut-Sénégal-Niger*, 3 vols. (Paris: Larose, 1912). See also relevant sections of D. Forde, ed., *African Worlds* (London: Oxford University Press, 1954); M. Fortes and E. E. Evans-Pritchard, eds., *African Political Systems* (London: Oxford University Press, 1940); and H. Baumann and D. Westermann, *Les peuples et les civilisations de l'Afrique* (Paris: Payot, 1962). A number of nutritional studies should be mentioned, including Bruce F. Johnston, *The Staple Food Economies of Western Tropical Africa* (Stanford, Calif.: Stanford University Press, 1958); S. D. Onabamiro, *Food and Health* (London: Penguin, 1953); M. and S. L. Fortes, "Food in the Domestic Economy of the Tallensi," *Africa* (April 1936); and K. M. Buchanan and J. C. Pugh, *Land and People in Nigeria* (London: University of London Press, 1955). To these should be added the massive geographic text of W. B. Morgan and J. C. Pugh, *West Africa* (London: Methuen, 1967), as well as the first recent attempt at a comprehensive economic historical analysis for Africa—A. G. Hopkins, *An Economic History of West Africa* (London: Longmans; New York: Columbia University Press, 1973).

5

FOREST CIVILIZATIONS

The Way of Life

Fragmentary were the reports by Saharan travelers telling of the great kingdoms of the western and central Sudan, yet these were riches indeed compared with the almost total blank that comprised the body of concurrent knowledge of the West African forest. Intrepid and inquisitive, the explorers from the north nevertheless failed to breach the forest frontier, resorting instead to secondhand accounts of gold mining in the land known as Wangara, to occasional and sometimes disastrous experiments with foodstuffs of forest origin, or to descriptions of characteristic forest products celebrated throughout West Africa for their nutritional, medicinal, or pleasure-giving capabilities.

There is a palatable root plant grown in Mali, the thirteenth-century Arab scholar al-Omari informed his readers, adding somewhat fancifully that its theft would cost a man his head, this grisly reminder invariably left to mark the place of execution as a deterrent to further larceny. His contemporary Ibn Battuta has a different story based on the personal experience that al-Omari had lacked. While visiting the western Sudan,

97

Ibn Battuta and six companions had made a meal of yam—for that was surely the plant in question—all of them falling ill and one subsequently dying.

This anecdote also contains its bizarre aspect since yams, though in some cases poisonous, were in their various forms the principal staple of the West African forest, serving for that region as millet and sorghum did for the savanna. The basic variety was, as it is today, the white Guinea yam *(Dioscorea rotundata)*, an indigenous plant that was possibly domesticated as far back as the third millennium B.C. when the desiccation of the Sahara forced peoples southward into the forest, bringing with them their taste for wild yam. These plants, though they grew tolerably well under the drier conditions of the savanna, thrived in regions of heavy rainfall; hence, the movement south was a triumph for the yam which soon became established as the basic diet of the forest people.

Who were these people? Written historical sources do not exist, and archaeological explorations have only begun to yield their first facts, but an analysis of present-day West African languages tells much. With some notable exceptions like Hausa and Songhai, the peoples who now inhabit the West African savanna and forest speak related languages, a circumstance of great significance for it strongly suggests a common ancestry. Moreover, analyses of linguistic differences among some of these groups indicate that they began to separate at least as far back as eight thousand years ago, thereby implying a long-lived process of migration and settlement across West Africa by growing numbers of descendants from a small ancestral body that existed far in the remote past.

It seems probable that the main lines of movement were south and west, partly because this would have followed from increasingly inhospitable Saharan conditions, but there is also the fact that so many traditions of West African peoples speak of a northern and eastern origin, and the evidence of more recent times that traces migrations along this general direction. Yoruba tradition claims kinship with the ancient Middle East, and similar origins have been argued at times for the Jukun, Ga, and Akan, among others. While such affiliations are usually regarded as fanciful, it is generally agreed that migrations did indeed take place, bringing the Yoruba down to the region of Oyo and Ife as recently as one thousand years ago and the Akan south into the forest of present-day Ghana at approximately the same time. The great Bantu migration, moreover, which covered subequatorial Africa during the two millennia following the birth of Christ, is also understood to have begun among West Africans along the Benue River who filtered southward into the Congo forest in the earliest stages of their vast movement.

The examples of Yoruba and Akan may be somewhat misleading, not as to the fact of their migrations which illustrated a widespread pattern, but in the size and complexity of their societies. The Oyo empire of the Yoruba and the Akan state of Ashanti, as well as several others, notably the kingdom of Benin or the latter-day slaving power of Dahomey, were atypical forest nations. Powerful, prosperous, and aggressive, led by rulers of unusual ability, and equipped with the administrative sophistication necessary for sustained control of large areas and many diverse subject groups, these nations in their very size and strength contrasted sharply in character with the majority of peoples inhabiting the rain forest of West Africa and the Congo basin.

By its very nature the forest bred isolation and rudimentary political organization. The typical community was the small, self-sustained village, a hamlet centered within a few fields cleared from the grudging growth of the surrounding forest. Such a grouping numbered perhaps but a few score inhabitants, farmers and their families, most related to one another in a tight-knit web of kinship. Life was simple, government largely limited to the settlement of disputes by family heads or elders, the basic economy scarcely more than the production and consumption of food, social life centered on the ceremony accompanying birth, death, and family alliance, recreation preoccupied with the eternal round of visit and gossip which were the main pursuits of leisure time. At varying intervals—every fourth, fifth, seventh, or seventeenth day, for example—there were markets held in larger neighboring villages, and these were social as well as economic occasions of great importance where news could be exchanged along with produce, a new marriage contracted, a family dispute settled, or a companionable afternoon passed at the stall of the palm wine merchant.

The forest villager lived a simple life, but his cuisine at any rate achieved a variety that would have been the envy of the more limited savanna dweller. To begin with, there was the ubiquitous yam, a heavy

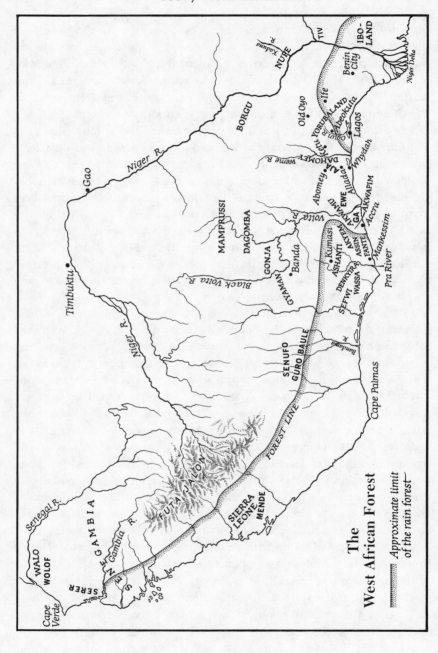

The
West African Forest

Approximate limit
of the rain forest

tuber as big around as a man's arm and sometimes growing so large that a single individual could scarcely lift its weight. To supplement this staple food, the farmer added other starchy crops—cocoyam, plantain, and banana. In some wetter regions such as the tidewater swamps of the western Guinea coast, rice was the basic cereal, and in most districts varieties of beans, okra, chives, onions, melons, and peppers filled out the roster of cultivated plants.

Hunting and gathering were not neglected, however, and added much to the diet. Fresh- and saltwater fishing by net, line, harpoon, gaff, trap, and poison contributed vital proteins, the fish supplemented in many regions by giant river snails and oysters found attached in clusters to the lower trunks of swamp trees. In the forest, hunting and trapping were limited essentially to small game such as porcupines, birds, hares, and monkeys, although larger quarry, including elephants, could have been pursued. Indeed, foraging seems to have been a more fruitful pastime, particularly because of the versatile palm with its milky wine and its oil that was as basic to the cooking of the African forest regions as the yams that each housewife converted into the doughy paste called fufu.

Here, too, grew the celebrated kola trees, their fruit prized widely, serving Africans as an antidote to fatigue and as a traditional sign of welcome in each village compound. The kola seeds were rosy red in color and chestnutlike in size and shape. They divided into four segments which, when chewed slowly and thoroughly, quenched thirst and quieted hunger. The bitter astringency of their flavor was widely appreciated throughout West Africa and the Congo region, but it was their caffeine content that helped sustain the weary traveler and built the reputation of this mild stimulant for curative powers, particularly, it was said, with liver ailments.

As in the savanna, flour was milled with mortar and pestle made of wooden pole and hollow log, but the ancient flat grinding stones were considered superior. The yam was cut into pieces and soaked in water, then placed between the grinders which were set on an angle so that the milled flour paste would fall away. The women worked the upper stone rhythmically, holding it by two ends that had been tapered to provide handles, stopping their circular motion frequently to add water. When finished they placed the grated material in bags where it was allowed to ferment in the sun for a day. It was then mixed with water, boiled and strained, the coarser batter set aside for goat and pig feed, the residue shaped into loaves of white dough which were wrapped in plantain leaves and stored for future use.

The yams were grown in fields which were cleared and cultivated in a pattern of mounds similar to that employed by the savanna farmer for his millet. Throughout these fields, and in the surrounding forest as well, were the palms, many growing wild, others planted and subsisting with a minimum of care, yet all greatly cherished by the forest people who had long appreciated the many values of this generous plant. In the forest, land tenure was practiced much as in the savanna; in both areas shifting cultivation, an abundance of land, and low population density combined to weaken the concept of individual land ownership. Such was not the case with the palm tree. In Dahomey, anyone who planted a palm using a wild sprout gathered in the forest could claim that tree for himself and his descendants regardless of who controlled the land it occupied, its yield of nuts and oil also becoming his property. Furthermore, it was under a palm tree that the umbilical cord of each individual was buried, and thus every Dahomean owned at least one palm which thereafter possessed for him important religious as well as economic properties.

The economic assets of the palm were multifarious. Some species, the raffia in particular, provided fibers used in the Congo River region for weaving cloth employed both as garment and as currency. Others were grown to form hedges and groves of shade trees, providing a tasty yellow plumlike fruit in the bargain. Still others gave forth a refreshing liquid when tapped—the celebrated palm wine, the finest varieties of which were reserved among Congo people for honoring the ancestors. Everywhere the gifts of the palm were apparent—in the walls and roofs of houses, in the traps of hunters and the snares of fishermen, in medicines, in cosmetics, in clothing, and in nourishment.

Of all the palm species, the most prized was that which produced the palm kernel and its palm oil derivative. The nutlike kernel, turned red when ripe, was sometimes eaten roasted but more typically was boiled in order to extract the oil. This was done in some areas by treading on the softened nuts in canoe-shaped wooden troughs, in others by kneading with the hands until the fibers had been broken down and the oil collected. The kernels were then put aside for livestock feed while the oil was strained and boiled in a further refining process. The oil impressed early European visitors, one remarking poetically that it combined "the odor of violets, a taste approaching our olive, and a color purer and more perfect than saffron." The final product was an oil or butter which might be burned in lamps or used to anoint the body but which was chiefly employed in cooking.

Palm oil and yam pudding were the staple elements of the forest dinner, which was garnished with a variety of wild and cultivated plants and less frequently with meat or fish. At day's end the women busied themselves before the cooking pots, preparing a mixture of oil and water into which went peas, beans, melon seeds, onions, okra, and whatever other seasonal growth the forest might offer, all laced with copious quantities of pepper which overwhelmed all but the hardiest palates. Salt, too, was added, frequently gained from the ashes of incinerated palm pith, and finally in went bits of meat and fish when these were available. Protein deficiency, endemic in the yam belt, led to a general craving for meat, which in turn widened the limits of what was conventional fare. Poultry was common, though limited largely to ceremonial occasions, and dog meat was consumed in many places. Small animals, sometimes including insects and reptiles, were acceptable, and the earth of termite nests was looked on in some districts as a dish for gourmets. No palate could afford to be so fastidious as to balk at the presence of putrescent flesh, for decomposition developed quickly in the hot forest climate and the pangs of hunger compelled response, whatever the means.

When the palm oil stew was ready, it was poured into a calabash platter which already contained a large loaf of warm yam fufu. Here each family gathered, sharing their meal from the same central dish and their water from a single enormous gourd, their solidarity expressed in this act of communion. Utensils were minimal, but etiquette was rigidly prescribed. Among some people, the women and children ate separately, but everywhere the diners attacked their meal with characteristic gesture. Squatting about the communal calabash, they took turns breaking off a lump of fufu with the fingers, rolling it into a ball which was soaked in the hot pungent oil with its floating bits of meat and vegetable. That enthusiasm for this dish was not restricted to Africans alone may be noted from the testimonial of a sixteenth-century Briton visiting Benin.

Speaking of yam bread, he paid it the highest compliment: "When it is well sodden," he explained, "I would leave our bread to eat of it, it is pleasant in eating, and light of digestion."

The palm tree fed the dweller of the forest. It also housed him, protecting him from enemies and sheltering him from the elements. In Dahomey the walls of the houses were made of mud but the roofing was thatched with palm leaves—first, ridgepoles of bamboo, then cross-stripping of palm leaf ribs, and finally the thatching itself made of the stripped-away fronds tied in bundles. With the Bakongo, the whole construction, walls and roofing, was manufactured from woven palm leaf, which was also employed to build a complex series of mazelike passages throughout the village, designed to confuse the stranger and protect the inhabitants against surprise attack. These dwellings were surely some of the earliest examples of prefabricated housing. Walls and roof were woven of interlaced palm branches, a process more reminiscent of the art of basketry than of architecture, then were quickly assembled at the chosen site where they were attached to stakes already driven into the ground. In short order the house was completed; a small rectangular structure lighted only by a low entrance, it was virtually bare of furniture, containing a few straw mats, some gourds and pots for storage, water, and palm wine. The royal or aristocratic residences in the larger towns were only slightly more pretentious, chiefly because they contained drums as well as ceremonial equipment for the performance of rituals necessary to ensure the general prosperity.

Congo villages appeared haphazard in plan, but in fact they were well-constructed mazes, designed for defense. A labyrinth of narrow paths ran in all directions through thick, tall grass which effectively screened the scattered homesteads, while each dwelling was further guarded by the live or fabricated hedges installed to thwart wild beasts or surprise slaving attacks. More formidable city walls were found among certain West African peoples. Benin City was reported by European travelers early in the seventeenth century to be protected by earthworks fronted by a broad ditch, a construction devised specifically as a defensive fortification. More commonplace, if less military in conception, were the barriers employed by such people as the Yoruba, Fante, or Ibo who normally surrounded their hamlets with mud walls, on the outer side of which a strip of forest was left standing to separate the village site from the farms and gardens beyond. A seventeenth-century variation of this pattern was the waterfront town of the Ijebu Yoruba who had provided themselves with a wooden wall. Fishing communities in the Niger Delta and coastal inland waterways built their palm leaf houses on tall platforms poised above the lagoons, their location making unnecessary the precaution of fencing to protect homes that were approachable only by boat.

The Yoruba compounds usually consisted of attached houses enclosing an interior courtyard, outer walls fronting on the village street with a blank exterior broken only by a simple doorway, living quarters facing inward on the courtyard which was shared by the members of the single or extended family. Some Yoruba put walls about their compounds like a miniature village, the houses standing detached within; but this was a pattern more characteristic of Ibo communities wherein each head of household presided over his own compound which contained the houses of his wives, unmarried children, and other dependents along with a meeting hall used primarily for the entertainment of visitors. Ibo architecture favored wattle and daub construction with raffia mat roofing, whereas the Yoruba buildings were normally made of large earthen bricks, the walls supporting thatched roofs.

More formidable still were the structures of Benin City and the Ashanti capital at Kumasi, perhaps befitting the importance of these royal metropolises. Seventeenth-century Benin was said to be laid out along some thirty main avenues, broad and straight, through which ran a network of small, intersecting secondary streets. The houses were set close together, single-storied structures equipped with verandas and balustrades supporting roofing of palm and banana leaf. Those of the nobility were large, containing many rooms with walls and floors of packed red earth; but these were modest compared with the royal palace, enclosed within its own walls on one side of the town. It consisted of numerous buildings containing apartments for the king's ministers, the rooms supported by wooden columns encased in copper on which were reliefs depicting historic military victories.

Benin was kept scrupulously clean, and municipal security was so effective that theft was unknown and houses had no doors. Ashanti towns visited early in the nineteenth century were also reportedly clean, at least in the main thoroughfares, although the back streets and the areas behind each dwelling were typically heaped with garbage. Housing ranged from simple bamboo huts to larger mud-brick dwellings with whitewashed walls sometimes embellished with sculpted reliefs. What distinguished Ashanti, however, during this period when her power and prestige were at a height, was the complex and artful architecture of the royal court.

The compound of the *asantehene,* or king, consisted of several large courtyards flanked by buildings, the main floor of each containing a series of chambers raised a few feet above the court level. Each of these rooms, variously furnished with gold embossed stools, silk-covered beds, and scattered regalia, was open to the courtyard, although provided with a drop curtain of plaited cane. Above these apartments ran a second story fronted by an arcaded gallery behind which were a series of smaller rooms employed chiefly as sleeping quarters and private residences. The walls were made of a gravelly clay poured between wattle molds and finished with mud facing and whitewash, their solid structure serving to support the second floor. The roof, which rested on squared wooden columns, was of typical thatch design laid on steep gables. The gallery arches were of bent cane construction, above which the entablatures were filled with mud and wattle and finished in fan and trellis motifs, while the whole facade was decorated with a series of intricate geometric patterns in bas-relief. The ground-floor chambers were approximately a dozen feet square and those above about eight feet in each dimension. When doors were used they were carved in solid pieces from silk-cotton trees and provided with locks imported from Hausaland. The upstairs accommodations included commodes which emptied by chute into the ground and were cleared by boiling water, a feature that was standard in most Ashanti town houses. The royal quarters fronted on one side of a large court but were screened from all profane gaze by a decorated wall. When holding audiences, the *asantehene* usually repaired to an outer yard, here surrounding himself with his courtiers, all bedecked in brightest cloth, all shaded by a dome of elaborately designed umbrellas, all equipped with the insignia of their exalted position—gold canes, spangled elephant tail fly whisks, embossed muskets, and gold-headed swords.

The Concept of Work

While it is difficult to generalize about the many peoples of a vast continent, it is safe to say that traditional African communities were fully conscious of the value and necessity of work, although they varied in how they apportioned the work load and in the emphasis they placed upon work in relation to other activities. This is a point worth making not only for its own sake, but also because of the observations of foreign visitors who repeatedly misinterpreted African societies in reporting variously that Africans were naturally lazy, that the men passed the day in drunken gossip while the women farmed and cooked, or that compulsion was the sole means by which the African could be induced to perform gainful labor.

Such misinterpretation emerged from differing views as to what constituted a functioning economy. To the traveler from the burgeoning capitalism of sixteenth- or seventeenth-century Europe, labor was a marketable production factor, essential and costly, and therefore to be utilized at maximum efficiency. To the African subsistence farmer, there was much work to be done, but there was no such commodity as labor, only the recognized duty of each individual to promote community prosperity, no market for labor, only the mutual privileges and obligations of productive members of the functioning group. Work was performed and understood in terms of social relationships. "Why do we work together? But isn't this our land? Aren't we brothers? Are we not as one man?"

Outside observers, moreover, were usually ignorant of those environmental imperatives governing village productivity. Everybody worked, and necessarily so, for labor as a factor of production was not infrequently in short supply. Nevertheless, so-called nonproductive activity claimed much attention. Marginal utility limited investment in labor beyond the absorptive capabilities of land and technologies; consequently, leisure-time pursuits could have been as much determined as desired. Those who condemned African labor as wasteful and inefficient scarcely understood this principle; neither were they aware of the disease factor—hidden and deceptive—which robbed the African of his incentive and capacity for productive work.

In one respect the African attitude toward work was as understandable as it was universal. Work was never regarded as a necessary evil to be endured in toil and drudgery, and it was not something to be performed in solitude. No doubt this view emerged originally from the economic necessity of the group hunt or the premium that heavy agricultural tasks placed on communal cooperation. In time, however, work developed social characteristics that stressed entertainment and recreation, thereby giving it another important distinction from the Western concept of labor. It could not be bought and sold, or made painful or distasteful. In the lexicon of traditional Africa, work was never the stated opposite of play. Indeed, work and play were more likely to be regarded as complementary, if not synonymous; their opposite in each case was indolence.

In the West African forest, as elsewhere, the essential working unit was the family, its many tasks distributed by traditional usage. For example, the men cleaned out brush and trees and did the heavy work of preparing yam mounds while the women cleared the grass. Both sexes might participate in planting and harvesting, weeding being widely regarded as women's work while cultivating was felt to be the responsibility of the men. Children who were old enough fell in with the work prescribed for their elders, while the younger ones were assigned the important task of warding off animal pests attracted by the ripening harvest.

When farming was organized around the compound, production was controlled by the family head who distributed food, tools, and even land and who was able to coordinate his resources and labor force with an efficiency that allowed for complex scheduling of crops and farming on a scale not accessible to the individual farmer. The compound head was typically a father, uncle, or eldest brother controlling a number of younger brothers or sons, unwed or only recently married. He determined which crops were to be planted in particular fields each year. It was he who assigned individual tasks and outlined the daily routine, making frequent inspection tours in lieu of the actual field work which he did not perform. He took charge of the total harvest and doled it to the compound members, planning its disposal in such a way that there would be surpluses for such expenses as the purchase of tools, the payment of bridewealth, or the cost of major repairs within the compound. Although these were cooperative enterprises, they retained a strong sense of individual participation. Pride in the efficiency of good teamwork was balanced by an awareness of what each individual worker had contributed to the whole; effective unity thrived on internal competition.

Some tasks, such as clearing new ground, roofing a house, or building a wall, required large-scale collective labor beyond the resources of the family or compound and were reserved to larger village groups, frequently organized by means of age grades. Depending on the job at hand, an invitation was sent out to the young men of the village to assemble on a certain day, perhaps to rethatch a roof or prepare a field for new yam plots. If it were a field that required clearing, the workers arrived early on the morning of the appointed day accompanied by a band of musicians who were an invariable feature of the occasion. The air was festive, the attitude of the participants an alloy of pride in status and pleasure in anticipation.

The staccato drums, the skirling flutes, and the chanting of the work songs quickly drew bystanders as the party divided into two competing groups which began at opposite ends of the field, moving slowly toward each other, each team accompanied by its complement of drummers. As the work proceeded, the tension mounted, driven by the rhythmic movement of the hoes, the deep, hoarse grunts of the participants, the compelling cadence of the drums, and the shouted encouragement of the spectators. Older men stood to one side, watching, commenting, criticizing; children romped and shouted; periodically a worker would rise to assess his progress, then uttering a piercing yell would fall to his labors with renewed vigor. As each participant finished a row, he looked about to compare his technique with others; then executing a little triumphal dance, he sang of his speed and dexterity, proudly comparing his achievement with what he saw as the clumsy pace of the others.

With the end of the project in sight, the pace quickened, the men overcoming their fatigue, driven by the pulsating rhythm, their own ambition, and the exhortations from the sidelines. Suddenly the two teams were together, the field was finished, and the contest was over in a hubbub of shouting, dancing, singing, and laughing. Great calabashes of yam porridge were brought for the breathless, sweating workers who fell on their meal with the same enthusiasm they had brought to their task, downing their food with draughts of palm wine as they retold and reargued their accomplishments.

The meal completed, the teams returned to their work, resuming their feverish pace throughout the rest of the day save for another meal and long break during the noon-hour heat. By dusk they had cleared and tilled approximately three acres, and it was now time for the competitive, sporting aspects of the affair to give way to a more purely recreational pastime. Everyone—musicians, workers, and audience—repaired to the house of the farmer for an evening of feasting and dancing during which the exploits of the day were discussed and analyzed endlessly amidst much boisterous but good-natured contention, chiefly on the part of the young men who were the heroes of the occasion.

Similar competitions were organized among the women for such tasks as hoeing and weeding in the fields, or packing the dirt floors of the houses and open areas around the compounds. Aside from the obvious advantages that working parties offered in meeting the needs of public works projects and large-scale jobs beyond the capacities of a single family, there were a number of additional economic assets. First of all, the practice offered a form of insurance to those members of the community too ill or aged to sustain the full rigors of farming. Heads of family groups whose sons had married and moved away could still call on assistance from other young men of the village in preparing their fields, this by right of their position of seniority and the fact that they had in their time also participated in working parties for others. Furthermore, at certain seasons when the timetable of seeding and harvesting called for close precision, the availability of a work gang was often crucial. Finally, if the working party came to the rescue of ailing farmers, it could also be made to assist the resourceful; in the case of a land dispute, for example, a trespasser might be obliged to give up control of the land he had occupied; but if these fields had already been sown and cultivated, perhaps through the shrewd employment of a work group, custom permitted him to retain control of the disputed plots until his harvest had been completed.

Of course, to call together such a group involved the expense of musicians and food, but this was a minimal cost more than offset by the advantages of a cheap, efficient labor supply. A day in the fields with a moderate-size party achieved as much as could be done in a week or more under normal conditions. Hence the farmer exchanged the price of a day's entertainment for many man-hours of essentially free labor. The workers received no remuneration, their payment being the pleasure of the occasion, and if the affair was judged a success, its sponsor gained the additional advantage of a much enhanced reputation within the community.

Social Order and the Division of Wealth and Labor

Most ancient communities in the rain forest were small, their economies essentially limited to subsistence agriculture and their societies generally egalitarian. Adequate land was the right of each family member; but social controls prevented excessive personal acquisition of land, for this might lead to neglect of group obligations. While the fruits of land and labor belonged first to each individual, reciprocal privileges and duties within the family prescribed a mutual sharing that discouraged personal differences in material prosperity. Communal labor was commonly employed, but its performance arose normally from general agreement, not through impressment or tribute imposed by chief or council of elders. Political authority within the village was also circumscribed, residing almost exclusively in each compound where the family leader held sway. Even here an arbitrary head who disregarded the advice of others would soon find himself bypassed or replaced.

Surplus wealth and political authority were thus accumulated with difficulty, but prestige could come to those who controlled the destinies of large families. Many dependents meant more workers and bigger farms with the possibility of an increasingly efficient division of labor. Large compounds gave the family head an immediate following, a greater voice in community affairs, influence in the disposition of produce, land, and labor, and important prerogatives in the arrangement of marriage contracts. Nevertheless, the influence of a family head had natural limits. The more land, the more claims thereto; the more family connections, the more lineage obligations; the more compound members, the more mouths to feed; the more children, the more loss of manpower, land, and property to other families through marriage.

Subsistence economies with minimum political or social differentiation existed in Africa alongside other societies which, by contrast, encouraged a concentration of political authority, social distinction, and accumulation of wealth. These communities were exemplified by such great savanna kingdoms as Mali or Songhai, the Luba and Lunda states of south central Africa, or forest powers like Ashanti and Benin. By and large they were the creation of peoples whose expanding population and growing economic complexity had achieved a degree of labor division permitting certain members to occupy themselves with affairs of state, craft production, or trade, thereby diminishing their share in the more usual pursuits of food production. Under such circumstances class lines developed along with aspirations toward improving individual status, power and prestige became linked with the accumulation of wealth, and tribute was an accepted means whereby the governing class sustained itself, in return providing security and policing for the community as a whole.

Whatever shape traditional African societies assumed, they all established a major division between the sexes for both wealth and labor. In all parts of Africa, specific economic responsibilities were assigned exclusively to men, others reserved to women, while each people had areas of work on the farm and in the compound in which both men and women might participate. With this division of labor went a corresponding allocation of controls over land and its products, participation in market activities, and obligation for household supplies of food. In these matters customs varied widely, making generalization difficult, but it may be said with some confidence that women in traditional African societies occupied a position of economic and social strength based securely upon the widespread belief in ultimate male dependence upon a female source of life.

This position may be quickly illustrated. In Kanem-Bornu the queen mother and other women of the royal house traditionally exerted a powerful influence in affairs of state, and the same was true among the Wolof who delegated major economic and judicial authority to women of royal birth. During the fifteenth century, the most important ruler of the Hausa kingdom of Zaria was a woman; in the caravan cities of Kumbi Saleh and Walata, women practiced a personal freedom that astonished Muslim visitors—in Kumbi they were entitled to forms of adornment otherwise reserved only for the king. Among the Ashanti, wives were inherited along with personal property, but this was more than offset by powerful sanctions that protected the standing, rights, and possessions of every woman, assured of her status by the full authority of her clan membership. The warlike people of Dahomey established a woman's corps within their army, the famed and feared "Amazons" whose exploits set the standards for Dahomean conduct in battle; in like spirit, it was the Egba Yoruba women who greatly assisted their troops in repelling the armies of Dahomey during a climactic battle in 1851 fought at the walls of Abeokuta.

Yoruba women in general were spared work in the fields, a freedom that enabled them to develop wealth and influence as traders, but the Ibo followed quite another pattern, dividing farm chores between the sexes and maintaining, in some parts of Iboland at any rate, a strong male domination in daily affairs. Some early European explorers in West Africa and the Congo made special note of the inequities of a system that relegated women to the heavy labor of planting and harvesting while the men entertained themselves in war making, hunting, and gossip, reinforcing their idleness with quantities of palm wine which their wives were bound to provide. While such accounts were exaggerated and incomplete, they suggested the burdens placed upon women in some societies as compared with the elevated status and respectful treatment they enjoyed in others.

Like the Yoruba, the Nupe women had no responsibility for farm work but were expected to embellish the staple family diet with spices, greens, and other ingredients, an obligation that drew them into trade as a means of supplementing household income. Among the Tiv, both work and ownership were divided between the men and women along lines that indicated a sensitivity to corporate needs and individual capabilities. Women controlled their own fields by right of marriage, but both men and women worked these plots according to well-established principles. The men surveyed the farms, performed the heavy clearing, and prepared mounds for the planting of yams. The women were responsible for planting, weeding, and harvesting but were assisted in the harvests by the men who also helped with planting on occasion. The yams and sorghum belonged predominantly to the women along with such side crops as beans, peppers, and okra, but from this stock they were obliged to feed their families. The men took charge of the millet which was reserved as a hunger crop but was also converted into beer, the making of which was the responsibility of the women. During the rains little farm work of any sort was performed, and activities centered on ceremonies and beer drinking. It may seem strange that, at this moment of potential preharvest hunger, there was the tendency to commit scarce and dwindling food resources to brewing. To the Tiv, the logic was inescapable—it was preferable to give the illusion of satisfaction to ten than to sustain one single individual, leaving no comfort for the rest.

This sense of group cohesion and responsibility was manifest in another aspect of African life closely connected with the allocation of labor. The institution of slavery was, by all accounts, long-lived and far-flung throughout the African continent and established a lowermost social stratum, even in otherwise classless societies, while providing a source of labor to supplement the more usual supplies, along with a solution to the problem of disposal for war captives, criminals, and debtors. A slave was essentially a stranger who had lost his right to return to his own people. Being a stranger he had no local status, but having been purchased or captured in war, he was obliged to remain in a foreign community, but under distinctly disadvantageous circumstances.

In theory the slave had none of the rights and standing enjoyed by those who belonged to the society through their lineage. He was a piece of property controlled by his master for whom he was compelled to labor in perpetuity. He could but infrequently claim legal protection; his very life lay in the hands of his owner who was usually free to destroy, sell, or maltreat him with impunity, who usually inherited his property on death, and who might lay claim to his children as the slave issue of slave parents. He was not infrequently the appointed victim of human sacrifice, and with the advent of the Atlantic slave trade he faced the additional hazard of sale to slave dealers for eventual disposal overseas.

In actual practice, however, a slave's condition was often much more promising. Though normally required to perform the more taxing, less pleasant tasks, he might become a full-fledged, albeit lowly, member of his master's family. He thus was given land of his own and spare time to work it and was frequently provided with a wife, sometimes freeborn, in which case his children by her were regarded as free. He could purchase his own liberty through work and saving, and if he was a person of ability, he had the opportunity to rise in wealth and influence among his adoptive kinsmen.

With most African people there was no stigma attached to slavery since it was regarded as a natural affliction, the result of unhappy accident which could befall anyone. Many slaves gained positions of great influence, particularly those attached to the houses of nobility or, best of all, to the royal court itself. Slaves in the households of princes might become trusted messengers, advisers, tax collectors, or body-guards, their loyalty based on the personal master-slave relation, their value augmented both by their ineligibility for succession to the throne and their counterpoise to the pretensions of a powerful nobility. In some societies, even the exalted position of king was not beyond the grasp of a slave. The large ruling houses of the Niger Delta city-states sometimes allowed slaves to rise to positions of control, and in the case of the celebrated Jaja, a former slave ultimately became founder and head of the powerful trading state of Opobo during the latter part of the nineteenth century.

Slavery was by its nature involuntary, but Africans also practiced a form of voluntary slavery called pawning in which a person was given over as security, usually to guarantee repayment of a loan. Slavery resulted from political insecurity as one individual lost his freedom while another gained a capital asset which bore interest in the form of productive labor. Pawning emerged from economic insecurity, the borrower exchanging the freedom of a designated pawn—usually himself or a close relative—for a loan needed to meet some extraordinary expense.

The economic implications of pawning were somewhat more complex than those surrounding simple involuntary servitude. In a subsistence economy, the limitations in family capacity to meet unusual expenses such as the cost of food procured in time of famine or the burdens of a heavy bridewealth were sometimes overcome by bonding a husband, son, daughter, or other member of the household. Unlike slavery, this was a temporary arrangement which obtained only until the loan was repaid. The pawn lost none of his family connections and enjoyed full customary and legal protection within the society, although he and his family usually lost social status by a public confession of poverty revealed through the degrading process of bonding. No interest was charged on the loan, the labor of the pawn being considered proper compensation, but if the pawn died before the debt was settled, custom obliged that another be substituted, since the pawn represented the principal of the account as well as security for its repayment.

Like the slave, the pawn was obliged to perform labor as directed; hence, an individual able to gain control over even a few slaves and pawns could, through their labor, substantially augment his productivity, an important consideration in those societies like the Ibo or Nupe in which wealth was an important means to enhanced prestige. At the same time, pawning was a rough-shaped system for redistribution of wealth. Among the Nupe a well-to-do man could not easily refuse to help a poor suppliant, even if the pawn offered as surety were but a child from whom little economic advantage could be expected. Such a pawn could be redeemed after a few months or years just when he had become productive, a poor investment compared with the outright purchase of an able-bodied slave of permanent utility. Moreover, by pawning a child to the household of a skilled farmer or craftsman, a father secured educational opportunities for his offspring not otherwise easily obtained.

In fact, pawning contained some similarities to the concept of clientship, which the Hausa called *bara,* or servant, and which was a common practice in many parts of the West African savanna. An impecunious peasant offered voluntary allegiance to a powerful, well-placed individual, receiving in return security against the uncertainties of village life. For his part, the patron provided legal and economic assistance while gaining a follower as servant and soldier or merely as a material sign of his exalted status.

The Uses of Surplus

In the kingdom of Dahomey, when a man died the size and lavishness of his funeral was considered a direct measure of his importance. The provident man, therefore, devoted his life to securing as many wives as he could and begetting as many children as possible so that they and their friends could provide him with the kind of funeral that assured his prominence both in this world and the next. Among the Ashanti, the chiefs supported themselves through a series of taxes levied on inheritance, legal transactions, and commercial activity, these substantial revenues being used to considerable extent in maintaining the open-handed hospitality that Ashanti convention demanded of Ashanti chiefs. Along the Gold Coast, early European explorers remarked on the custom of acquiring musical horns made of elephant tusks which were collected and played by families in public performance, the number of horns and the leisure to perform reflecting the wealth and prestige of the players. In like wise, these same peoples strove to impress one another through elaborate feasts and the acquisition of decorated battle shields, fabricated purely for purposes of display.

The societies of precolonial Africa were geared to a subsistence agriculture, but traditional African economies were not in any literal sense subsistence economies, for they were quite capable of accumulating and utilizing small but measurable quantities of surplus wealth. The ancient farming communities of Africa organized their land occupation without reference to private ownership, but the principle of private ownership was understood and practiced full well. The motive of personal profit, so intimately associated with the history of capitalism in western Europe, is said to be foreign to the economic concepts of traditional Africa. In fact, the desire for personal profit was equally powerful in Africa. In Europe the accumulation of capital was economic; in Africa it was social.

The farmer who could afford slaves or pawns gained both increased leisure and the prestige which that leisure reflected. The man who could provide lavish feasts for his kin and invest substantial payments in bridewealth sought and received the approval of his community as a person of means and therefore of standing. Throughout the West African savanna, the horse was the mark of a warrior, a widely accepted external sign of distinction that was acquired, where possible, by members of all social groups. In the kingdom of Kongo, dress was an immediately identifiable badge of status, as it was in ancient Ghana and Mali, the richer and more elaborate dress being reserved for nobility and the wealthy. According to William Bosman, the seventeenth-century Dutch trader, the soldiers in some Gold Coast districts were so loaded down with jewelry and finery that they could scarcely march, and more generally he concluded that, in the areas he visited, it was wealth rather than rank that was most honored.

Wealth, therefore, offering the opportunity for display, for open-handed entertainment, or for generous support of family and lineage membership, was a direct means to enhanced prestige and elevated status. In this context, it is not surprising that property played an important role in the achievement of influence and political authority. Rights of inheritance were carefully defined in many societies, since a legacy involving slaves, houses, money, fruit-bearing trees, or magic charms bequeathed a control over resources that could and did introduce substantial changes in the social position of individuals or families within their community. In Ashanti inheritance was an important source of chiefly wealth, and in Dahomey to inherit a man's claim to his wives was to inherit the potential wealth and prestige that the numerical enlargement of his family would bring. Even in more egalitarian societies, where Western concepts of property and accumulation of wealth are not so easily identifiable, surplus production was guided toward the enhancement of prestige. Among the Tiv, goods to be inherited like seed yams and clothing or rights in women were distributed to preserve equity; yet Tiv women were ever hopeful of increasing their supply of yams by inheritance or otherwise, while prestige and influence were accorded that individual most successful in expanding the size of his compound and the number of his dependents.

Quite aside from the satisfaction in display provided by the disposal of surplus production, the social and economic systems of traditional Africa employed their surpluses to establish a form of welfare insurance for the less fortunate or provident. In their several ways, the large compound of the egalitarian Tiv, the clientship system among hierarchic Nupe, or the open houses of Ashanti chiefs helped feed hungry mouths and redistribute some of the resources in the land. Thus was essential human motivation diverted to serve broader social ends.

SUGGESTIONS FOR FURTHER READING

As with the West African savanna, sources for the forest areas may be divided broadly into traveler accounts and recent anthropological and other studies. Among modern studies shedding light on forest economies, see P. A. Talbot, *The People of Southern Nigeria*, 4 vols. (London: Oxford University Press, 1926); Melville J. Herskovits, *Dahomey: An Ancient West African Kingdom*, 2 vols. (New York: J. J. Augustin, 1938); R. S. Rattray, *Ashanti* (Oxford: Clarendon Press, 1923); S. F. Nadel, *A Black Byzantium* (London: Oxford University Press, 1942); and Paul and Laura Bohannan, *Tiv Economy* (Evanston, Ill.: Northwestern University Press, 1968). Also useful are J. Richard-Molard, *L'Afrique occidental française* (Paris: Berger-Levrault, 1949); H. Baumann and D. Westermann, *Les peuples et les civilisations de l'Afrique* (Paris: Payot, 1962); J. Vansina, *Kingdoms of the Savanna* (Madison: University of Wisconsin Press, 1966); G. Balandier, *Daily Life in the Kingdom of the Kongo* (New York: Pantheon Books, 1968); Raymond Mauny, *Tableau géographique de l'ouest Africain au moyen âge* (Dakar: Institut Français d'Afrique Noire, 1961; Amsterdam: Swets and Zeitlinger, 1967); Melville J. Herskovits, *The Human Factor in Changing Africa* (New York: Knopf, 1962); G. I. Jones, *The Trading States of the Oil Rivers* (London: Oxford University Press, 1963); I. M. Lewis, ed., *History and Social Anthropology* (London: Tavistock Publications, 1968); W. R. Bascom and M. J. Herskovits, eds., *Continuity and Change in African Cultures* (Chicago: University of Chicago Press, 1959); and Melville J. Herskovits, *Economic Life of Primitive Peoples* (New York: Knopf, 1940). See also A. G. Hopkins, *An Economic History of West Africa* (London: Longmans; New York: Columbia University Press, 1973).

Among traveler accounts, see John Adams, *Remarks on the Country Extending from Cape Palmas to the River Congo* (London: Frank Cass, 1966); J. A. Barbot, *A Description of the Coasts of North and South Guinea* (London: Churchill, 1732); W. Bosman, *A New and Accurate Description of the Coast of Guinea* (London: Frank Cass, 1967); R. F. Burton, *A Mission to Gelele* (London: Routledge and Kegan Paul, 1966); Archibald Dalzel, *The History of Dahomey* (London: Frank Cass, 1967); O. Dapper, *Description de l'Afrique* (Amsterdam, 1686); J. Dupuis, *Journal of a Residence in Ashantee*, 2nd ed. (London: Frank Cass, 1966); and T. E. Bowdich, *Mission from Cape Coast Castle to Ashantee*, 3rd ed. (London: Frank Cass, 1966). See also T. Hodgkin, *Nigerian Perspectives* (London: Oxford University Press, 1960); and Freda Wolfson, *Pageant of Ghana* (London: Oxford University Press, 1958).

Part Three

THE HERDERS

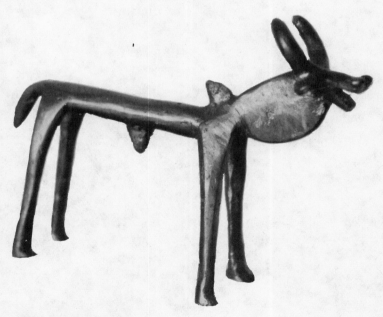

Bronze figure, Dahomey.
Photo courtesy of the author.

6

THE BANTU

Occupying the Subcontinent

The vast peninsula of subequatorial Africa, a third of a continent, is the Africa of the Bantu. Here, in almost limitless variety, they are to be found—forest dwellers like the equatorial Fang and Bangi; East African plainsmen such as Gogo and Hehe, Nyamwezi or Sukuma; savanna farmers called Shona, Luba, Lunda, or Malawi whose forebears fashioned empires in their time; Swahili-speaking traders of the eastern coast; amphibious Lozi cultivators on the Zambezi floodplain; proud Zulu, Ndebele, Ngoni, or Basuto descendants of warriors and statesmen; and many others, imperious or humble, celebrated or anonymous. Differing in way of life, appearance, and history, they all share a common origin and the common heritage of having derived from one of the world's great migrations. In short, at one time they were a single people occupying a small portion of what is today the eastern districts of the state of Nigeria.

Such an astonishing assertion is based almost wholly on data provided by linguistic analysis. Documentary sources are fragmentary and enigmatic, while archaeology, through widely scattered evidence, grants but few glimpses into the daily lives of these peoples and is silent as to who

123

they were and whence they came. Only two relevant written accounts survive. One, called the *Periplus of the Erythraean Sea*, was composed as a guide to the ports and the trade of the Indian Ocean, probably early in the second century after Christ. It deals at some length with the commerce of the East African coast but its references to the inhabitants are disappointingly meager. The coastal dwellers, we are told, were unusually tall and given to piracy. Even at this early date they were intermarrying with Arab traders, but if they were blacks, as one might suppose, considering the locale, the *Periplus* makes no mention of the fact. Indeed, its silence concerning their appearance has led some scholars to conclude that these Africans were possibly light-skinned, or at any rate near enough to visiting seamen in coloration to be unremarkable in their eyes.

The second written source, Claudius Ptolemy's *Geography*, was well known in the ancient world and contained information dealing with East Africa said to represent knowledge compiled in fifth-century Byzantium. Like its predecessor, the *Geography* concentrated its attention on identification of landmarks and the sailing time between trade centers, but there was brief mention of the people—Ethiopians, says the author, living along the Tanganyikan coast behind which arose a great snow-capped peak, "the Mountain of the Moon," later to be known the world over as Kilimanjaro.

From these meager clues, historians have made the necessary deduction that black men had occupied the East African coast by approximately A.D. 400 but need not have been there three hundred years earlier. Black men, but which black men and from where? Responding with evidence from a smattering of sites in eastern and central Africa, archaeologists have been able to identify a certain similarity in pottery designed by peoples whose middens also yielded indications of iron-working, the earliest finds dating from the first few centuries of the Christian era. These could have been the Bantu, and so it has been suggested, although clay pots usually tell more of a people's culture than of their identity and origins. Nevertheless, these pottery sites and their carbon 14 dates spread broadly across the map of subequatorial Africa may well be related to the great migration of the Bantu-speaking people.

To these frail shreds of evidence the study of African languages has added information of the greatest importance. Scholars long ago noted

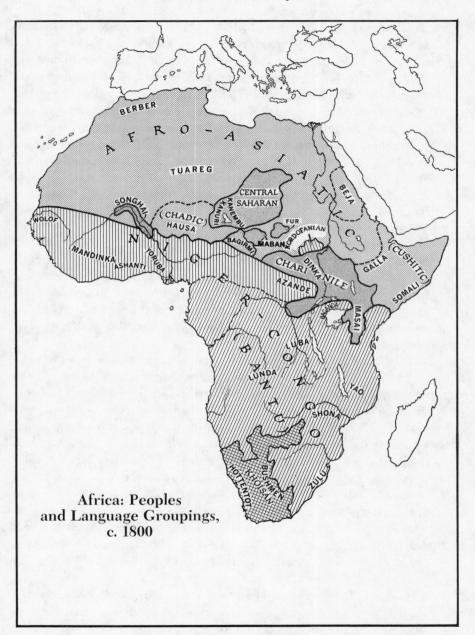

Africa: Peoples and Language Groupings, c. 1800

the close resemblance among the Bantu languages which today blanket subequatorial Africa. Through a technique known as glottochronology which measures changes in language structure and usage over time, it has been possible to hypothesize that all present Bantu languages are descended from an ancestral Bantu tongue dating from about two thousand years ago or possibly somewhat earlier. Furthermore, though differences of opinion still exist among linguists, there is substantial acceptance of the view that this ancient proto-Bantu was a branch of the vast Niger-Congo family of languages found today throughout much of West Africa and was especially related to the ancestors of those Niger-Congo languages now spoken by peoples living in the central Benue River valley. Since all these related tongues except Bantu are located in West Africa and since Bantu is so closely connected linguistically to a particular Niger-Congo group situated in eastern Nigeria and adjacent areas of Cameroun, it is argued that the original Bantu speakers came from the Benue River watershed. Beginning about the time of Christ they presumably moved out of their homeland, eventually fanning across subequatorial Africa in a vast migration that endured through virtually two millennia into the middle of the nineteenth century.

The linguistic evidence is persuasive and ingeniously presented. The migration has been described as a rapid initial passage through the equatorial forest of the Congo watershed by small bands who followed the waterways and eventually established themselves in the lightly wooded region of what is today the northern Katanga athwart the upper reaches of the Kasai and Lualaba rivers. Once they had broken clear into the Katanga south of the rain forest, these Bantu travelers began a major population expansion based in part on cultivation of cereals which were obtained from Cushitic speakers whom the Bantu early encountered along the eastern edge of their nuclear position. To these staples were added the yams, taros, and bananas that had come to East Africa from Asia. Finally, the tending of livestock which had already been established on the eastern plains, probably by Cushites or just possibly by herders from the central Sudan, now assumed a new importance among a number of Bantu groups. Thus, with a varied and flexible food supply, the Bantu were equipped to deal effectively with a wide range of environments. Eventually their growing population spilled completely across eastern and southern Africa, reaching the climax of its expansion with the arrival of the Xhosa people along the southeastern continental coast during the sixteenth century and possibly even earlier.

Unhappily, this explanation fails to accommodate certain inconsistencies, some of an economic nature. First of all, a quick thrust through the Congo forest seems problematical, partly on technological grounds and partly because it appears to lack any clear motivation. The migrants probably understood the use of iron which, it is felt, was essential to their penetration of the forest, but such knowledge would not necessarily imply the speedy movement conjectured. Neither is there any clear compulsion for a quick migration through difficult terrain, for no evidence exists of unusual pressures to the rear or enticements ahead that would have kept the Bantu moving. Moreover, if these ancestral Bantu had followed the waterways as has been suggested, they would have drifted downstream to the Atlantic coast. Instead they seem to have traveled overland across the drainage pattern, using the rivers, if at all, only for a difficult passage upstream in order to reach their staging position in the Luba country of the upper Katanga.

Further complications emerge from recently obtained carbon dates for pottery sites associated with the Bantu movement. These dates range from the late first century to the mid-fourth century after Christ, although most fall within the third century A.D. Despite this near contemporaneity, the sites are scattered across an immense area from the Zambezi River above Victoria Falls to Rwanda in the north and the Mombasa area to the east. When added to the fifth-century evidence of coastal "Ethiopians" reported in Ptolemy's *Geography*, this archaeological evidence permits little time stretch, which in turn raises questions concerning the source and direction of the Bantu population movement.

Finally, the swift penetration of the difficult Congo region is complicated by the fact that these early migrants were savanna farmers whose native sorghum and millet were ill adapted to the rain forest. At the time of their initial movement they had no access to the Asian yams and bananas which would have eased their passage, for these crops were only then making their appearance along the East African coast, brought by the mariners from Indonesia.

Such objections are difficult but not insuperable. For one thing, knowledge of ironworking was not a necessary prerequisite to breaching the forest. West Africans were well established in the forest belt of present-day Nigeria as long ago as 8000–9000 B.C., or long before the advent of iron in that area. Thus, the Bantu could have been Stone Age peoples and still penetrated the forest, and if so, they might have gained their eventual knowledge of metallurgy in East Africa where it had been introduced by the Indonesians along with their Asian crops.

What is more, the Bantu had no need for the banana and taro while in the forest. The farmers of the Benue watershed undoubtedly raised yams along with their cereals, just as do latter-day residents such as the Tiv. Their yams, which were indigenous to West Africa, would have been ideally suited to a shifting forest agriculture and could easily have been supplemented by extensive hunting and gathering which many farmers in Africa still practice today. Once free of the forest, the Bantu could have resumed their cultivation of sorghum and millet, adding the Asian food crops to their arsenal as these moved inland from the coast along trade routes.

With or without iron and whatever the nature of their food complex, however, the Bantu moving so rapidly through the Congo rain forest are difficult to envision; no less so is the quickness of their dispersion following the establishment of a nuclear region in the northern Katanga. Skepticism becomes particularly intense when it is realized that these lightning movements were accomplished by extremely small numbers, while there followed a much more leisurely expansion across eastern and southern Africa despite the pressures of an admittedly rapid population growth during this ensuing period. It seems improbable that only four hundred years were sufficient to bring the Bantu from the Benue to the Katanga and then on to the Kenyan coast when an additional thousand or twelve hundred years were to be consumed in the movement of land-hungry settlers across subequatorial Africa, between the Congo forests and the rolling hills of Uganda, from the slopes of Mount Kenya to the foothills of the Drakensberg range.

Much more credible is a development that began along the Benue at an earlier time, which therefore allowed for the slow and painful penetration of the Congo region and the subsequent spread across the eastern and southern plains, which permitted adaptation of man, animal, and food supply to new conditions—in short, a development that grants the modern observer a plausible hypothesis for describing one of the world's major movements of population.

The Migration of Peoples

What, then, stirred the Bantu to move and to continue their wanderings until a third of a continent had been occupied? What has driven other Africans at other times to leave their abodes for distant lands—Nilotes, whose own great journeys were surpassed only by those of the Bantu; Fulani, in their ancient peregrinations across the West African savanna; Galla, pressing inexorably into the mountain fastness of Ethiopia; Songhai and Hausa, Ashanti or Yoruba, whose early travels are largely lost in time and myth; Tuareg in their ageless movement through the Saharan wastes; and countless others who have crossed and recrossed this continent of migrations? What attractions have overcome fear of the unknown, what disabilities at home have forced men to abandon their familiar fields for the uncertainties and potential dangers beyond the next rise of land?

The answers, though difficult to identify in particular instances, are surely related to broad economic factors such as availability of land, soil fertility, population pressures, epidemic and endemic disease, and agricultural productivity. Immense in territory, Africa is nonetheless a continent of widely varying receptivity to human habitation. An abundance of land is counterbalanced by poor soils, insufficient water supply, and a surfeit of enervating and mortal maladies. A severe death rate has negated the effect of high fertility and birthrates, while economic productivity has been compromised by low population densities, nutritional deficiencies, and a minimal technology for agricultural production.

Africa as a continent has always been sparsely populated and remains so today; yet overcrowding exists and population pressures are severe in certain regions. Many areas can sustain but limited numbers. In water-scarce Kenya only 17 percent of the land is cultivable; Niger with its large tracts of Sahara possesses barely 2 percent farmland; while

South Africa, despite its wealth and technological sophistication, can commit but 5 percent of its land mass to productive agriculture. Such vast areas of limited utility push Africa's peoples into regions of more favorable character, where increasing numbers soon bring forth a deteriorating standard of living in a progressively exhausted terrain.

Taken overall, more than 30 percent of the African population today exists on 1 percent of the total area, at densities in excess of three hundred per square mile. In the highlands of Rwanda and Burundi, to choose a particular example, a high average rainfall and comparatively good soil have combined with a relative freedom from tropical disease and a total absence of tsetse fly to create a heavy population concentration in an overcultivated and overgrazed territory characterized by soil erosion and widespread poverty. Again, generally good soils, abundant rainfall, and a tropical climate permit year-round cultivation in the forest areas of West Africa, but resultant population densities have exceeded four hundred per square mile in some areas of Nigeria, rising as high as seven hundred in parts of Iboland, where human ingenuity has offset the limitations of local soil deficiencies only to fall victim of the poverty and disease caused by too many hungry mouths. Such severe overcrowding has forced the Ibo people outward into other parts of Nigeria where they have sought economic deliverance, but often they have found not the relief they have craved but political resistance and hostility.

It is not unreasonable to speculate that similar pressures have triggered past population movements. For pastoral groups such as the Beja, Fulani, and Masai, or desert nomads like Tuareg or Somali, migration was the pattern of life as each group followed the seasons in search of forage and water. Other peoples have been obliged to leave their homes each year at the time of flooding; this is still the rhythm of the Dinka along the upper Nile or the Lozi far to the south in the Zambezi floodplain. Indeed, cyclical movement of another sort has been the pattern for most African farmers, their style of husbandry based from the beginning upon intensive cultivation for a limited period, followed by a longer interval of fallow and regeneration while the village moved on to occupy a succession of new sites.

If seasonal or cyclical migration was the lot of many, there were others who were forced by recurrent disaster to evacuate their homes, to abandon their fields, and flee to safety and survival. Epidemics such as sleeping sickness or rinderpest, yellow fever or smallpox, were a periodic scourge; persistent and unforeseen periods of drought rendered otherwise habitable land untenable; and warfare, often accompanied by widespread slavery and loss of life, was a potential threat to stability and security. Since wars, plague, or the vagaries of the weather usually meant a drastic loss of food supply and productive capacity, these natural or man-made disasters frequently set people in motion in search of economic survival. Even in earlier times when the overall continental population was no more than 15 or 20 percent of its present total of approximately 330 million, pressures could easily have become excessive in local areas, where drought, disease, famine, and civil violence placed their mark on the land and stirred its people to move on in quest of greater fortune elsewhere.

It is probable that the Bantu expansion was stimulated by such factors as these. The Saharan dry phase, beginning in the third millennium before Christ, brought a major movement of peoples outward in search of moister climates, a movement that introduced new settlers into the West African savanna and forest regions. During much the same period, the spread of agriculture across the Sudanic belt below the desert probably added the pressure of rising population. The process that unfolded may be envisioned as a series of migrations by small groups, each tending to jostle and displace those ahead, each in turn being pressed forward by those who followed behind. In most of West Africa this movement ended at the ocean front, but for the ancestral Bantu in the Benue region there was no such impediment and they were able to continue their migration southward into the Congo region.

These early Bantu were most surely agricultural and probably iron users as well, but their shifting cultivation required continuing access to new, unused lands, an economic imperative that suggested migration, and if their population was rising in response to growing prosperity, this factor too would have brought pressure for periodic displacement. For the most part, their movement must have been peaceful for there seems to have been plenty of unoccupied land for the taking, the only competitors those small groups of pygmoid hunters in the Congo forest or bands of San (Bushmen) roaming the southern and eastern plains.

Both in timing and direction the expansion of the Bantu was a complex of small shifts and eddies in various directions, although the main lines described a fanning-out process across subequatorial Africa. If the movement was largely peaceful, there appear to have been periodic outbursts of violence, probably caused when local circumstances deprived an expanding population of access to new lands. Such is a possible interpretation of the spasms of death and destruction that marked the brief appearance of the marauding, cannibalistic Zimba in East Africa and the analogous depredations of the Jaga in Angola during the sixteenth century. In any event, land shortage in the face of population pressures seems the most likely explanation of the Zulu *Mfecane* which exploded among the Nguni-speaking Bantu during the early nineteenth century.

This spectacular climax to the Bantu migration had been preceded by several centuries of equilibrium as the Bantu vanguard crossed the Limpopo probably by 1000 A.D., the Sotho groups subsequently spreading across the interior plateau as far south as the Orange River while the Nguni channeled into the narrow coastal shelf that separated the Drakensberg Mountains from the eastern sea. While the Sotho country was not especially inviting, the Nguni corridor was a fertile land where millet and maize could be grown and cattle thrived on good pasture and a merciful lack of tsetse.

Despite chronic warfare and tribal division, a basic ecological balance endured among the Nguni for several centuries, but all the while overall population steadily increased under the stimulus of a genial environment. Finally, the critical density for a livestock economy was exceeded and the equilibrium of a restricted terrain shattered. What followed was the *Mfecane*—warfare of unsurpassed ferocity and devastation which destroyed or captured the weak, established large centralized states of military character, and sent remnants of population reeling outward in a series of shock waves which eventually were felt as far away as the plains of Tanganyika. As with the Zimba and Jaga, the explosion turned Bantu against Bantu and set in motion migrations that ran counter to the main southward thrust of the dispersion. By the time the *Mfecane* and its ramifications had subsided, an array of new nations of novel political form had emerged, and the ecology of eastern and southern Africa had been changed forever.

The Question of Iron

Among Africa's substantial mineral resources iron has long held a respected place. Its use first appeared in a number of scattered points during the last centuries of the pre-Christian era, whence it gradually spread thereafter to all parts of the continent, sustained by the technological superiority it introduced and the relative accessibility of workable ores in many, though not all, regions. It played a fateful role in the fall of Egypt before the armies of Assyria; it served as the basis for the great Sudanic civilization of ancient Meroe; it helped the Bantu to occupy a subcontinent and the Swahili civilization of the East African coast to come into flower. Everywhere it introduced a mechanical efficiency that banished Stone Age cultures and brought new levels of productivity, even as today the production of iron ore contributes a major economic thrust to the modernization efforts of a number of Africa's developing nations.

Although it seems reasonable to conclude that the knowledge of iron first came to Africa from the Middle East, there is considerable speculation as to the routes and timetable followed by this skill in its spread throughout the continent, as well as uncertainty over the identity of those directly concerned in the diffusion process. The ancient Egyptians were early workers of bronze, but they did not know iron until after its initial appearance in Asia Minor, and it did not become common with them until introduced through the Assyrian and Persian invasions of the Nile valley in the seventh and sixth centuries respectively. From there, ironworking spread up the Nile to Nubia where it became established as a major industry at Meroe, probably during the first century before Christ but possibly as much as five hundred years earlier.

The extent of iron manufacturing at Meroe, evidenced by the massive slag heaps which today mark the site of that ancient metropolis, has formed the basis for a widely held theory that Meroe was the likely point of dissemination from which knowledge of iron spread west and south eventually to cover the rest of the continent. Such a hypothesis might be most persuasive were it able to take account of several troublesome factors. One is the total lack of undisputed Meroitic remains yet to be found west of the Nile. Another involves the ambiguous nature of oral traditions among West African peoples who speak of eastern origins; still others relate to uncertainties over the ostensible affinities in artistic styles or social and political institutions between ancient Egypt and several West African societies.

Most serious, however, is the fact that knowledge of ironworking in West Africa is now thought to date as far back as the fifth century B.C., at which time it appeared in the celebrated Nok culture, located just north of the middle Benue, its practice roughly contemporaneous with the earliest iron manufacture far to the east at Meroe. If iron technology was a closely guarded secret at Meroe, as has been suggested, it is difficult to escape the conclusion that the Nok people either developed this skill independently or received it from some source other than Meroe. This last possibility has been argued by those who point out that knowledge of iron arrived in North Africa with the advent of the Phoenicians who founded a trading center at Carthage, probably in the ninth century B.C., and thereby made possible the spread of ironworking to West Africa. Once again precise dating is difficult, but iron was known to desert Berbers before the time of Christ and may have been brought into the West African savanna via trans-Saharan chariot routes about the same time that this skill came up the Nile from Egypt to Meroe.

Whatever the origins of iron in West Africa, its use in that region seemingly preceded the expansion of the Bantu who have been credited with the knowledge of iron as an important prerequisite to their penetration of the Congo rain forest. This hypothesis rests in part on the logic that iron tools would have been necessary for dealing with a forest environment and partly on the existence of processed iron scattered from the Zambezi to the East African coast at sites that have been associated with the early Bantu migrants. Ironworking need not have accompanied the Bantu passage, however, since there is ample evidence of Stone Age forest cultures in Africa.

Beyond this, it must be understood that neither iron ore deposits nor the knowledge of smelting were common in Bantu Africa during the early centuries of the dispersion, and acquisition of iron tools likely emerged from trade as much as from local manufacture. This suggests that many early Bantu groups may have been but infrequent iron users and may have picked up the knowledge of smelting after their arrival in southern and eastern Africa. Thus, the appearance of early iron sites in East Africa could represent a technology introduced by Bantu migrants but could alternatively have followed the arrival of Iron Age Indonesians along the Indian Ocean littoral during the initial centuries of the Christian era. Movement from the coast inland might have filtered along early lines of trade, a not unreasonable hypothesis judging from the extensive exchange that later developed between coast and interior, with particular emphasis on inland mining of gold and copper. Whatever the source of iron technology, however, Bantu communities slowly gained skill in the refinement of iron ore and the manufacture of simple tools, drawing their supplies from widely scattered ferrous deposits and disseminating their iron artifacts throughout the Bantu territory by means of extensive interregional bartering networks.

Economy and Polity—The Force of Necessity

One hundred years ago, the British missionary and explorer David Livingstone remarked on village life among the Bantu people living in the vicinity of the Kwilu River on the edge of Lunda country. "The country is full of little villages," he noted, adding, "Food abounds, and very little labor is required for its cultivation . . . . When a garden becomes too poor for good crops . . . the owner removes a little farther into the forest, applies fire round the roots of the larger trees to kill them, cuts down the smaller, and a new, rich garden is ready for the seed." Here, in this brief comment, is contained the essence of the Bantu migration and, indeed, the whole process of migratory agriculture which characterized most indigenous African societies. It is also suggestive in tracing the political shape of these early precolonial African communities.

What is the relationship between economic necessity and political configuration? In Africa, as elsewhere, man strove toward survival, even toward affluence, organizing his activities in response to this basic thrust within the restraints of environmental limitations. His political and social institutions, therefore, were in part attempts to ensure some sort of orderly process for the production, distribution, and consumption of life's necessities. It might be supposed that the same set of economic circumstances would have brought forth similar political solutions, and, broadly speaking, this was the case with the traditional societies of Africa. Most were subsistence food-producing societies showing little labor specialization and minor differentiation in standard of living. Communities tended to be small in size and independent from one another politically, their limited scale a reflection of the territorial impermanence among cattle-keeping groups or migratory farmers, their autonomy engendered more by poor communications than by an essential independence of spirit. Material culture was simple, even meager, conditioned in part by climatic considerations that placed small premium on elaborate dwellings or numerous personal possessions and in part by the evident convenience of unencumbered travel.

Nevertheless, these early African civilizations were by no means identical in form or static over time; moreover, the particular shape they assumed was not always predictable in terms of their economies and environment. Some organized descent and inheritance through the female line, others through the male. Some kept neat villages, others, adjacent, quite the opposite. Some sorted out economic activity into clearly defined crafts controlled by particular family groups according to well-defined rules; others practiced little economic differentiation. Among the Nguni speakers of southern Africa it was taboo to eat fish, though many varieties were in plentiful supply in nearby ocean waters and were prized by Khoikhoi (Hottentot) herders and San (Bushman) hunters living in the same regions. For their part, the San groups held steadfast to their ancient hunting and foraging practices despite the lessons to be drawn from Khoikhoi herds or the millet harvests of neighboring Bantu.

In West Africa the Bandama River bisecting the modern Ivory Coast marked a sharply defined boundary between rice-eating peoples to the west and the yam culture to the east, both territories mutually exclusive in terms of the institutions and practices of their various resident peoples. What caused this total difference in diet and culture among forest dwellers living within a seemingly uniform environment? Again, what extraeconomic factors enabled the Ibo nation to prosper despite a home region of insufficient natural resources? Why were the Shona compelled to create their imposing monuments at Zimbabwe? How can be explained the genesis of the Mali empire in a few obscure Mandinka villages, or the artistic flowering within the great bronze-casting centers of Ife and Benin?

These are imponderables which set historians talking about the indefinable quality of the human spirit; yet, in balance, clear lines of association are generally traceable between economic necessity and political configuration. Traditional African societies were organized along two basic patterns—some were states headed by a ruling prince who governed through a hierarchy of public officials; others were so-called stateless tribal complexes, their cohesiveness a web of mutual obligations resting upon consanguinity. In either case the essential unit was the family, a social, biological, and political grouping that also performed important economic functions. Village life relied heavily upon mutual assistance in agricultural production which each household maintained under the direction of the family head. Economic cooperation was greatly strengthened by kinship ties of blood, tradition, and familial loyalty, but kinship sentiments were not likely to prevail for long when they clashed with antipathetic economic interests, and a family-based labor group tended to disintegrate once its productive efficiency had disappeared.

Among the Nupe, for example, the traditional family work unit lost coherence during the era of colonial control as the pressure for tax payments and the appetite for new town-based attractions overcame the authority of old loyalties. At the same time, those Nupe households which succeeded in converting their fields to a lucrative commercial agriculture were able to maintain the ancient family work group, for it provided the young men with needed tax money or bridewealth. Economic factors also determined to an extent Nupe friendliness toward strangers who were taken into the village and, if they proved themselves to be substantial citizens, were granted land and became adopted members of established local families. The motive of this commercially vigorous people was the attraction of individuals with new techniques or knowledge that could be added to the crafts and agriculture of Nupeland.

The Nguni Bantu also provided for strangers, usually members of alien clans who attached themselves to a particular chief and settled in his territory. Such freedom of allegiance was understandable among people whose livestock kept them on the move, but the character of each new attachment was political and economic alike—the need of the individual cattleman to protect his herds from raids by predatory neighbors, the desire of each local chiefdom to attract able-bodied defenders.

Among the stateless Nuer of the White Nile and its Bahr al-Ghazal tributary, community life has always been heavily influenced by geographic considerations. Nuer country, which alternates seasonally between a parched savanna and a flooded plain of high grass, has conditioned both the pattern of family living and the size, location, and makeup of each village. During the rains the villages perch on raised knolls or ridges, their people subsisting on cereals and separated from one another by vast stretches of flooded grassland. In the dry season these sites are abandoned in favor of camps along streams or poolsides where cattle may be watered, but in the process the village membership often scatters among a number of water sites while larger camps attract individuals from many different villages. Neither village nor camp has any direct bearing on political relations which are governed primarily by lineage connections. Such conditions have not always brought forth the same political response, however. Among the Lozi, whose Zambezi floodplain exhibits similar seasonal variations, an analogous population movement takes place, although the Lozi nation is governed as a conventional kingdom, complete with king and counselors, nobility and commoners, castes and serfs.

The Economics of *Mfecane*

African history contains many examples of societies whose development was strongly influenced by economic considerations. The case of Dahomey comes readily to mind, evolving under the stresses of the Atlantic slave trade during the eighteenth and nineteenth centuries. Ashanti provides another ready illustration, the growth of her empire and military power nurtured in no small measure by her determination to gain access both to the rich commerce of the savanna and to the

European trade which had come to West African shores. Certainly Bugandan expansion can be but dimly understood by those who ignore the influence of local geography and the impact of long-distance trade. Many other instances might be introduced—the trading states of the Niger Delta or the international emporiums along the East African coast; pharaonic Egypt, her glittering civilization conceived in the Nile's life-giving waters, and ancient Axum, linking the Mediterranean traffic to the Indian Ocean trade; the great empires of the western Sudan and of Mwene Mutapa in Central Africa, whose gold brought merchants from faraway Europe and the East.

Perhaps the most instructive illustration of all is found in the events that took place in southern Africa during the early years of the nineteenth century. Here exploded the phenomenon called *Mfecane* by the Nguni, or *Difaqane* in Sotho parlance—the wars and disturbances that marked the rise of Shaka and the appearance of the Zulu kingdom; the flight to safety on the part of many peoples seeking asylum from death and devastation.

It was the start of a new way of life but it was also the last act in the unfolding process of the Bantu expansion, the Nguni groups in the coastal strip and the Sotho spread across the interior plateau. Among the Sotho there was a pronounced preference for large villages, many numbering thousands of inhabitants, their purpose possibly defense, possibly the need to remain near limited sources of water. By contrast, the Nguni lived in scattered homesteads, a lack of concentration that bespoke a plentiful and well-dispersed supply of spring water for every family herd. In like manner, Nguni political organization was decentralized. Chiefdoms were small and given to easy division arising from disputes over succession, for royal wives, located in different parts of each realm, produced competitors to the rightful heir and a consequent temptation to revolt, secession, and a new tribal grouping.

Yet economic factors appear to have been decisive in shaping events, the evidence circumstantial but persuasive. Within the coastal corridor the Nguni thrived, fattening their herds on fine pasture and supplementing their assets in livestock with ample harvests of maize and millet. Expanding population encouraged further migration; then by the beginning of the nineteenth century the Nguni found themselves caught between the Drakensberg scarp and the sea. Expansion into new territories was limited by geography and by growing numbers of *trekboer* cattlemen migrating eastward along the southern continental limits from their colony at Cape Town. At the same time, traditional agricultural techniques were unable to effect the regeneration and reutilization of soils necessary for increased productivity within already occupied fields and ranges. Under such circumstances the ancient Bantu solution of fission and migration was no longer possible, for there was no new place to go; hence, the process of political decentralization and isolation of homesteads was checked and replaced with new forms of consolidation seeking more effective organization and utilization of now limited land and food supplies. Concurrently, warfare converted from a quasi-recreational pastime to a deadly contest for survival.

The innovations were developed by a series of remarkable individuals —first, Dingiswayo, leader of the northern Nguni people known as Mthethwa, then Shaka, the great Zulu conqueror, and finally, Moshesh, a minor Sotho chief whose destiny it was to create the Basuto nation. Shortly after his accession to power late in the eighteenth century, Dingiswayo did away with the traditional circumcision rites, providing in their stead a new and demanding proof of manhood by conscripting the young men of his kingdom into military regiments based upon age grades. This imaginative reshaping of customary practices gave the Mthethwa a substantial advantage over their neighbors and enabled Dingiswayo to conquer and absorb a number of nearby groups into a new and powerful federation capable of controlling an extensive range area with its supplies of grain and cattle. Others quickly paid him the compliment of imitation, particularly the Ndwandwe led by Zwide and an assortment of Nguni and Sotho communities which were eventually to form the Swazi nation under their chief, Sobhuza.

Of even more significance in this respect, however, was Shaka whose military and political reforms greatly extended what Dingiswayo had begun. As Dingiswayo's lieutenant and protégé, Shaka succeeded to the Zulu chiefdom on his father's death, drilling its army into a small but murderously effective fighting force. When Dingiswayo was killed fighting the Ndwandwe, Shaka and his Zulu cohorts absorbed the Mthethwa and defeated the Ndwandwe, thus establishing Zulu preeminence throughout what is today northern Natal. Not only did he bring into being a powerful Zulu state, he also caused the substance of his reforms to be spread broadly throughout southern Africa by means of tribal groups who migrated to escape Zulu conquest but who adopted Zulu tactics for the evident strength they produced. Shaka's most spectacular innovations were military in the form of the short, stabbing assegai, the unbending discipline among his thoroughly drilled regiments, the total mobilization of a nation's young manhood for military service, the ingenious battlefield tactics and campaign strategies that brought wealth and power to this irrepressible king and his legions.

Nevertheless it was the shape of Shaka's political reforms that provided the most abiding change. His military exploits brought into existence a large centralized state consisting of peoples gathered together from many disparate tribal groups, all henceforth to be converted into Zulu nationals by the stresses of the times, the bonds that join comrades in arms, and the dawning pride of national accomplishment. Shaka's emphasis on a conscript army organized by age grades made novel use of the traditional African ceremony for initiation of adolescents into adulthood. First, it created a new kind of military machine; more than that, by this device Shaka drew individuals from many parts of his kingdom into a personal relationship in which each subject looked directly to his prince as an object of loyalty, receiving from him at the same time the proud identity of Zulu warrior, economic support during his soldiering years, and eventually a wife when he was mustered out and returned to his regional homeland within the Zulu state.

Concurrently, chiefs, whether hereditary or appointed, served at Shaka's pleasure and by consequence looked to him for direction and support. The royal herds became the largest and most important in an economy increasingly subject to centralized control; moreover, by the time of his death in 1828, Shaka had been moving toward the establishment of trade links with the British, both at Port Natal (present-day Durban) and the Cape, a commerce that certainly would have been conducted as a royal monopoly.

This type of political centralization based upon military need and strength was adopted by many others, most notably the Ndebele who eventually established their own kingdom north of the Limpopo during the 1830s, and the Ngoni who projected the Shakan revolution far beyond the Zambezi into the high plains of East Africa. Much closer to the Zulu eruption, a Sotho chief named Moshesh reshaped traditional usage in other novel ways to stem the tide of destruction, in the process developing his own centralized state as another, quite different, means to survival and a new way of life.

On the South African high veld west of the Drakensberg scarp, the Sotho encampments had often been located on hilltops that formed natural defensive positions. Flat at the summit, which was guarded by steep cliffs, these sites were approachable only by occasional passes, their narrow entry easily blocked by an entrenched determined force. After the initial outburst of the *Mfecane* within the Natal corridor, a number of Nguni groups came over the Drakensbergs in a flight for survival that quickly converted into a series of predatory attacks of their own on the less military Sotho. Gradually, organized life broke down over wide areas as each group became both pursuer and pursued and the normal peaceful occupations of daily life gave way to warfare and brigandage. Death and destruction obliterated whole communities while populations were scattered and decimated in the face of disease, starvation, and, eventually, cannibalism. Some Sotho people, like the Tlokwa, survived by adopting and mastering the military aggressiveness of the Nguni, but it was Moshesh who was able to give birth to a permanent center of stability in the otherwise widening chaos and thereby to establish a nucleus of orderly existence where civilization might survive and eventually regenerate.

Establishing himself on a mountain stronghold called Thaba Bosiu, he attracted refugees from Sotho groups crushed and scattered by the *Difaqane,* gradually fusing them into a Sotho, or Basuto, nation which has prevailed to the present. Where Shaka created the Zulu state by force, Moshesh achieved the same goal through suasion, attracting diverse peoples to the defensive strength of his position and holding their allegiance with tact and a careful respect for differences in custom. His statesmanship disarmed such belligerents as the Ndebele and Zulu, and his military prowess, sparingly used, nevertheless defeated the intractable Tlokwa among others. News of his enlightened rule brought adherents even from Nguni country, the recruits remaining to become part of a new nation inspired by the gifted leadership of an unusual man.

Left to himself, Moshesh might well have constructed a strong and wealthy state on the ruins of traditional Sotho society. Unhappily, his success against the onslaught of the *Mfecane* had scarcely been achieved when he was faced with a new and more dangerous threat, and it was before this growing European presence of Boer and Briton that his powers did indeed finally waver. But this was a new force of quite different character and magnitude in the face of which even the massive *Mfecane* and all of its consequences were eventually obliged to bend.

SUGGESTIONS FOR FURTHER READING

Theories concerning the Bantu migration are summed up in Roland Oliver, "The Problem of the Bantu Expansion," *Journal of African History*, vol. 7, no. 3 (1966), but others should be consulted. See, for example, Merrick Posnansky, "Bantu Genesis—Archaeological Reflections," *Journal of African History*, vol. 9, no. 1 (1968); Jean Hiernaux, "Bantu Expansion," in vol. 9, no. 4 (1968), of the same journal; and G. P. Murdock, *Africa: Its Peoples and Their Culture History* (New York: McGraw-Hill, 1959). The linguistic argument is set forth by Joseph Greenberg in *Languages of Africa*, 2nd rev. ed. (Bloomington: Indiana University Press, 1966); again in "Historical Inferences from Linguistic Research in Sub-Saharan Africa," in Jeffrey Butler, ed., *Boston University Papers in African History*, vol. 1 (Boston: Boston University Press, 1964); and in "Linguistic Evidence Regarding Bantu Origins," *Journal of African History*, vol. 13, no. 2 (1972). To these should be added M. Guthrie, "Some Developments in the Prehistory of the Bantu Languages," *Journal of African History*, vol. 3, no. 2 (1962).

For a general introduction to tropical populations, see Pierre Gourou, *The Tropical World*, 3rd ed. (London: Longmans, 1961), which may be supplemented by geographies of Africa such as those by L. D. Stamp and Mountjoy and Embleton mentioned in the bibliography for chapter 1. More particularly, however, see William A. Hance, *Population, Migration, and Urbanization in Africa* (New York: Columbia University Press, 1970). Judgments concerning the spread of iron in Africa appear strongly conditioned by the origin of the observers involved. French scholars working chiefly in Saharan areas have leaned toward a North African origin. British investigators, familiar with the Egyptian Sudan, have favored Meroe. See, for example, R. Mauny, *Tableau géographique de l'ouest Africain au moyen âge* (Dakar: Institut Français d'Afrique Noire, 1961; Amsterdam: Swets and Zeitlinger, 1967), and the same author's "Histoire des métaux en Afrique occidentale," *Bulletin de l'Institut Français d'Afrique Noire*, vol. 14 (1952). By contrast, see A. J. Arkell, *A History of the Sudan*, rev. ed. (New

York: Oxford University Press, 1961). P. L. Shinnie in *Meroe* (New York: Praeger, 1966) is cautious as to origins. Also to be consulted is P. L. Shinnie, ed., *The African Iron Age* (Oxford: Clarendon Press, 1971).

The relation between political institutions and economic conditions is found in the myriad anthropological studies of traditional African societies. Among many examples, see E. Colson and M. Gluckman, eds., *Seven Tribes of British Central Africa* (New York: Humanities Press, 1959), and M. Fortes and E. E. Evans-Pritchard, eds., *African Political Systems* (London: Oxford University Press, 1940). For material dealing more particularly with the early history of the southern Bantu, see M. Wilson and L. Thompson, eds., *The Oxford History of South Africa*, 2 vols. (New York: Oxford University Press, 1969, 1971); J. D. Omer-Cooper, *The Zulu Aftermath* (London: Longmans, 1966); and L. Thompson, ed., *African Societies in Southern Africa* (New York: Praeger, 1969).

7

THE CATTLEMEN

Nilotic Migrations

Bantu farmers were dedicated colonists, yet it may have been the African herdsmen who were the more inveterate migrants, drawn by a continuing need for new ranges, capable of greater mobility in reaching them. Even among the Bantu, though many remained farmers, many others became devoted cattle keepers, while a wide variety of non-Bantu African peoples were made up of herdsmen whose way of life kept them constantly on the move. In West Africa, it was the Fulani, a herding people, who, from the thirteenth century onward, spread their cultural and political influence across the savanna from the Senegal country to Lake Chad. Within the African deserts, moreover, nomads have long been dominant—Tuareg, Teda, and Arab camel herders in the Sahara or warlike Beja, Somali, and other Cushitic peoples inhabiting the parched wastelands and foothills surrounding the Ethiopian massif. Finally, it has been suggested that cattle-keeping migrants could have reached eastern and southern Africa even before the advent of the Bantu. These would have been those peoples who speak central Sudanic languages, a population at one time much more widely distributed but now limited to sections of southern Chad, the Central African Republic, and northeastern Zaire.

Beyond these examples, there are the Nilotes, a predominantly pastoral people whose movements over the centuries led them to occupy large sections of eastern Africa where they found the open stretch of high plateau as attractive for their stock as it had been for the great herds of wild game preceding them. Among Africa's earliest known inhabitants, Nilotes can trace their beginnings possibly as far back as three thousand years before Christ, their original homeland the dry plains west and south of the Ethiopian massif and their economy very early associated with a pastoral life. As with the Bantu, the evidence for Nilote origins is primarily linguistic, for such antiquity lies far beyond the reach of oral traditions, while archaeology remains silent, perhaps permanently, regarding a people who traveled much and traveled light.

Today Nilotes are scattered across the eastern plains, from the White Nile and Bahr al-Ghazal region of southern Sudan down through Uganda and western Kenya into Tanzania, following in a rough way the lines of the Rift fault which splits east and west of Lake Victoria. Linguistic variations among Dinka and Nuer of the Bahr al-Ghazal, Luo on Victoria's Kavirondo Gulf, Turkana near Lake Rudolf, or Masai in the eastern Rift Valley suggest that the ancestral Nilotes may have been located along the lower stretches of the southern Ethiopian highlands from the Lake Rudolf area west and north toward the Nile. Slowly, much more slowly than the Bantu, they moved outward to achieve their present extent. The movement must have been very gradual since analysis of Nilotic languages suggests initial differentiation possibly as much as five thousand years ago. By early Christian times, the Nilotes had split into their three major groupings of Western, Eastern, and Southern, the first containing Dinka, Nuer, Luo, Burun, and others; the Eastern branch including such representatives as Karamojong, Teso, and Masai; and the Southern Nilotes exemplified by Nandi, Kipsigis, and Pokot among many others.

Even in this early period most Nilotes had emerged as confirmed cattle keepers, some of whom, at least, understood the use of iron. Their languages at that time contained such terms as "forge" and "branding iron" as well as numerous references to livestock, these last traceable linguistically as far back as 3000 B.C. With the passage of time, further

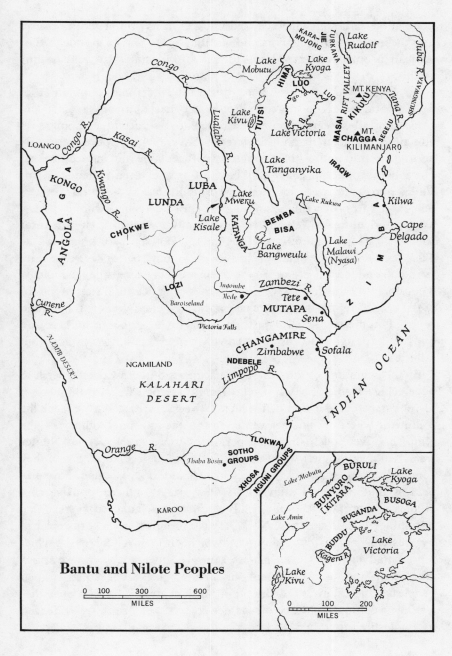

Bantu and Nilote Peoples

0 100 300 600
MILES

0 100 200
MILES

population variations emerged, reflecting both environmental pressures and the influence of neighbors and resulting in a complex mosaic of East African peoples and a widespread mix of cultural traits and genetic strains.

To begin with, there was a resident bushmanoid population of hunter-gatherer groups spread through the East African savanna and woodlands, their early presence attested to by ancient camping sites containing stone tools and sheltered by overhanging rocks frequently adorned with paintings of characteristic Bush style and subject matter. Next, about one thousand years before Christ or even earlier, the Rift Valley and its adjacent highlands were infiltrated by Cushitic speakers descending from the Ethiopian highlands, cattle keepers who may have known agriculture as well and who eventually spread their culture as far south as the lower end of Lake Tanganyika. This southern branch of the Cushites arrived in small groups over a long period of time and eventually added the use of iron to their original Stone Age technology. They are also thought to have built a series of agricultural sites noted for the presence of irrigation ditches, terraced fields, graded roads, and revetted homesteads, all constructed in fitted stone technique and apparently designed to sustain relatively dense populations in low-rainfall areas.

By the beginning of the Christian era these Southern Cushites seem to have achieved their greatest extent; from that point forward they began to retreat before the Bantu tide that flowed into East Africa from the southwest where its nuclear center lay in the savanna country of the Katanga. Over much the same period of time, cattle-keeping Nilotes were also making their way into the Rift area, and after 1000 A.D. they commenced an expansion that occupied many of the regions formerly held by the Southern Cushites. First it was the Southern, or Highland, Nilotes who expanded dramatically within a few hundred years; then, beginning about 1700, these Nandi-related groups were in turn replaced by Eastern, or Plains, Nilotes of which the Masai were the chief representatives. The Cushites were severely squeezed by these various movements and today are found only in a few pockets occupied by such peoples as the Iraqw and Murungi of north central Tanzania; nevertheless, their cultural influence on the newcomers was strong, as evidenced by linguistic borrowings and adaptation of economic and social practices, developments that probably imply a substantial population mix as well.

Indeed, slow migration by small numbers and complex interpenetration linguistically, culturally, and genetically among major peoples became the characteristic pattern for the settling of East Africa, the combinations and the degree of mix varying widely according to circumstance. Southern Nilotes, for example, took over Southern Cushitic customs along with their ranges, while the Masai, who followed the Southern Nilotes into the Rift Valley region, adopted much of the culture of these Nandi-related peoples they supplanted. The Bantu, who eventually occupied the large share of East African territory, often developed institutions and linguistic variations showing clear marks of the cultures they had superseded; witness the strong Cushitic influence upon the Bantu Hehe and Gogo of Tanzania or the Nilotic strains found among Bantu dwelling along the eastern shores of Lake Victoria.

This interplay of populations and cultures is further illustrated by the example of Nilotes and Bantu founding the great states that took shape to the west of Lake Victoria beginning in the sixteenth century. Basically this was Bantu country, but the Bantu-speaking population had for some time been ruled by a pastoral minority called Hima or Tutsi, depending upon its location, a group that in the territory northwest of Victoria had given rise to a royal clan known as Chwezi, presiding over a kingdom named Kitara. These aristocratic clans may have been Cushites or possibly even central Sudanic peoples; in any event, while taking on the tasks of government they had also adopted the Bantu languages spoken by their subject populations.

In the late fifteenth or early sixteenth century, there came into what is today Northern Uganda a migration of Western Nilotes—Luo who had moved south from their original home along the White Nile in a complex migration that helped fix the modern populations of such peoples as the Acholi, the Alur, and the Lango. Pressing on farther south, small groups of Luo reached the region of Kitara where, despite their modest numbers, they were able to oust the Chwezi and establish themselves as a new ruling clan called Bito. The Luo have sometimes been styled as conquerors, sometimes as peaceful migrants, but in either case they appear to have been culturally less sophisticated, though politically more vigorous, than the Chwezi. Their clans had long been based upon centralized rule through a royal family, and this type of political organization was at once employed by the Bito to convert the loosely formed kingdom of Kitara into a more structured state called Bunyoro.

Domination by a Luo royal house led to the introduction of Luo clan patterns and political organization, but the small numbers of the invaders and the virility of the resident Bantu farming society caused the Luo to set aside their own language for Bantu and to convert their culture and economy from pastoralism to crop cultivation. Much the same process emerged in a series of peripheral states which the Bito established near Bunyoro—most notably Buganda, Buddu, and the Busoga principalities. Farther to the east, other Luo finally came to rest in the neighborhood of Kavirondo Gulf; in this instance, however, although they abandoned pastoralism for farming, they retained the use of their Luo language.

The Luo impact induced a number of variations among other peoples in the Victoria area. Those Luo speakers who helped form the Acholi people also brought a strong interest in cattle along with their language. By contrast, the Lango, originally Plains Nilote cattlemen, adopted the Luo tongue but transformed themselves from pastoralists to sedentary cultivators after the Luo contact, probably because resultant population pressures had forced them to move into regions where farming was economically more feasible than pastoralism.

For their part, sections of the displaced Hima appear to have retreated to the south of Bunyoro where they formed a ruling clan called Hinda which gained control over a number of Bantu groups near the western shore of Lake Victoria. The Hinda were cattle keepers, but their practice of parceling out their stock to peasant farmers greatly increased, through animal fertilization, the production of bananas which eventually became the staple crop from Bunyoro to Rwanda. In the case of Buganda, the ubiquitous and easily cultivated banana provided an essential economic base upon which her energetic people were able to build a powerful and influential state during the eighteenth and nineteenth centuries.

The Plainsman

He stands motionless in the middle of his cattle, a tall, slender figure watching as the herd moves slowly past. All is quiet over the great plain; nature hangs between day and night, the afternoon's warmth already touched with the first chill of evening. Beyond, in the distance, the tawny hills deepen into purple, their summits still touched with gold, the evening shadows advancing up their slopes before the retreating sun. Overhead, the big sky is filled with great sculptures of clouds, ever changing shape and color in a wondrous phantasmagoria that fills the heart with the joy of living and touches the spirit with a sense of the infinite.

The herdsman sees none of this. Neither does he make conscious note of his charges' familiar scent, mixing with the odor of grass and dust as the herd eddies about him, unhurried in its passage to the safety of the kraal. Yet he too is filled with a sense of well-being; he too feels communion with the infinite. He reaches out to rub a moist muzzle thrust toward him, pats a scrawny rump, tickles a twitching ear. He knows each animal as friend and companion and each knows him in like manner, an unspoken bond that transcends explanation or, indeed, understanding. It is simply that this is the stuff of life, a man watching his cattle come home. There is no other way.

For Africa's pastoralists cattle have always occupied a major place in religious expression and in social order; more than that, they are the essential prerequisite to individual psychic well-being. Cattle are sacrificed to bring the life-giving rain or to ward off the threat of plague. Cattle are slaughtered to mark the ritual of adulthood or to celebrate a new marriage. Cattle form the basis of a complex system of exchange whereby a man establishes his economic and social position in the community.

But, most of all, cattle are the ingredient that fulfills, in their sufficiency making one life rich and satisfying, another empty and frustrated in their absence. Cattle are music, art, philosophy. Each man has his favorite ox whose horns he shaves and pounds into fanciful shapes to be admired and envied, whose hide he scarifies with elaborate banded patterns, building the skin up around the head in an ornamental crest, whose baritone bellow he imitates in songs dedicated to its honor. He gives his ox a name which he himself takes as one of his own; in battle he shouts out this name, and later his animal's ear he slits, one cut for each victim, so that the ox will know what enemies his master has slain and together they may rejoice. For the pastoralist, cattle contain the very meaning of life. "If you don't have cattle," he says with finality, "you won't be a person."

Stock raising in Africa began early, probably not as a transition between hunting and farming, as once was thought, but more likely as a concurrent development with agriculture, awareness of the utility of animals growing with the knowledge that their domestication often complemented the cultivation of plants. Farmyard animals aside, early domesticates included cattle, sheep, goats, and donkeys, these last employed as pack animals by the great Egyptian explorer Harkhuf in his journeys to the south near the close of the third millennium before Christ. Much later horses and camels were introduced from Arabia, the former usually associated with the Hyksos invasion of Egypt in the eighteenth century B.C., the latter, though early known, not coming into general use until the Christian era.

The first cattle to be domesticated in Africa were indigenous to the continent, the celebrated *Bos africanus* whose graceful lyre-shaped horns adorned the funerary reliefs of royal Egyptian tombs, appearing as well in Neolithic cave paintings scattered across the Saharan vastness. Another possibly indigenous strain, the shorthorn *Bos ibericus,* became popular in some areas, but much more important was the humpbacked zebu which arrived in numbers from India about the time of Christ and eventually spread from East Africa across the savanna to the western Sudan. Crossbreeding gradually introduced additional complexities of type, but broadly speaking the longhorn *africanus,* with its greater immunity to trypanosomiasis, was able to establish itself throughout the sub-Saharan continent, while the zebu, with its ability to subsist on minimum moisture, came to occupy the more arid reaches along the desert edge.

Like the African farmer, the African herdsman has always borne the deep mark of the African environment. To begin with, pastoralists have gravitated toward that dry steppe country inhospitable to cultivated plants but attractive to livestock for its wild grasses and shrubs. These sparse ranges, moreover, are repellent to insect pests that thrive in areas of permanent vegetation; especially in the higher plains of eastern and southern Africa there are extensive regions quite free from tsetse infestation.

Protection against livestock disease was bought at a price, however—the nomadic life, involving both seasonal migration, or transhumance, and a daily movement in search of adequate pasture and water. This was a difficult existence graced with few of the physical comforts enjoyed by the more sedentary farmer. Nevertheless, despite the poverty and elementary living conditions, the cattleman was obliged to deal continually with technical questions that demanded much of judgment and experience—what pasture best suited his various charges, how nutritional were different grass types, where could water be found in a dry stream bed, or when a distant range with good pasture and water was preferable to a more proximate location that avoided fatiguing travel but yielded poor sustenance in return.

Marginal supplies of food and water carried the threat of annihilation —a herd expiring of thirst, wiped out by epidemic, or badly depleted by malnutrition. Consequently, the plainsmen diffused their holdings across their territories, partly to maintain low population density, but also in support of a system of loans and gifts which distributed the beasts of any particular individual among many herds located at widely separated points. Decentralization was achieved in various ways. Some, like the southern Bantu or the Kipsigis, billeted their stock with their wives in scattered homesteads. Among the Fulani of West Africa, it was normal for members of a lineage to borrow and lend stock as needed for such purposes as breeding, milking, or refurbishing diseased herds, in the process thoroughly dispersing their property.

Perhaps the most systematic hedge against disaster was practiced by Nilotic groups like the Jie and Turkana through a system of property exchange whereby individuals accumulated cattle from many sources upon request, possibly to amass a bridewealth, sometimes for purposes of ritual sacrifice, or perhaps merely to build up a particular herd. The loan was gladly, even eagerly, made, supported as it was by the sanction of custom. He who received gained the use of many cattle while the giver created an obligation of future value, establishing a bond that ensured the moral and material support of a new friend. More than that, he gained social approbation and consequent status, endowments for which he was more than willing to part with some of his property. Finally, as this exercise in property exchange unfolded, each owner gained back from others what he had given. In the process all were able to spread their liabilities and minimize their susceptibility to misfortune.

Common to the nomadic life was the sharing of range land. "We can move anywhere, everywhere. Are we not all Turkana? You own stock and things; you do not own the country." In this the Turkana spoke for all pastoral people; yet in practice individual families or sections tended to move within certain areas and resented intrusion by others, a latent hostility that could greatly intensify in times of stress. Normally the stress could be eased through migration to new lands, and indeed the process of migration was a population safety valve as well as an engine for the great movements of peoples throughout Africa.

Even more was population controlled by drought and disease. It is estimated that pastoralists in Africa have maintained a population density of between two and seven individuals to the square mile, subsisting on herd animals at a ratio of twelve or fifteen cattle per person. Under ideal conditions cattle might have increased at a 4 percent annual rate, an expansion that would have doubled the need for land at twenty-year intervals. Clearly, such growth unchecked would have quickly encumbered all available land, but, as ever, population concentrations in Africa soon came under assault from natural enemies.

During the late decades of the nineteenth century, for example, the Masai greatly expanded within their Rift Valley home south of Lake Rudolf, pressing other peoples into less attractive locations through their energetic war making. In 1884, however, their herds were attacked by rinderpest, and this misfortune was soon followed by famine. In 1890 another outbreak of rinderpest combined with a smallpox epidemic that wiped out three-fourths of the Masai pastoralists, thereby effectively terminating their tribal expansionism. During much the same years, rinderpest destroyed the herds of the militant Ndebele north of the Limpopo, while locusts devoured their crops. Such disasters drained their strength and greatly complicated their capacity to resist the incursions of Europeans who coincidentally had pressed into their territories.

Unable to cope effectively with plague and famine, the African cattleman was more successful in standing off the onslaught of man or beast. During daylight hours the herds could be defended with shield and spear, and at night they were lodged in the security of the kraal. These enclosures were remarkably similar, whether designed by Sotho Bantu or Nilotes like the Dodoth of the northern Ugandan plains. The latter built large circular kraals approximately ten thousand square feet in area, containing both living quarters for the herders and an open yard for the cattle. The perimeter was constructed of stout poles standing well above the height of the average man, driven solidly into the ground, and interlaced with a heavy tangle of branches, their dense, thick barricade broken only by the cattle gates and occasional well-protected entrances. One-half of the enclosure was divided into pie-shaped segments containing the mud and thatch dwellings of individual families, and all these were separated from the cattle pen by a fence which was the symbolic center of the Dodoth universe, the line of contact between the people and their beloved stock.

Many pastoral people conducted their most serious business in or about the cattle pen. There the men met for secret discussions on affairs of state. There important individuals were buried, wrapped in the hide of a freshly slaughtered ox. Nearby was the meeting place of the men who would sit about the fire in discussion or dispute, administering justice, arranging marriages, receiving strangers, or simply indulging in the gossip of the hour.

Although customs varied, in some areas access to the cattle enclosure was denied to women, but this did not necessarily mean that women retained no rights pertaining to stock. Fulani women, for instance, could gain ownership through inheritance, and though female ownership generally was not countenanced, the utilization of cattle products by women was universally recognized, particularly in connection with food preparation. The use of milk and its products was obvious. Among the Nilotes—Jie, for instance—the women also claimed the blood and the occasional meat available. When an animal died, it was a wife who received the hide, an important concession in a subsistence economy. It is true that some Nilotes, like the Luo and Bari, made cattle strictly taboo to adult women, but many others, including Nandi, Dinka, Karamojong, and Masai, delegated their milking responsibilities to the women. In general, while overall ownership and maintenance of herds fell to the men, women controlled livestock at the domestic level. Each wife was given a number of beasts to help feed herself, her children, and, to the extent she shared the responsibility, her husband.

Among the pastoralists meat was rarely consumed. Stock was precious and infrequently slaughtered, the only other opportunity arising when animals died of disease or age. More important in the diet were milk and blood which appeared in a variety of dishes, some of which were created by adding vegetable products, others by mixing the blood and milk. Milk was normally permitted to ferment—among the Nguni of South Africa, it was set out in a calabash or an untanned leather bag hung in the sun. The result was a thick, sour curd eaten separately or mixed with boiled porridge. The Kipsigis often let their milk stand as long as a month in calabashes rubbed with wood ash. This resulted in a hard yogurt of greenish color and pungent smell. The Dodoth, like the Kipsigis and many others, made butter, but they also produced ghee and a salty cheese prepared by curdling the milk with cow's urine.

Judging from the extent and uniformity of its usage, fresh blood has long served as a dietary staple among most Nilotes, the surgery of its extraction performed in characteristic fashion. The ox or cow is held by horns, legs, tongue, and tail, its neck corded to produce a vein, and a small arrow shot from short range into the neck, the shaft blocked to control the degree of penetration. When withdrawn, the arrow is followed by a stream of blood caught in a calabash or other container, approximately two quarts at a time. The blood is normally drunk raw after the clots have been broken by squeezing them between the fingers, but other more complex dishes are also produced. The Dodoth mix blood with green millet flour to provide a light pudding, while the Kipsigis often cook it with greens.

It is estimated that two cattle would have been sufficient to feed a family of five over a single day. Since an animal could not be safely bled more frequently than every five or six weeks, the family herd in this instance required about seventy-five or eighty head to sustain normal living, a very substantial number of beasts for the human population involved. Presumably this estimate makes no allowance for consumption of milk and dairy products, but these may have been available only during the wetter periods when sufficient lactation was assured. Indeed, it has been suggested that the uncertainty of a milk supply may have been the origin of bleeding as a regular element in the diet.

Of course, livestock produced much more than food. Cowhides provided sleeping mats and clothing, utensils and weapons. Among the southern Bantu, skins were prepared for clothing by first stretching and drying them on pegs; then, after scraping clear the fleshy and fatty tissue with an adze, the hide was softened by a device made of iron spikes, each process alternated with applications of milk, butter, and brain tissue smeared over the surface to ensure a soft texture. When hides were to be converted into shields they were hammered to a dry stiffness before being affixed to a frame for proper rigidity. Masai, Nuer, and others used hides as well for such diverse needs as housing or carrying utensils. Along with mats and straw, skins served as a covering for huts, but the Masai also plastered the walls with a mixture of dung and mud, while cattle droppings were employed by the Dodoth for flooring and were widely used as fuel. Urine, which was an ingredient in numerous dairy dishes, being sterile, was also the standard soap for washing.

The Symbiotic Society

Pastoralism in Africa has long been the ideal for many peoples. Not only is it an idealized image of a perfect world; it also reflects the fact that most cattle-keeping peoples are obliged to be part-time farmers, while even the proudest pastoral Masai, Turkana, Fulani, or other herders must maintain relations with despised cultivators in order to support their economies.

Whatever the origins of pastoralism, either as a transition from hunting to farming or as an offshoot or parallel development to crop production, it appears probable that many one-time nomads, facing famine and plague, chose survival through the more efficient economy of crop production. Just as the hunter, requiring five to ten square miles to sustain himself, was forced to give way to the cattleman, so the latter, his herds supporting a scant half-dozen souls to the square mile, could scarcely compete with the far greater productivity of the farmer. Given optimum conditions, the nomad might have succeeded in his simple existence at the edge of the settled world, but each temporary disaster of drought or plague necessitated some expedient—even farming—to ward off catastrophe, and each successful recourse to crop production forced another step in the retreat of unadulterated pastoralism. A food supply based upon agriculture quickly led to rising birthrates and increasing population densities, but these, in turn, denied any escape back to the simple beauties of pastoralism, with its freedom and its joys, but also with its incapacity for feeding so many new mouths.

Those like the pastoral Masai who succeeded in resisting such change were loud in their contempt for the apostates, but the many who made the transition have taken a somewhat less dismal view of the matter. Kipsigis mythology tells of the time that famine virtually blotted out the herds and threatened the people with extinction, the nation being saved when some women discovered eleusine growing in elephant dung, tasted its goodness, and promptly sowed the remaining grain. "From that day," the Kipsigis claim, "we have become a stronger and a better people than any of our neighbors"—a claim that has been disputed by the Masai who regard the Kipsigis as degenerate and fit victims for cattle raiding. Whatever the merits of the argument, pastoral Masai require some eighteen or nineteen cattle per person for survival, whereas the Kipsigis, part cattle keepers and part farmers, sustain themselves with an average of between two and three animals to an individual.

The Masai attitude, romantic and intractable, takes little account of the essentially symbiotic relationship that has developed over the centuries between cultivators and pastoralists, a relationship spelling cooperation and mutual assistance much more than antagonism and competition. Such cooperation may be observed both within the nation and between pastoral and farming peoples. If it is sometimes grudging and marred by assertions of cultural superiority, this is, in part, the measure of an inadequate economic system. The passionate devotion to cattle on the part of so many peoples whose survival nonetheless rests on farming gives eloquent testimony that economic necessity, not cultural preference, determines how people will live.

These stresses between the "should be" and the "must be" were well exemplified by the Fulani of Hausaland, both within their own families and between their pastoral habits and the farming life of their Hausa neighbors. Fulani nomads began arriving in Hausa country from the west during the thirteenth century or earlier; in time they became permanent settlers—herders whose seasonal migrations did not transcend the Hausa area, and full- or part-time farmers wholly or partially assimilated into Hausa culture. The Fulani have never been more than a substantial minority in Hausaland; recent census figures assign them about 14 percent of the total population in the Sokoto region, but the same statistics go on to show that only one out of five Fulani is a true pastoralist, the rest having permanently lost their herds and turned to farming for a livelihood.

Such figures reflect the shattering impact of the great rinderpest epidemic of the late nineteenth century, but they also indicate long years of attrition which have made the pastoral life an unattainable ideal for the great majority of the Fulani population. Even those who succeeded in maintaining their cattle were obliged to turn to farming on occasion, for their herds were often insufficient to produce the supply of dairy products needed to sustain life.

When the Fulani cattleman resorted to farming, it was regarded as a temporary expedient until full-scale pastoralism could be resumed. Usually a few meager fields were prepared near the large mobile bush encampments of the herdsmen, these fields planted at the beginning of the rains with quick-maturing bulrush millet which had the advantage of both limiting the length of time that had to be devoted to cultivation and making possible an early harvest before the families scattered to the wet season ranges. The grain was consumed primarily during the dry months when milk supplies tended to run out. Basically the Fulani relied upon milk and its products, for meat was rarely available and blood was not drunk as it was among the Nilotes.

During the early nineteenth century, the Fulani *jihads,* or holy wars, led to the conquest of the Hausa states and converted the Fulani from a subject to a governing people. The long years of warfare forced them to abandon their camps for walled villages, their fields and herds now tended by slaves. Later still, the more affluent Fulani hired Hausa labor to care for their farms, their distaste for agriculture unabated, their hopes fixed on the day when the purely pastoral life might be resumed. Against such happy expectations was balanced the apprehension that farming might become a permanent occupation, the herds decreasing in size and the family unable to follow the cattle in their seasonal movements because of growing commitments to the permanent homestead. This was a specter indeed—that one might lose one's cattle and "become *Habe,*" that is, degenerate into sedentary cultivators like the Hausa they held in such contempt.

However scorned, the Hausa were an essential accessory to Fulani prosperity, just as far across the continent pastoral Masai and Kikuyu farmers lived in symbiotic relationship, frequently engaged in warfare and cattle raids but also trading with each other and sometimes marking their truces by marrying one another's women. The cattle-keeping Masai allowed themselves to take nothing from the soil; hence, they relied upon Kikuyu for red ocher and gourds and preferred Kikuyu spearheads as superior in quality to their own. These items were exchanged for sheep, either by Kikuyu traders who entered Masai country protected by a safe passage or by Masai who came to Kikuyuland with similar assurance that they would not be molested in the course of these necessary transactions.

Hausa and Fulani were bound together in similar interdependence, their relationship poised between the mutual dislike of two antithetical cultures and the mutual reliance of economically complementary societies. Before the *jihads* there had been relatively little contact between Hausa and Fulani; yet there is indication that some Hausa have practiced permanent cultivation for centuries, making use of manure to revitalize their fields. While there is no direct evidence available, it is an intriguing presumption that there early developed an arrangement whereby Fulani herders were invited to graze their animals on Hausa farmland, the cattle gaining forage in exchange for the fertilizing effects of livestock droppings.

Certainly, in more recent times, this relationship has developed to mutual advantage. The herds are brought to Hausa farms, usually located near large villages, the arrangement providing dry season pasturage for Fulani cattle and grain for the herdsman and his family, the Hausa gaining the enrichment needed to maintain his fields under permanent cultivation. Beyond this, Fulani herders have come to rely on Hausa markets for a number of products such as calabashes, knives, clothing, salt, kola nuts, and grain, all exchanged through the sale of milk. Even the fully pastoral groups have gradually adopted maize as their staple food and are therefore largely dependent upon the Hausa farming economy, their nomadic ways giving only the illusion of an independence that they may still feel differentiates them from less fortunate sedentary kinsmen.

In Quest of Security

Like the African farmer, the cattleman lived simply—doubtless even more so, since his nomadic existence put no premium on personal possessions while his standard of living permitted few luxuries for himself and his family. The pastoral Fulani typically dwelt in rudimentary camps, which were little more than cattle enclosures designed primarily to protect the stock against hyenas but which also included some rough bed shelters and cooking areas. So well camouflaged as to blend into the surrounding countryside, these sites could easily escape detection, their residents coming and going, as it was said, "as the wind which blows through the bush," leaving no more than a few cut branches and a patch of bare earth to mark their passing.

Modest domestic accommodations were also characteristic across the eastern plains. Homesteads were frequently located on hilltops or along ridges, sometimes clusters of round mud and wattle huts surrounded by a palisade, sometimes no more than simple brush enclosures for temporary occupancy. The men equipped themselves with bow, arrows, and long wooden spears tipped with iron, weapons that accompanied them everywhere, resting at their side as they slept, remaining always in hand during the daily activities. They bedecked themselves with bracelets, necklaces, anklets, and other ornaments, culminating the display with an elaborate headdress topped by a jaunty feather. The usual garment was a cloak of skins worn off one shoulder in toga fashion and doubling at night as a blanket to keep off the chill air. Though some owned leather sandals, the men were otherwise naked; the women, however, supplemented this modest wardrobe with a leather apron and quantities of beading. Utensils and containers were normally made of hides, but basketry and mat manufacture provided additional domestic equipment, while those who were part-time cultivators also possessed the characteristic short-handled hoe.

These few articles defined the extent of personal and family possessions, giving little indication even of the meanest comfort or of variations in individual affluence. Yet within the limits of a subsistence economy there was wealth and the power and prestige that went with it, and there were those whose possessions put them well beyond others in material and spiritual resources. The difference was measured in cattle.

Among the pastoralists cattle were life's very essence; yet their exalted mystical and aesthetic strength rested ultimately on their mundane, material function as the foundation of the pastoral economic system. Cattle were currency and a medium of exchange. They were an investment and a way to capital accumulation. They sustained the population with food and equipment, but they also bound families together in marriage and linked friends and acquaintances through their mutual exchange. They eased the way for social relations, established fortunes, and salvaged the impecunious, the unlucky, or the inept. They were at the root of warfare and sport; equally they influenced external relations with other peoples and domestic affairs at each hearth. They brought wealth through inheritance and power through possession. They dominated the life of their master, dictating where he might live and when, designing the style of his architecture, and even providing the material for his winding sheet.

Essential to economic, social, and psychic stability, cattle and their accumulation became a natural preoccupation of the herdsman, even extending to those peoples who had long since divided their energies between pastoral and agricultural pursuits. In a menacing environment the overwhelming instinct was to increase and augment, not to concentrate on a few vulnerable beasts of genetic strength or fine milking qualities. The big herds formed during the good seasons could smother catastrophe with their numbers—so the logic went—the survivors checking the onset of famine and providing the basis for eventual regeneration of the stock. Similarly, if crops failed, the farmer who possessed cattle prevailed, his success secured by diversification. This was no idle romance, some passionate attachment to obsolete custom; this was economic pragmatism rooted in long-lived experience.

Beyond sheer survival, livestock was regarded as a good investment for it provided a sizable return in offspring and offered reasonable protection against loss and deterioration caused by climate and vermin. Cattle, moreover, were no mere symbol of wealth; they were wealth itself, as valuable and negotiable to the herding peoples as gold bullion or a well-stabilized currency in today's modern world. By attempting to accumulate cattle, the pastoralist was the classic economic man engaged in augmenting his capital to the fullest, his investment preferences of course involving social as well as economic motivation.

Frequently, social and economic objectives complemented and reinforced each other. The pastoral Fulani, for example, saw their destiny in the vigorous growth of individual families, but these could prosper only when they owned expanding herds of healthy livestock. "If the cattle die the [Fulani] will die," went the saying, and their conventions governing marriage and inheritance were specifically designed to forestall this unhappy eventuality. It was customary for the unmarried sons to help with the herd; in this way they gradually increased their rights in the family stock, each finally inheriting his share on marriage. In marriage, moreover, a wife was typically chosen from within the lineage; thus any inheritance, of which cattle were the chief corpus, would not be lost to the lineage—this was the traditional morality, but the motivation was basically economic.

The Masai practiced a similar custom, the family head granting animals from his herd to his sons, beginning at an early age and continuing until each had a considerable collection of his own. Thus responsibility was securely linked to the ownership of cattle and the concept of increase affirmed as the natural order of things. For these and other Nilotes, as well as for the cattle-keeping Bantu, livestock also figured prominently in marriage contracts; unlike the Fulani, however, the object was to offer a substantial herd to the father of the bride, the accumulation of cattle therefore accruing to families of many daughters.

Each bridegroom gave as many head as he could afford—the more he gave, the greater his prestige in the community; the closer he came to the true limits of his capability, the warmer his welcome by the family of his father-in-law as a sober and trustworthy person. The amounts varied greatly from people to people and between individuals. Among the Nilotic Jie or Dodoth one case might involve twenty cattle, another twice that much and more with an additional hundred goats or sheep thrown into the bargain. With the southern Bantu the *lobola,* or bridewealth, was much more limited, but everywhere the amount seems to have been determined by the ability to pay rather than by any notion of the exchange value of the bride. During the rinderpest epidemic of the 1890s, for example, bridewealth among the Jie was reckoned for a time at one or two beasts, while famine periods in southern Africa have occasioned token *lobola* in the form of stones or mice.

Bridewealth payments thus appeared to be social in definition, public approbation their primary purpose; yet, in fact, their object was essentially economic. The payment of cattle legitimized a man's marriage and assured his authority over his children, but it also brought him a wife who would take responsibility for managing his household. Marriage offered motherhood and the support and protection of a husband, but it also guaranteed important rights in the bridegroom's herds, both for the wife and for her children. In some societies the women cared for the calves, and where agriculture was practiced they tended the gardens and saw the crops through to the table. A man's sons were his labor force, but their labor was well recompensed through inheritance, an inheritance that would be employed in its turn as bridewealth to secure the fortunes of the next generation.

Most importantly, the bridewealth pattern established an extensive web of property among members of two families including friends and associates of each. When a man married he normally assembled his bridewealth by adding to his own herd livestock begged and borrowed from relatives and acquaintances who may have felt some obligation toward him and who henceforward would have a direct concern for his welfare. At the same time, the father of the bride distributed the payment widely among members of his own family, thereby further augmenting the number with personal interest in a successful marriage. The total transaction described a substantial reapportionment of animals among many individuals while introducing complex new alignments of mutual obligations and privileges. Those kin of the husband who contributed toward his bridewealth would eventually be repaid in part from the bridewealth obtained upon the marriage of his sister or daughter. Furthermore, his new wife would be expected to assist his family in their various domestic tasks, and in time they might even receive some of her children for adoption if they happened to be childless or their work were exceptionally heavy. Her family, moreover, would make her gifts of food and clothing and would treat her children with great respect, performing certain ceremonial rites on their behalf and contributing toward the *lobola* of her male children at the appropriate time.

Livestock, therefore, served many functions. It was food supply and standard of value; it was an emblem of prestige and the measure of all social relations of importance. Finally, it was the medium through which a people, needing the closest cooperation in the face of actual or potential disaster, were able most effectively to join forces in their quest for security. The Fulani, though they practiced no bridewealth, regularly united within each lineage to ensure that all households maintained adequate supplies of stock and labor. The lineage was a close-knit group, usually living and pasturing together; hence, exchange of livestock and mutual support were easily achieved.

Among Nilotes livestock exchange was undertaken on the grand scale. Not only were substantial numbers reapportioned through marriage; cattle also changed hands informally, sometimes between kin, sometimes simply between friends and acquaintances. In these closely-knit societies, recourse to blood relatives was understandable, but the system of exchange with individuals outside the family or lineage was also widely practiced, chiefly, it would seem, as a means for broadening the base of support to the full extent of individual economic resources. The arrangement was more like a business undertaking than an act of friendship, its motivation practical, its consummation a measure of the material assistance each individual hoped to gain. The process was informal, usually initiated by a gift offered and received and sustained over the years by the principle of reciprocity on which the whole system rested. Genuine friendship might, and often did, flower in the course of such an alliance, but cordiality was not normally the basis for the initial transaction. Thus, wealthy men with large herds had many such associates, for they were much in demand; poor men, on the contrary, were obliged to seek out one another, for the uncertain aid they could render offered little attraction to the more affluent.

There were numerous advantages to these informal associations not always available through clan relations. Lineage members might be concentrated in particular areas and unavailable in others; hence, a choice of associates based on convenience could ensure support from all quarters—an essential in a land where water or pasture might fail in one region while remaining sufficient in another, where disease or cattle raiders might strike one community but leave its neighbor in peace. Moreover, a man was always welcome at the homestead of an associate where he could obtain scarce food or seed as well as water or forage for his stock. The number of livestock associates would have varied according to circumstance; a recent count among the Jie and Turkana ranged from seven or eight to as many as fifty, with an average of about thirty. Numbers could be important for more than simple reciprocity in cattle. In days when disputes were likely to be settled by force or its threat, the support of a large body of stock associates was an essential prerequisite to a successful position in the community.

The Exchange of Gifts

In Nilotic societies the exchange of property in livestock appeared to have as much force for kith as for kin. Indeed, even where kinship served as the initial basis for reciprocity, it came to be the exchange rather than the kinship tie that dominated the relationship. The bond of blood remained significant when it involved the fulfillment of past obligations and the acceptance of future commitments in livestock payments; without these practical expressions of continued interest, it atrophied. "If he does not give you stock, you do not give to him," explained a Turkana, adding, "He is not like your mother's brother now." Against this was the pleasure taken in an active alliance between two unrelated individuals, their reciprocity in livestock leading to cooperation in work and leisure, to mutual affection and esteem, and ultimately to a kind of naturalized kinship status. "Your bond-friend gives you a beast; and he comes to beg and you give him a cow. He is like your own people . . . like a cousin."

Whatever the starting point, therefore, it was reciprocal exchange of domestic stock that finally defined individual relationships and ultimately the shape of the whole society. Close personal bonds rested on mutual gifts of cattle, not as the symbolic manifestation of an association otherwise conceived but as the practical reason for the existence of that association—to provide a man with animals he needed and to create the obligation for repayment whenever the need was reversed.

Thus, for the pastoralist it was the gift of his most precious commodity, and essentially his only form of property, that brought about the movement of goods and services, propelling the economy and giving form and purpose to the society. A Jie or a Masai, a Nuer or a Kipsigis, a Nandi or a citizen of any other cattle-keeping community, sought and gained cooperation, assistance, friendship, security, power, or the pleasures of life primarily through the offer to exchange his assets and his property for those of others. Theoretically the more affluent might have maintained themselves using cattle from their own herds, but such a self-centered system could not have prevailed in a parlous world where cooperation was the foundation stone of all societies and virtually the sole means of survival.

Indeed the employment of the gift as an engine to accelerate distribution and consumption was broadly characteristic of all traditional African societies, both agricultural and pastoral, even of those that engaged in local or long-distance trade. Markets normally provided insufficient impetus to increased productivity in subsistence economies, for there was little familiarity with the idea of profit or the accumulation of goods beyond immediate need.

Such an image fitted the large and powerful state fully as much as the smaller community. Buganda, for example, all conquering during her apogee in the eighteenth and nineteenth centuries, conducted a lucrative trade with the emporiums of the East African coast, but her economy was classic in its reliance on gift exchange, its trade doing little to increase production either for export or for internal consumption. The principal exports of slaves and ivory were obtained primarily through raids on neighboring peoples, the Buganda economy sustained by its staples, the banana and plantain. The exchange of gifts bound the community together in its social relationships, but it also provided the main thrust behind economic intercourse within the Buganda state. Relations between chiefs and their people, as well as conventions governing hospitality, marriages, births, and deaths, were all governed through the institution of the gift. Generosity was the rule and public scrutiny the compulsion; to give too little was to risk censure while liberality was always smiled upon as a sign of wealth and prestige.

There were, however, deeper forces at work. Buganda's parent and predecessor was Bunyoro, which dominated the region northwest of Lake Victoria in the sixteenth and early seventeenth centuries. Like Buganda, Bunyoro drew strength from a centralized monarchy, the *mukama,* or king, holding the threads of power through a number of devices, several of them economic in substance and linked to the institution of gift exchange. It was the custom for all who visited the king, chief or commoner, to come with an offering—women, cattle, beer, or grain—but it was also obligatory for the *mukama* to distribute these riches among his callers with an open hand and to preside over frequent and lavish feasts as well.

In the royal palace, moreover, there were large numbers of retainers drawn widely from among the clans throughout the kingdom, far more than were needed for practical purposes, thereby binding many lineages to the crown through benefit of the royal largess. Finally, the king frequently went on tour, remaining for extended periods in different parts of his realm. While he was in residence, it was the duty of the local population to provide an appropriate palace for their monarch and his entourage, stocking it fully with food and supplies. In return the king was expected to entertain his subjects with numerous feasts. By all these devices the *mukama* was able to establish loyalties that sustained the kingdom politically, but in the process his office also served as a major channel for the interchange of goods and services, thereby ensuring a level of prosperity commensurate with the productive capacity of the Bunyoro state.

Always the economic imperative was reciprocity. African communities had a keen sense of private property and gave clear definition to ownership in herds, agricultural products, or personal gear. There was no legal compulsion in the modern sense to dispose of cattle through gifts, to contribute to the bridewealth of a relative, to provide a spouse with certain crops or fields, or to donate labor to public works. No sanction compelled the suppliant to present his chief with an offering, and no prince was obliged to respond with a favor. Yet all did, for custom dictated thus. Each offered the gift in order that he might receive in like manner, and all participated in the tightly integrated system of reciprocity because they knew no other way and because it worked.

SUGGESTIONS FOR FURTHER READING

Information on Nilotic migrations comes primarily from linguistic materials and oral tradition. The works to consult are B. A. Ogot, *History of the Southern Luo* (Nairobi: East African Publishing House, 1967); C. Ehret, *Southern Nilotic History* (Evanston, Ill.: Northwestern University Press, 1971); J. P. Crazzolara, *The Lwoo* (Verona, Italy, 1950, 1951, 1954); J. Greenberg, *Languages of Africa*, 2nd rev. ed. (Bloomington: Indiana University Press, 1966); G. P. Murdock, *Africa: Its Peoples and Their Culture History* (New York: McGraw-Hill, 1959); and the relevant chapters in R. Oliver and G. Mathew, eds., *History of East Africa*, vol. 1 (Oxford: Clarendon Press, 1963). There are also informative chapters in B. A. Ogot and J. A. Kieran, eds., *Zamani* (Nairobi: East African Publishing House; New York: Humanities Press, 1968).

There is a great deal of information available on African cattle-keeping peoples and their customs, most of it anthropological in focus. See, for example, E. E. Evans-Pritchard, *The Nuer* (Oxford: Clarendon Press, 1940); P. H. Gulliver, *The Family Herds* (London: Routledge and Kegan Paul, 1955); D. J. Stenning, *Savannah Nomads* (London: Oxford University Press, 1959); C. E. Hopen, *The Pastoral Fulbe Family in Gwandu* (London: Oxford University Press, 1958); and J. G. Peristiany, *The Social Institutions of the Kipsigis* (London: George Routledge and Sons, 1939). M. Fortes and E. E. Evans-Pritchard, eds., *African Political Systems* (London: Oxford University Press, 1940), also deals with certain cattle people, albeit briefly, while I. Schapera, *The Bantu-Speaking Tribes of South Africa* (London: George Routledge and Sons, 1937), is a survey of all southern Bantu peoples. The sections dealing with cattle in William Allan, *The African Husbandman* (New York: Barnes and Noble, 1965), are also useful, while much information is scattered through works by travelers of former times such as Livingstone, Barth, Caillié, Burton, and others.

For Buganda and Bunyoro there are J. Roscoe, *The Baganda* (London: Macmillan, 1911); Lucy Mair, *An African People in the Twentieth Century* (London: George Routledge and Sons, 1934); and J. Beattie, *Bunyoro; An African Kingdom* (New York: Holt, Rinehart and Winston, 1960).

There is no information dealing directly with the economic aspects of gift giving in Africa. The classic work in the field is Marcel Mauss, *The Gift* (Glencoe,

Ill.: The Free Press, 1954), and references may be found in many of the works cited above as well as in others. An interesting discussion of the economics of the gift as it occurs in Bunyoro is contained in J. Beattie, "Bunyoro, an African Feudality," *Journal of African History*, vol. 5, no. 1 (1964).

Part Four

THE TRADERS

Bronze figure, Dahomey.
Photo courtesy of the author.

8

❦

THE GOLDEN TRADE

Across the Vast Sahara

Almost twenty-five centuries ago, the Greek historian Herodotus spoke of the Garamantes, a people who dwelt on the northern edge of the great desert and chased down black men from the deep interior with the aid of four-horse chariots. Long did this appear to be another of the famed historian's tall stories, but eventually his assertions came to be fully substantiated. Only very recently, numerous rock drawings of horse-drawn chariots have been discovered in various sites throughout the Sahara, including, finally, a rendition in the Garamantes' own Fezzan country of the four-horsed vehicle that Herodotus had reported.

How far the Garamantes traveled to reach the land of the blacks is not entirely clear. It may have been to the mountains of Tibesti or the hills and canyons of Tassili, both in the full Sahara, but many other sites have yielded their renditions of chariots, including some far to the south along the Niger River; hence it must be inferred that some system of transport and communication existed clear across the desert between North Africa and the Sub-Saharan savanna. The contact must have been an ancient one as well. The testimony of Herodotus applies to the fifth century before Christ, but related evidence concerning the introduction of horses into Egypt more than ten centuries earlier still, suggests that the desert chariots could have been in service as long ago as 1000 B.C.

The rock drawings were found to describe patterns of travel along two recognizable routes—one from the Tripoli coast southwest through the Fezzan and Tassili to the top of the Niger bend, the second descending from the Moroccan coast in a long, southwesterly arc paralleling the continental shore, then turning east along the savanna to reach the Niger near the site of what was later to become the great entrepôt of Timbuktu. Surely, such well-defined routes with their implication of repeated journeys presupposed an ancient trans-Saharan commerce. For one thing, there is the reasonable presumption that Garamantian forays against the blacks—probably the Teda people of Tibesti—were prompted in part by a search for slaves. Furthermore, it is known that, in Carthaginian times, carbuncles were systematically brought out of the interior as an article of trade; later the Romans obtained ivory from the Garamantes, supplementing dwindling North African supplies with shipments that must have originated in the Sudan.

The suspicion persists, however, that what trans-Saharan commerce there may have been was of no great consequence, at least not to the North Africa of ancient times. Carthage was a maritime power oriented outward toward the markets of Europe and the East, while Rome seems to have been interested mainly in the foodstuffs and wild animals available north of the desert. Gold, that resource of tropical Africa that should have greatly attracted the ancients, is barely mentioned in classical texts, while an almost total lack of Mediterranean artifacts in West Africa is further testimony to the absence of any serious trading contacts. It must be concluded, therefore, that a minor, intermittent trade existed, probably conducted by Berber groups, its products largely absorbed in North African markets, its international ramifications yet to come.

This was in the nature of things. The indifference of the Mediterranean world reflected, at least in part, the hazards of a difficult and unknown land; the uncompromising Sahara still awaited the touch of ingenuity that would convert its sometime chariot trails into the broader avenues of a major international commerce. During the final years of the pre-Christian era, such a breakthrough did indeed occur and the ecology of the desert was forever altered. It was at this time that the camel was introduced into the world of the Sahara.

The Desert Ecology

Like the horse, the camel came from the East, first to Egypt, then to North Africa, and finally to the Sahara. The horse had spread quickly across the Mediterranean littoral, not as a humble pack animal but rather as the prestigious drawer of chariots. His martial role gave rise to a romantic image that obscured his doubtful economic value, especially when he was compared with the lowly but useful donkey or to the camel which in the desert proved superior in warfare as well as in commerce. Yet he held on, at least along the edge of the desert, a symbol of social status and martial strength, adding the swiftness of cavalry to the armies of savanna empires and the imposing presence of a thoroughbred mount to every royal entourage from ancient Ghana to modern Nupe.

By contrast, the camel was an unlovely creature, bizarre in appearance, stubborn and irritable in manner, and surprisingly fragile in the face of careless treatment. Perhaps this is why he was so long disregarded in Egypt; although he must have been well known there from Arabian contacts; he did not pass westward across the Nile until the close of the pre-Christian era—unprepossessing in the wake of the handsome Mongolian or the spirited Arabian steed. Nevertheless, in the Sahara he quickly proved his value, profoundly influencing human habitation and desert ecology, in the process elevating the old chariot routes to major thoroughfares of economic exchange and cultural intercourse.

The difference rested with the camel's ability to thrive in places denied to other creatures by lack of water. Whatever his aesthetic appeal, the horse needed daily watering and ample supplies of food; by contrast a camel could forego water over long periods, provided he had access to lush pasture. Where this was not available, he could still maintain a normal work load for several days on end without water or, indeed, without norishment of any kind. Such a performance was possible because of a low rate of liquid elimination, including sweating, and an ability to store substantial quantities of water outside the fabric of tissue cells so that draughts on this reservoir had no ill effects on intracellular protoplasm.

Under these circumstances, a camel could carry a rider or a full load during an extended desert journey without any loss in efficiency. If he was the long-legged, graceful saddle camel, he would proceed at a normal rate of five miles per hour over a six-hour day, but in extreme circumstances he might double his speed and cover as much as one hundred miles in a fifteen- or twenty-hour sprint. The pack camel was capable of similar prodigies, supporting five-hundred-pound burdens on daily marches of fifteen or twenty miles.

Outstanding effectiveness under severe conditions was contingent upon careful husbandry, a treatment that desert people like the Tuareg were at pains to provide. The more extraordinary the demands upon strength and stamina, the more time was required for relaxation and recuperation. The camel deprived of proper water or forage over protracted periods necessarily drank and ate heavily when the opportunity presented itself, and forced marches had to be followed by long idle intervals to ensure total rehabilitation. The daily caravan regimen was usually broken by a lengthy noon hour during which man and beast alike sought repose and refreshment, and in the evening each camel was carefully unloaded that his energies be not needlessly taxed. Camels normally could work only four months each year; pushed beyond these limits they would sicken or die, sometimes dropping of exhaustion on the march, more often degenerating into pitiful shadows of their former selves, their strength broken, their poor labor scarcely worth the cost of their upkeep.

The camel's unusual capabilities, so uniquely attuned to the desert environment, permitted a degree of human habitation hitherto impossible. Each desert oasis, despite its gardens, its arbors, its date palms, and its flocks, could not have prospered without the mobility provided by the camel. Indeed, in the desert all wealth was reckoned in camels—to cite his personal importance, a noble or prince typically made note of the size of his herds rather than his holdings in gold or other properties.

The utility of the camel did not end with the capacity to move people and goods across otherwise impassable wastes. For the desert folk, camel milk was often their only beverage, butter and camel meat a major part

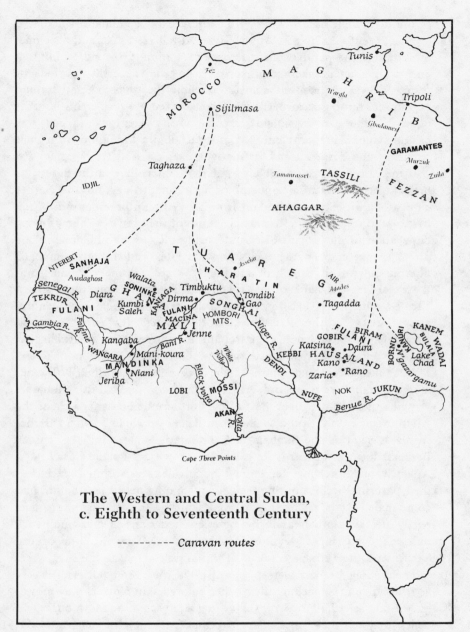

The Western and Central Sudan, c. Eighth to Seventeenth Century

---------- Caravan routes

of the diet, while camel skins were employed by a number of nomadic groups as tenting material. Among desert dwellers, a man and his camel mount were inseparable, their activity a continuous round of hunting and raiding enemy herds, broken only by the necessary periods of respite. It was the camel that made possible the trans-Saharan trading expedition, but on occasion he was obliged even to sacrifice his life that others in the caravan might survive—when water gave out it was customary to slaughter camels in order to obtain the liquid from their stomachs in a desperate bid for survival.

If the camel was responsible for altering the ecology of the desert, he brought his talents to a population long resident—negroid and Berber cultivators, probably descendant from the Saharan hunting and fishing folk of earlier times, who remained to adapt themselves to the growing desiccation as the Sahara dried out during the closing millennia of the pre-Christian era. To these groups were later added Berber nomads filtering down from the north and finally Arab herdsmen, pressing into the desert on the flank of the vast Arab occupation of North Africa effected during the seventh century and again in the eleventh century after Christ. Together with the pastoral Berbers, the Arabs came to dominate the oases and to control the expanding caravan traffic that grew up once the camel had become established in the Sahara.

After the eleventh century the Saharan Arabs were primarily Bedouins, originally from central Arabia, their warlike habits ultimately bringing them control over most of the northern desert as far west as the Atlantic shore. In the process they eventually overwhelmed major Berber segments such as the Sanhaja in the western Sahara, but the Tuareg Berbers, located primarily in such central desert uplands as Tassili, Ahaggar, and Air, remained largely independent of Arab influence. For their part, the Berbers during their long-standing desert occupation had commingled with remaining negroids, partly through intermarriage, partly in a symbiotic relationship between herder and farmer, and partly in a major sharing of territory as between the Tuareg in the central Sahara and the Teda pastoralists of the Tibesti massif to the east.

The Tuareg Berbers were pastoralists, tending their flocks of sheep, goats, and camels, packing their ocher-colored skin tents as they moved in constant search of the wiry yellow grass and scattered thorn bushes on which they fed their stock. These were no peaceable herders, however,

for existence in a hostile land bred tough, pugnacious warriors. Raiding
was a way of life, practiced with equal enthusiasm on sedentary villagers,
passing caravans, or the herds of rival groups, the love of booty for its
own sake matched by eternal needfulness and an urgent sense of
survival.

The Tuareg on his camel was as formidable in appearance as he was
lethal in war. Clad in folds of loosely cut trousers, long gowns, and
copious shawls, he perched majestically atop his tall, white beast, his face
masked by the *litham,* a combination turban and veil of dark blue cotton
cloth wound in such a way as to allow only the narrowest slit opening at
the eyes. Thus reminiscent of the helmeted jousting knight, he moved
quickly to the attack, his armament bristling with spears and javelins for
long-range assault, his sword and dagger ready for the eventuality of
closer hand-to-hand conflict.

Successful raiding depended largely on speed and surprise. Caravans
not already equipped with Tuareg guides and armed escorts were fair
game for sudden strikes out of ambush. Quick attacks in quest of slaves
were also aimed periodically at savanna farming communities, but in
fact the most common raids occurred among the pastoralists themselves.
The victim was usually a group several hundred miles distant, chosen to
complicate retaliation, the raiders singling out an isolated herd to be
surrounded and driven off with utmost speed, preferably over a difficult
terrain that would discourage pursuit. It was here that the capabilities of
the desert camel shone most brilliantly; in some instances mounts were
able to move as much as four hundred miles during a six-day forced
march.

Such skirmishing was chronic, not so much from political necessity or
sporting instinct as from well-established economic need. Livestock raids
revitalized herds decimated by disease or drought; more than that, they
helped to maintain the range rights of particular groups through an
energetic belligerence that controlled limited water and forage and
ensured that the modest resources of the desert were not overtaxed with
resultant disaster for all. This delicate economic balance of power
extended beyond the desert to adjacent regions where the nomads
migrated each year during the hot, dry months. In normal times the
seasonal movements were peaceful—the Arabs of the northern desert
pasturing in the Atlas highlands, the Tuareg drifting southward to the

valley of the Niger—but when the ranges failed or the water holes gave out, migration turned to armed attack and hit-and-run raiding to militant occupation. Thus were the Tuareg always an uncertain factor to the great savanna kingdoms, periodically taking and holding emporiums like Timbuktu and regularly overrunning the peaceful savanna country-side. Successful retaliation required occupation of desert strongholds such as Agades in the region of Aïr; in any event, the ebb and flow between desert and savanna, like the intramural raiding among the Tuareg, was essentially a response to economic pressures.

For all their independence, Tuareg and other nomads could not have sustained themselves without established desert stations, oases where water, foodstuffs, and other goods were available. In Tuareg country these consisted of small farming centers where sedentary negroids collectively known as Haratin tended small, irrigated gardens as sharecroppers on Tuareg plots, raising wheat, barley, and millet along with fig trees, grapevines, and the ubiquitous date palm. The Haratin were a serf class to be distinguished from household slaves of the Tuareg; in the northern desert their role was taken over by Berbers tilling the plots of Arab landlords.

North or south, these oasis towns maintained a characteristic appear-ance, despite substantial variations in size. In some locations the gardens were encircled by stone or palm branch walls with the farmhouse located inside each enclosure. More commonly, the town buildings were crowded onto some easily defended point, possibly a rocky outcrop, the fields and orchards lying some distance away on the flat. Oasis houses followed certain essentials dictated by circumstance—square design with a flat roof terrace, thick stone or brick walls shutting out the hot, dry desert air, an open central courtyard where most domestic work and recreation took place, and a series of small rooms surrounding the court used for sleeping, storage, and livestock areas.

Similar in aspect, these oasis communities shared a common function as caravan way stations. Most of the bigger centers, like Wargla and Ghadames in the north and Agades in the south, lay near the desert edge, serving as exchange points where goods could be obtained for the Saharan trip while those just arriving might be disposed of in the market. Mid-Saharan settlements such as Kufra in the Lybian desert or Adrar and Tamanrasset in Algeria also contained markets, but more particularly they were the resting places where weary caravans might pause to refresh and restock.

Where Arab and Berber groups controlled the caravan routes passing through their territory, it was sometimes commerce rather than tribute that occupied their attentions. This was exemplified by the Massufa Berbers who held the desert town of Taghaza, famed for its salt production but in itself a dismal hamlet where a population of slaves eked out the meanest existence in the mines while their masters reaped vast profits in the hungry markets of the savanna. Two celebrated Sahara travelers, Ibn Battuta and Leo Africanus, passed through Taghaza, the former in the middle of the fourteenth century and Leo approximately 150 years later; yet there is remarkable consistency in their observations.

Taghaza is an unattractive village, wrote Ibn Battuta, set in the full sandy wastes where no tree takes root and where the inhabitants live in houses made of salt blocks roofed with camel skins. The local water is brackish, he continued, and the place plagued with flies, while the population subsists on a miserable diet of dates, camel meat, and millet, all brought in by caravan. Leo Africanus added further depressing details. From time to time, he stated, the caravans are late in arriving, and when they finally appear they frequently find the unfortunate miners in their cheerless homes dead from starvation. More than that, he went on, the summer wind blows so severely as to injure the eyes and many of the miners have thereby been blinded. Both Leo and Battuta noted, however, the high value placed upon Taghaza salt in the savanna, a circumstance that ensured the continued operation of the mines, however wretched the working conditions. "The business done at Taghaza," concluded Battuta, "for all its meanness, amounts to an enormous figure."

The Caravans

The camel made possible both habitation and travel in the desert of a magnitude previously unimaginable. Nevertheless, it was the Arabo-Berber merchants of North Africa who elevated the Saharan crossing from an uncertain venture to a regular commercial enterprise, in the process inventing the camel caravan. Unlike the Carthaginians and Romans, these entrepreneurs showed great interest in the lands to the south, a mercantile interest that was shared equally by northerner and southerner. "Why have you ceased to send to our country?" complained the ruler of Bornu, writing in 1440 to the chief of a northern desert oasis. "I swear . . . I will do you no hurt. . . . Come then as you were accustomed to come . . . for the country is yours as it was your father's."

If there was reluctance in this particular instance, it was less likely the result of indifference than of doubts raised over the difficulties of the voyage. The initial terminus was normally a northern oasis town such as Sijilmasa, Wargla, or Zuila, although on occasion expeditions were formed farther north beyond the Atlas Mountains in cities like Fez and Tlemcen. From there the caravans crossed the Atlas range by horse and mule, sometimes beginning their journey in disaster if they were unluckily engulfed by a killing mountain snowstorm but perhaps more happily reaching the desert without mishap. Poised for the Sahara passage, the trains were fully outfitted and restocked—camel transport arranged, drivers and outriders hired, and goods assembled for the long journey. A great deal of preparation preceded the actual beginning of the expedition. Merchants usually had correspondents in southern cities like Gao or Timbuktu to advise them on local demands and price changes, on commercial competition and political complications. The camels were bought or leased from desert Berbers who also provided guides and messengers, information on routes and desert pasturage, and, above all, protection against attack—protection, that is, from the protectors themselves—all for a stiff price. To these expenses were added export duties, normally assessed at 100 percent *ad valorem,* and additional tolls were to be expected en route and upon arrival in the south.

Such formidable expenses implied a large-scale operation backed by substantial financial resources, and, indeed, the Saharan caravans were enormous affairs, the main limits to their size being the capacity of desert wells or the purses of the sponsoring merchants. Large size tended to discourage attack, and caravans of as many as twelve thousand camels were reported in the fourteenth century, such mammoth expeditions containing the goods of numerous merchants banded together for the desert crossing.

The scale and complexity of business enterprise was illustrated by the al-Maqqari family firm from Tlemcen which flourished during the thirteenth and fourteenth centuries, its members established permanently at the sensitive points of the trans-Saharan trade. One branch of the family remained in Tlemcen shipping goods south; a second lived in the savanna city of Walata, dealing with the southern markets and gathering local products for the return trip; and a third settled in Sijilmasa, engaged largely in keeping track of price changes, market information, and the machinations of competitors. Such thoroughgoing activity meant wealth both to the terminal cities on the caravan routes and to the merchants themselves. It was businessmen like these who were largely responsible for the growth and importance of the commercial centers, north and south, and who therefore were much smiled upon by local rulers profiting from their efforts. Despite the heavy duties and dangers of the trip, moreover, their own individual profits were enormous; witness the tenth-century promissory note of a businessman covering a sum of 6,000 gold ounces, the fifteenth-century merchant whose fortune was estimated at 12,500 ounces, and those sixteenth-century traders from Jenne whose annual shipments in the gold trade were worth 7,500 ounces while their yearly traffic in salt was valued at a substantial 1,250 ounces of gold.

Such high finance reflected high risk, both to capital and to personnel. At worst, the journey might end in disaster; at best it was arduous and unpleasant, marked by such desert afflictions as oasis lice, serpents, and scorpions, brackish water when water was available, and the celebrated desert heat by day combined with bone-chilling nighttime cold. "The desert is haunted by demons," testified Ibn Battuta, who knew it well, "nothing but sand blown hither and thither by the wind."

The outward journey from the north was normally made in the winter to avoid the hottest season if not the sandstorms that sometimes struck the caravans with their fury or, equally disastrous, drifted mountains of sand over the wells, filling them and covering them from view. The daily routine was designed to minimize the difficulties and discomforts of the march. The camels were loaded and the train set in motion at dawn, proceeding until the sun's heat became insupportable. At this point tents were pitched and a long siesta ensued during the heat of the day, the march being resumed in the cooler afternoon hours and continuing until darkness. At times when the heat was too great, the expedition set forth late in the afternoon, marching through the night and resting by day.

All activities were conducted under the strictest of discipline. Laggards and wanderers were abandoned without pity, for survival lay with unity and the ability to press forward with measured haste. Among the greatest dangers were buried wells counted upon to replenish supplies of water or navigational errors that set an expedition on a fatal tack toward the wilderness and eventual disaster. It was customary for expeditions to Walata to send word ahead so that water could be brought out to meet the caravan, but the bones of men and beasts along the route testified that the messengers did not always succeed in getting through. Leo Africanus tells the pathetic story of the rich merchant who, tortured with thirst, bought a drink of water from a driver for ten thousand ducats. In the end they both died, their common grave surviving to mark the site of their fate, mute eloquence to warn those who followed.

Equally dangerous were the attacks of desert peoples through whose territories the caravans ventured or of bandits attracted by the prospect of loot. The attacks of brigands helped force abandonment of the main southern route between Egypt and Ghana as early as the tenth century, and Arab raiders later so disrupted one of the main trails south to Walata that it was necessary to substitute an alternate farther east. The attrition bore heavily on both sides, for the caravans and their allies fought back with an obstinate determination. One observer made note of the leather carpet at the palace in Sijilmasa covered with the heads of slaughtered brigands. Another told of the bandit who died in a daring attempt to capture the wealth of the Mali sovereign *Mansa* Musa by cutting the well ropes when Musa and his gold-laden pilgrimage passed through. This desperate adventure ended violently at the bottom of the well where Musa's retainers trapped and dispatched the unfortunate highwayman.

In the desert, then, the law lay with those who were strongest, but once the caravans had reached the savanna, they found a far different situation in which the fiat of a powerful sovereign in a mighty state was supreme and his word spelled peace and order. In Ghana and Mali, unarmed travelers moved about freely and safely. The king of Ghana was always available to hear complaints of injustice, Mali's rulers dealt harshly with criminal behavior, while Songhai maintained the tradition of peace and security until the final days of her collapse.

Special care was taken to guard against violence and fraud in the markets which were established on consecrated ground under the protection of a local chief. Among many regulations were those forbidding access to armed individuals or persons suffering from contagious diseases. The king's men or the town fathers were at pains to see that strangers were fully protected—in Ashanti the court sent buyers to check for fraud, and unhappy was the merchant found cheating for he was obliged to make up weight shortages with the flesh of his own body.

The desert passage normally covered about two months, the caravans ending their journey at one of the great market towns of the savanna. Kumbi Saleh, the royal seat in ancient Ghana, is the earliest known of these, but in time it came to be challenged by others—the Sanhaja Berber center of Awdaghost; Walata, sited on the edge of the desert; Timbuktu, perched at the top of the Niger bend; Gao, the Songhai stronghold lying 250 miles downstream to the east; Kano, Katsina, and the other towns of Hausaland; and the Kanem-Bornu market centers near Lake Chad. Here the caravans ended their labors, their merchandise sold or unloaded for transshipment through the next stage of an economic conduit that channeled goods ultimately between the most modest of forest and savanna villages of West Africa and the markets of Europe and the East.

Goods arriving at Timbuktu were usually loaded in mammoth canoes with a capacity of twenty or thirty tons and taken three hundred miles upstream to Jenne, once more sold and reloaded on donkey trains driven by Dyula merchants or marched south toward the forest on the heads of human porters. Donkeys operated in wide areas of the savanna above the line of tsetse infection, for they were strong and easier to maintain in moister areas than the camel. In tsetse country, however, human portage was the basic transport, and individuals could carry one hundred pounds twenty miles in a day over terrain frequently too difficult for animals. These baggage trains were normally manned by slaves belonging to Hausa or Dyula merchants, their heads becoming bald, it was said, because of the constant friction of their heavy loads. In this fashion, trade goods moved widely throughout the savanna and forest, and it was the mean village indeed that did not receive at least an occasional visit from the itinerant peddler, the measured dignity of his leisurely approach along the forest path conditioned by the pace of his slave or apprentice who followed with the goods piled high on his head.

The Markets of West Africa

In the big West African cities—Benin, for instance, or Kano—the market was likely to be near the physical center of town, even as it was a focal point for much of the economic and social life of the metropolis. Several highways converged on the city, continuing through the gates to intersect typically in a large square in the middle of town. Along these avenues were residences, frequently open-faced in the forest community but in the savanna cities turning their blank facades of sun-dried clay toward the daily traffic, with only an occasional door or window to betray the life of the compound within. At the square might be found the mosque and probably as well the palace of local ruler or highly placed deputy for a distant emperor. Here too was the market, standing perhaps opposite the mosque, running along one complete side of the square near the royal residence and, during its busy hours, spilling out to take over virtually the whole of the available open area.

The large urban market operated daily and, though physically ephemeral, was as established an institution as anything in town, its stability marked not only through official benediction but also by the changeless pattern of its wares and the predictable location of its stalls. Near the palace entrance might be found the cloth merchants with their blue batik-style Yoruba cottons, Hausa blankets made of narrow woven strips stitched together in parallel, fine *kente* cloth from Ashanti, and many other regional fabrics. Nearby the leatherworkers set up shop and next to them the makers of straw mats, while across the square the horse traders were established along with the saddle makers and dealers in other forms of livestock. The butchers had a large display at a distance to the right of the mosque, and there could be heard the characteristic rhythm of their drummer announcing that meat had been freshly slaughtered that day. There were many others—barbers and potters, ironworkers, tailors, scribes, women selling hot food and others selling uncooked yams, millet, rice, or greens, some hawking animal skins or kola nuts, others offering the makings of magical charms with their monkey skulls, vulture heads, certain kinds of bones, bits of leopard pelt, dried herbs, or special pieces of iron.

All stalls and displays were highly portable for they would be packed up and taken away at day's end; spread out, the establishments were tightly crowded along narrow paths through which prospective buyers were forced slowly to pick their way. These were not the only pedestrians, for along the thoroughfares moved small bands of musicians, their drums and gongs delighting bystanders and stimulating an occasional impromptu dance step, itinerant peddlers balancing their wares expertly on wide calabash trays carried upon their heads, groups of young men preoccupied with flirtations, furious rushes of children at play, and a motley assortment of dogs darting about underfoot in search of scraps of garbage.

At its height the market was a concentration of order in apparent disarray. Out of the undulating mass came the vast, inarticulate half-roar, half-babble of many people; from the sun-baked square rose the undifferentiated though characteristic odor of decay, cooking, dust, sweat, and large numbers; across the dusty expanse the milling crowd pulsed with seeming aimlessness, the only sense of purpose belonging to the clouds of flies swarming about the food displays and the vultures perched on nearby trees waiting with impassive patience for what eventually would be theirs.

Yet here there was design, ambition, and planning aplenty, many affairs attempted and many consummated, much that went beyond the basic commercial exchange of goods and services. For each shouted argument ending in a satisfactory purchase, there was the friendly gossip exchanged over a gourd of millet beer, a marriage contract finally and happily negotiated, important mercantile deals contracted, political affiliations pledged, and perhaps even a prospective evening's diversion arranged by a fleeting, whispered word.

In the great savanna and desert cities like Kumbi and Awdaghost, Agades and Gao, Jenne and Timbuktu, these markets catered to an international trade, their size and importance keeping them busy almost constantly, so crowded and noisy at all hours, as reported by the eleventh-century Arab geographer al-Bakri, that one could scarcely hear the speech of a companion seated alongside. Here the great caravans arrived; here the large export-import houses thrived; here the major shipments of gold, salt, horses, and other valuables changed hands wholesale along with more modest everyday commercial exchanges.

There were, however, other West African markets—some regional and some purely local in importance. Regional markets arose at natural communication points such as major crossroads or resting places, at distribution centers for important local products like kola nuts, and at government seats with their concentration of prosperous courtiers. At these locations were certain to be found families of professional traders, frequently Dyula, a numerous and widely spread Mandinka clan that controlled regional trade over large areas throughout the West African savanna and forest. Like the Arab and Berber merchants from North Africa, the Dyula maintained close family and commercial connections among themselves, thus enabling them to move goods in coordinated fashion over long distances and to relocate themselves in far removed places when the occasion demanded. Nevertheless, the Dyula mixed easily with the local inhabitants wherever they settled, intermarrying and adopting parochial customs, adapting their Muslim faith to their surroundings, influencing their neighbors and being influenced by them in turn, yet always making certain of the continuing cohesion of their trading network.

So widespread was this Dyula network that the very term *dyula* came to be applied indiscriminately to any group of merchants, Hausa or Soninke, for example, moving about the West African region. While Dyula were to be found in many locations, their biggest concentrations occurred along the main trade routes, such as those running from Jenne south to Kumasi and east toward Hausaland, or in areas producing important trade goods. Thus in the kola nut region of Worodugu and main-line towns like Bobo Dyulasso, Salaga, and Yendi, the Dyula were an actual majority of the population, and from these centers they were able to export along with their trade goods their Islamic theology, a faith that thus circulated widely among the animist people of the surrounding territories.

Regional markets were held weekly or at some other appropriate interval, and when these were not in session their activity was normally preempted by purely local village markets. These were no diminutive versions of the regional entrepôts, however, for they were designed primarily to meet the special needs of the smaller, more self-contained parochial districts. Itinerant merchants visited the village exchanges, but the predominant trader was the farming wife seeking to barter the occasional surpluses from a subsistence farm. Individual transactions were small in scale and so was the total business in any given day; nevertheless, these markets provided the base line upon which was built the wider activities of regional and international exchange. Not only did they antedate and then stimulate the rise of that exchange; they also long represented in their aggregate the major share of total trading activity as it existed during these earlier times.

Articles of Commerce

Still another type of market long thrived in West Africa, reported first by Herodotus in connection with Carthaginian trade along the Atlantic coast, then fifteen centuries later by the Arab chronicler al-Masudi, whose account, in turn, was followed by many others. "On the other side of a great river," reported al-Masudi,

> lies the gold country where lives a people who trade without showing themselves or otherwise communicating with foreign merchants. The traders leave their goods and retire; the next day they find beside each bundle of goods a quantity of gold. If they accept the offer, they take the gold and leave; if not, to show that they seek a higher price, they retire without touching either the gold or the merchandise.

Thus the process continued until a bargain was struck in this, the celebrated silent trade of the West African gold miners. Their timidity was notorious, related no doubt to a desire to protect their source of supply, a not unnatural precaution considering the value of their exports and the strong desire of their clientele to learn the whereabouts of their mines. Indeed, monopoly control was an economic principle early understood and long maintained among West African traders. The salt of Taghaza was jealously guarded and zealously fought over, and kola nut production was tightly regulated in many areas. Much later, on the eve of the European scramble for colonial territories in Africa, Niger Delta merchants were to resist by force the efforts of European traders to break past their coastal controls, for they correctly interpreted this as a move to destroy their monopoly of the interior markets.

Prohibitions such as these were exceptional, however, and most products found their way to market in response to normal pressures of supply and demand. Furthermore, articles of commerce were many and varied, meeting the myriad demands arising in West Africa's markets. With the village market the emphasis was on consumer goods often sold in minute quantities. Foodstuffs such as yams and palm oil in the forest or millet and sorghum in the savanna, varieties of fowl, goats and sheep, spices, beans, and fruit, possibly dried fish near the seacoast and milk from savanna cattle—all these were found along with such items as cotton cloth and thread, palm mats, calabash bowls, straw hats, iron hoes, many types of pottery, and cooked foods offered by women tending tiny portable stoves.

On occasion the local markets also offered salt, kola nuts, glass beads, and possibly a little gold; normally, however, these were products more commonly associated with the regional exchanges, that is, with markets displaying goods that arrived by way of the long-distance trade routes. The main routes were by no means exclusively north-south; although this was an important orientation, there was much transverse movement across the savanna and through the forest—by donkey train in the hot, dry north, along southern forest paths by head portage, and down the big rivers to the sea by canoe.

In the Niger Delta, in fact, canoes were both transport and trading items, while fish and salt were shipped from the coast to the interior in return for agricultural produce impossible to grow in districts dominated by mangrove swamps. The movement of goods was rarely a simple transaction between two points—southern smoked fish, for example, in exchange for northern leather. More typically a Hausa donkey caravan would bring beans to Nupe country, taking back kola nuts previously brought up from the south. The beans might then move south to be traded against palm oil ultimately dispatched to the savanna along with local Nupe rice or cloth for Hausa cattle and horses. Rice sent down the

Niger to Ibo country could be traded against palm nuts or salt—in any event, all products of this complex exchange network eventually found their way to the major regional entrepôts, or in a lesser degree to the countryside village markets. In the process merchants filled many roles, from exporter to broker, from shipper to importer, from wholesaler to retailer.

There was no sharp line of distinction between regional and international exchange, and many of the goods moving about West Africa were later shipped across the desert to Mediterranean Africa and eventually to Europe and the Middle East. The gold of West Africa was, of course, its most celebrated and coveted commodity, but it was certainly not the only product making the desert journey. Foodstuffs were rarely taken because of spoilage, but spices, particularly the much esteemed malaguetta pepper, were a regular export, and kola nuts found a steady market in North Africa. The gum of Awdaghost was used in Europe as a fabric sizing, while Kano cotton cloth was a favorite throughout the continent, from the Atlantic to Bornu and from the southern forest to the shores of Tripoli. Tanned hides and leatherwork also were sent in quantity from Kano to North Africa; the other major export was slaves, second only to gold and maintaining its importance down to the middle of the nineteenth century.

Many goods came south in exchange. Slaves dispatched to Egypt or Tunisia paid for fine Barbary horses imported by the thousands to sustain the cavalries of the great savanna states and provide mounts for their royalty and nobility. These were esoteric items of limited utility save for warfare or display, but demand and the difficulties of the desert passage pushed the price high, and a good mount was certain to cost between fifteen and twenty slaves. Equally esoteric were the fine Arabian and Egyptian silks, the elaborate brocades, and North African woolens imported by savanna princes and their courtiers to add splendor to their glittering palaces. To be sure, such extravagances were not for the common peasant, but city dwellers in Walata, Awdaghost, or other towns near the desert could satisfy their taste for exotic foods with the North African dates, wheat, dried grapes, and nuts that also came across the desert.

Many other riches arrived in the caravan cargoes. Glass and coral beads were a great favorite everywhere, while copper from North

African and Saharan sources was in steady demand throughout both the savanna and the forest. In Benin and Yorubaland, copper fed the active and artistically productive bronze-casting industries, while from the fifteenth century onward it made possible the manufacture of copper and brass "manilla" bracelets which became an important medium of exchange along the West African coast. The ubiquitous cowrie, that currency propelling the exchanges of West Africa from Senegal to Lake Chad, was also imported across the desert in enormous quantities. Already known in the Sudan by the eleventh century, cowries arrived after a long voyage from Indian Ocean sources, surviving a dangerous sea passage to Egypt as well as the attacks of Arab brigands established in the Libyan desert.

Salt and Gold

Despite the variety of goods flowing north and south across the desert, it was salt and gold that were the major engines of the trans-Saharan trade. At first acquaintance, this juxtaposition of common mineral and precious metal seems bizarre, but in fact it was good economics, secured by inflexible patterns of supply and demand. The gold, reasonably plentiful and easily obtained in the Sudan, went north to feed the chronic hunger for bullion in Mediterranean Africa and Europe. The salt, so abundant in mid-Sahara, brought its life-sustaining qualities to communities throughout West Africa where local scarcity added its measure to the struggle for survival.

In coastal areas, salt was obtained by evaporating seawater, and in the forest it was extracted from vegetable matter or from soil, but the quantities were modest and scarcely capable of meeting more than local needs. The main source of supply, then, was the mineral salt of the Sahara, laid down in ancient lake beds and preserved by protective layers of clay at sites such as Nterert and Idjil in Mauretania and the great mine of Taghaza lying in the full desert, halfway between the northern and southern trading centers, a good three-week march in either direction.

Although it is not known when the deposits at Taghaza were first uncovered, the mines were operating by the eleventh century and their product shipped both to the savanna markets of Awdaghost and Ghana and to the Mediterranean terminus at Sijilmasa. The salt was mined in large two-hundred-pound blocks, cut out of the bed much as marble is quarried; in the mid-fourteenth century these blocks were reportedly loaded two to a camel and hurried five hundred miles across the desert to Timbuktu, at that time the principal salt market in the Sudan. From Timbuktu the blocks were transshipped to a number of other points, some sent by canoe to Jenne and some by camel train five hundred to six hundred miles south into the heart of Mali.

In either case, the salt was destined for that most desirable of markets—the gold-producing region of West Africa known as Wangara. Because of the air of secrecy surrounding the gold trade, the exact location of Wangara long remained unknown, but in fact it took its name from one particular region while representing in a generic sense the several productive fields located within the West African savanna and forest. First of all, there was the area called Bambuk, located along the Falémé tributary of the Senegal River. Part of this district was known as Gangara, which the Arab chroniclers converted to Wangara, and thus originated the fabled term synonymous with West Africa's golden wealth.

In fact Bambuk did not contain especially abundant deposits, its yields only a fraction of the much richer Bure fields lying nearby athwart the tributaries of the upper Niger. Nevertheless, both these areas attracted the Dyula slave caravans, long lines of men toiling across the rough scrubland, each carrying on his head a slab of salt cut from the great blocks that had been imported into Mali. Together, Bure and Bambuk comprised the essential Wangara—indeed, the Dyula, whose homeland lay near the upper Niger, were widely known by the name Wangara—but other gold-producing regions also existed farther east and south, and these were reached by the trade that moved through Jenne.

Coming south from Jenne, the Dyula caravans, comprising as many as two hundred porters, marched to the Lobi region along the upper Black Volta River and thence beyond to Bonduku, an important commercial center on the way to the abundant fields of Ashanti. Like Bambuk and Bure, these districts, rich in gold but deficient in salt, commanded the best that Taghaza produced, but the price was high—reported by al-Bakri and others as an equal exchange of gold for salt by weight, surely an exaggeration, but nevertheless eloquent testimony to the inflated price structure. Some of the salt was also shipped into the southern forest where it was offered for kola nuts. In this event the salt was broken into standardized pieces which not only were traded against the nuts but also became monetary units and local measures of valuation.

In its multiple locations, Wangara was West Africa's most important source of wealth, providing economic support for the savanna states and sustaining the hazardous trans-Saharan commerce. Though evidence is meager, the gold trade appears to have begun early, perhaps during the first millennium before Christ; but the volume must have been slight, the contacts intermittent, for no further word of West African gold was heard until much later, during the eighth and ninth centuries, when Arab and Berber merchants introduced the great age of the trans-Saharan trade.

No doubt the first merchants to visit Awdaghost and Kumbi greatly stimulated production, until then absorbed locally and confined primarily to the mines of the nearby Bambuk area. With the rise of Mali, the growing demand would have encouraged exploitation of the Bure pits, their success, in turn, leading to the opening of the Lobi region and adjacent territories, extending eventually as far south as Ashanti. All this activity generated a substantial annual production of gold, much of it for export but much remaining south of the Sahara, particularly in the hands of savanna princes who used it to maintain national strength and to add luster to their royal image.

In this respect the position of the king was somewhat ambiguous. In Mali, he controlled the gold but not the miners, and when he made attempts to coerce the mining societies—for example, to force pagan peoples to embrace Islam—production dwindled and the mighty monarch was obliged to relax his pressure and allow the miners to pursue the trade on their own terms. Nonetheless, these were trifling vexations. "The king of Ghana is the richest monarch in the world" was the tenth-century judgment of Ibn Hawkal, and one hundred years later, the great Arab geographer al-Bakri gave vigorous support to this astonishing assertion:

> The king is adorned with collars and bracelets . . . . he sits in a
> pavilion around which stand his horses caparisoned in cloth of gold;

behind him stand ten pages holding shields and gold-mounted
swords; on his right are the sons of the princes of his empire,
splendidly clad and with gold plaited into their hair . . . . The
entrance to the pavilion is guarded by thoroughbred dogs . . . .
they have gold and silver collars with bells of the same material.

The king also possessed a lump of gold weighing thirty pounds which, it
was said, he used to tether his horse.

Such opulence characterized the court of Mali as well. The royal
weapons, the bird atop the king's parasol, the bracelets, necklaces, and
toe rings with which bravery was rewarded—all these were of gold. In
the court, the windows of the audience chamber were decorated with
gold, while the sword scabbard of the royal interpreter, the instruments
of the king's musicians, ceremonial sabers, lances, and arrow quivers,
were similarly embellished. At Gao the supply of gold so far outstripped
the availability of imported goods that many rich buyers were obliged to
leave the markets unsatisfied, their gold still in hand. In Bornu the
trappings of the royal horses were trimmed in gold, the royal dinner plate
was largely of the same precious material, while even the palace dogs
were supplied with leashes of gold, fashioned from the finest wrought
links.

Tales of such wealth filtered across the desert along with the golden
shipments, but on occasion the Mediterranean world received firsthand
witness of the spectacular value and authority of the West African gold.
When the *askia* Muhammad Toure, ruler of Songhai, made a pilgrimage
to Mecca late in the fifteenth century, he brought three hundred
thousand gold pieces which were used not only for the expenses of his
entourage but also as contributions toward the upkeep of the holy places.
A century later, when Moroccan troops crossed the desert and threatened the existence of great Songhai, the kingdom, its military strength
spent, was still able to mobilize its wealth as the *askia* offered the
invaders a ransom of one hundred thousand gold pieces and one
thousand slaves.

This lavish offer was refused and Songhai soon expired, but more
effective were the activities of another celebrated Sudanic ruler, *Mansa*
Musa of Mali, whose pilgrimage to Mecca in 1324–25 dazzled the
sophisticates of the East with its openhanded extravagance, a spending

spree that also shook the Cairo bourse. Musa's train, an army in itself, was led by five hundred slaves, each bearing a golden staff weighing sixty ounces. Within the train were one hundred camels carrying loads that totaled some half-million ounces of gold, a fortune that the king disposed of with prodigal generosity, eventually supplementing these riches with a loan of fifty thousand dinars to finance his return home. Musa made generous contributions to the holy sites, but much of his largess was disposed of at Cairo in the form of gifts which, when added to the purchases made by his followers in the Cairo markets, so flooded the exchanges that gold suffered a severe drop in value and did not recover its former level for over a decade.

Such spectacular events aside, the gold reaching North Africa arrived more conventionally, a steady supply purchased by professional merchants, processed and transported by well-tested methods. In Ghana and Mali, all nuggets belonged to the king, but gold dust from the mines was brought to regional centers, usually by Dyula and Soninke traders, and from there shipped to the major terminals before its passage across the desert. The dust was typically transported in hollow feather quills, but sometimes it was converted into rings or other forms of jewelry. At Awdaghost, Kumbi, Timbuktu, and other markets, the local merchants sold their supplies to the trans-Saharan exporters who normally refined the dust, converting it into coins, twisted thread, ingots, or jewelry for easier transport and accounting. Although the gold was debased as much as 8 percent in the process, its quality remained high and its value in these more convenient forms was actually enhanced in the northern markets.

The gold crossed the desert by camel, each beast carrying between 250 and 300 pounds. With such a highly concentrated commodity, dozens of animals sufficed where thousands had been required for the southward journey. An incidental by-product of this transport imbalance was a lively southern market in camel meat, for caravans arriving in the Sudan typically sold their excess to local slaughterhouses. Those that did make the trip north, however, brought an estimated five tons of gold each year, a figure approaching two-thirds of the estimated annual West African production of eight tons.

The Mercantile Civilization

Discussing Timbuktu, the seventeenth-century Sudanese historian es-Sadi spoke with a glowing lyricism. "That exquisite city," he exclaimed, "delightful, illustrious, and pure, a blessed city, lush and lively—this is my home and my dearest possession." Allowing for hyperbole, the enthusiasm of as-Sadi nonetheless reflected the prestige, the affluence, and the cultivation of a great metropolis, possibly in its heyday the most sophisticated center representing the mercantile civilization of the Sudan. Timbuktu was not the first of its kind; that distinction probably belonged to Kumbi Saleh, government seat for the kingdom of Ghana, and to Awdaghost, its western neighbor along the desert edge. First or last, however, the savanna cities displayed many qualities in common, their way of life a mingling of two diverse cultures, brought together and fused in the heat of their mutual commercial interests.

This fact was at once demonstrated by their size. In a region of small farming villages, Kumbi at its twelfth-century peak probably contained fifteen to twenty thousand people; three hundred years later Timbuktu numbered twenty-five thousand or more, while Kano and Gao both reached the impressive total of seventy-five thousand during the sixteenth century. Of greater significance, however, was the physical plan of the towns which normally presented two separate quarters, one occupied by immigrant merchants from the north and the other by West African tradesmen surrounded by the dwellings of local craftsmen and laborers. This self-imposed segregation by neighborhood was accentuated by differences in architectural design, these in turn reflecting cultural and economic disparities between the two communities.

The merchant houses were two-storied stone structures, crowded together in their quarter, varying somewhat in design and size but resembling the buildings of the Saharan oases to the north, their ground floors given over to storage and merchandising, their upper stories to family living. The walls were very thick, making possible numerous rectangular and triangular niches used for storage. The interior surfaces were covered with a yellow plaster on which were traced geometric patterns and Quranic inscriptions in red and white. Furnishings were sparse and beds often cut into the heavy walls, but some homes possessed detached beds of matting on pottery legs. Earthenware dishes and ornaments were common as were finely worked red leather saddlebags and, presumably, rugs of wool, cotton, and camel hair. Many of these homes contained fine libraries—all in all, despite the mercantile preoccupations of their occupants, they conveyed a cultivated atmosphere, formal but intellectually stimulating, where leisurely meals combined with the ceremonial drinking of sweet green tea and good conversation went in easy companionship with prayer and contemplation.

This foreign quarter usually contained the city market as well as a main thoroughfare given over to additional commercial transactions, while the predominantly Muslim character of its inhabitants assured the presence of one or more mosques. Across town in the West African districts, a different ambience prevailed. Here, very likely, was the royal palace, and here the houses consisted both of single-storied, slab-sided mud structures topped by flat beam and reed roofs (except for the vaulted buildings in Hausaland) and the plain, round mud and thatched-roof dwellings of the simple countrymen. This was pagan territory to counterbalance the self-conscious piety of the commercial districts; here, both in the streets and at court, a more relaxed atmosphere signaled greater exuberance in expressing the joy of living.

Dancing and music making were a common pastime, particularly at late hours, when processions typically gathered to serenade the town. Public nudity was conventional among women, with royal princess no less than with slave girl, but such informality reflected freedom more than license. Women were highly respected socially and in numerous areas held important government positions. In Walata, where Ibn Battuta remarked their beauty, they were at liberty to have lovers without fear of censure; possibly their exalted status was linked to the frequent custom of uterine descent which shocked the Muslim northerners but which offered the clear advantage of linking family and inheritance to blood, thereby ensuring the purity and survival of the clan line.

At first the two societies touched only in their commerce. The savanna kings sought the horses, tempered steel, and other esoteric products—even northern slaves—providing their celebrated justice and order to encourage a healthy, growing trade. Gradually, however, there developed a taste for other imports, less tangible but more abiding. In Ghana the women alone had been permitted to wear the same ornaments as the king, but by the time Leo Africanus visited Timbuktu early in the sixteenth century he found them veiled in the streets, a sign of the shift toward Islamic customs of subservience and seclusion. Even during the ascendancy of Ghana, whose Soninke kings remained staunchly pagan, there was the beginning of a reliance on the northerners which eventually was to lead toward a much closer integration of the two societies. The Muslims were literate in a preliterate world and many were experienced in statecraft as well as commerce; hence, they served pagan kings well as scribes and advisers, in the process gaining access to the royal ear which listened increasingly to their religious arguments along with their mercantile overtures. Eventually they were able to convert the royal lines of Mali and Songhai, a conversion that produced such fervent displays of orthodoxy as the pilgrimages of *Mansa* Musa and *Askia* Muhammad.

This is not to suggest that traditional custom was abandoned to an irresistible alien culture. At court, the kings were still saluted by the ancient practice of prostration and dusting of the head, while Sudanic monarchs, for all their professed loyalty to the true faith, were capable of persecuting Muslims when the occasion arose. This was particularly apparent in the career of *Sunni* Ali, the great conquerer from Songhai. Though nominally a Muslim, he was also chief of a state whose people still held to their traditional faith. While exhibiting genuine respect for Muslim scholarship, he was also renowned as a magician whose powers, it was said, caused horses to fly, soldiers to become invisible, and their king to appear in the guise of a vulture. During his many campaigns, *Sunni* Ali consistently harried the Muslims, and his persecutions of the scholars and holy men of Timbuktu were so ruthless that, for a time, no one in the city could be found capable of reading Arabic. Such atrocities have been described as the excesses of a bloodthirsty tyrant, but they may also be seen as the political actions of a Sudanic monarch, uneasy over the rising influence of outsiders and ever mindful of the sources of his own power, which he knew to be firmly planted in the traditional way of life.

The ultimate thrust of history did not support such parochialism, however. Cultural fusion within the savanna cities pointed more surely to the future, first in the joint profit of commercial partnership and then with the eventual emergence of West African societies as an authentic idiom for the expression of Islamic civilization. *Sunni* Ali's Songhai empire finally collapsed when military invasion later followed the traders south from Morocco; but the cities did not expire until the trade had passed them by, and the civilization they created lived on, disseminated across the broad plains into each rural hamlet by the missionary exertions of Usuman dan Fodio, *al-Hajj* Umar, and those many other indigenous West Africans whose philosophies first arrived with the commercial shipments of the trans-Saharan caravans.

The Volume of Trade

Any discussion of the trans-Saharan trade can scarcely evade the question of total worth for the goods moving across the desert; yet an examination of the volume of trade must rely upon the most scattered and sketchy information, supported uncertainly through an analysis hampered by that very lack of information.

The problem of estimates begins with the gold trade, its overall importance affirmed by all accounts, its actual dimensions and value seriously clouded by incomplete and conflicting production figures. It has been calculated, for example, that the Bambuk fields gave approximately 75 pounds of gold each year during the sixteenth and seventeenth centuries, that figure rising to 130 pounds in the eighteenth century and finally to 220 pounds by the beginning of the nineteenth. This modest yield appears to have been roughly comparable with production in the Lobi region, modern statistics for two different years showing only 55 and 115 pounds a year respectively. By contrast, the Bure mines were much richer and during the era of colonial control furnished an estimated 90 percent of the total output of French West Africa. Even more fertile were the fields of Ashanti and the Gold Coast, as reflected in the commercial records of such coastal emporiums as Elmina and Axim.

At the beginning of the sixteenth century, the Portuguese were exporting from Gold Coast trading centers a reported 216,000 doubloons of gold each year, a sum that reflects a yield by weight of 2,250 pounds if the Quranic rate of 4.729 grams per doubloon is used. This Quranic rate, which applies as well with a rough equality to the ducat, mitkal, and dinar, is admittedly higher than most other calculations and its validity may be further shaken by the prevalence of adulteration in some areas, despite occasional reports of quality as high as 23 carats. If the Quranic figure is accepted, however, and if it is further reckoned that Dyula merchants dispatched across the desert an annual volume comparable to the Portuguese exports, this amounts to a total of 2.25 tons a year leaving the Gold Coast. During the early eighteenth century, the Dutch on the coast reported annual shipments of 1.92 tons. Assuming that the Saharan traffic continued to equal the quantities leaving by sea, Gold Coast exports would have risen to an approximate 3.85 tons a year.

Unsatisfactory as these data may be, the figures are even more uncertain for the other West African areas. Totals for Bambuk and Lobi suggest an approximate equality of production, although the Lobi estimates refer to actual yields whereas for Bambuk they indicate exports only. Taken together in a range of annual production beteen 150 and 200 pounds, they permit calculation of a ninefold Bure output, giving a grand total covering Bambuk, Bure, and Lobi of between 1,500 and 2,000 pounds per annum. When the Gold Coast and other scattered sites are added, the overall annual exports for West Africa might have thus approached 5 tons, or about 150,000 gold ounces.

This still does not represent total production, however. Perhaps as much as one-third or more remained in West Africa for local use, in which event West African gold mining would have reached an annual total of between 7.5 and 8 tons. It seems pointless to give these figures a monetary value, for this would involve choosing a currency, ancient or modern, calculating the effect of changing purchasing power and price levels over time, and making allowance for differences between nominal and real values of currencies. By any standard, however, it is easy to see that gold exports were substantial for their time, even if today the estimate of 5 tons would represent only about 0.005 percent of the total known world production.

The second most important trans-Saharan export was slaves, and once again valuation is difficult, given the available data. There are of course no statistics covering exports; only occasional comments by travelers before the beginning of the nineteenth century at which time the estimates become more frequent if not more reliable. Sifting these materials, some present-day observers have suggested an annual export of twenty thousand slaves moving across the Sahara, but some would accept only half that figure and others might insist upon much more. Whatever the volume, there is the further problem of valuation, not in currencies with their infinite variation, but in ounces of gold. Taking the estimate of twenty thousand for want of a better, a rough conversion can be made, first, by translating numbers of slaves into ducats or mitkals at the rate of ten to fifteen per head and then by translating the ducats into gold ounces, using the ratio of 4.729 grams per ducat. This calculation works out to a valuation ranging between thirty-three thousand and fifty thousand ounces a year, or one-fifth to one-third of the value of the gold trade.

The remaining exports seem relatively minor. Spices, animal skins, kola nuts, fabrics, leather, and a few other items were regularly sent north, but their quantities and valuation are unknown. Possibly a reasonable estimate lies between 5 and 10 percent of the total gold trade. In sum, then, exports across the desert amounted to the equivalent of 190,000–215,000 gold ounces each year—150,000 ounces of gold, slaves calculated at the rate of 33,000–50,000 gold ounces, and 7,500–15,000 gold ounces covering miscellaneous goods. Substantial though this trade may have been, it does not seem to have succeeded in stimulating West African economies much beyond their traditional preoccupation with subsistence-level production.

SUGGESTIONS FOR FURTHER READING

There is extensive literature available on the subject of the trans-Saharan trade in its many ramifications, but the basic material is contained in the numerous Arab and European traveler accounts which begin at the close of the first millennium after Christ. A useful selection among these might include al-Bakri, *Description de l'Afrique septentrionale*, translated by de Slane (Algiers: A. Jourdan, 1913); H. A. R. Gibb, tr. and ed., *Ibn Battuta: Travels in Asia and Africa*, 2 vols. (London: G. Routledge, 1929; New York: Cambridge University Press, vol. 1 (1958), vol. 2 (1962); Ibn Khaldoun, *Histoire des Berbères*, 3 vols., translated by de Slane (Paris: P. Guenther, 1925); Leo Africanus, *Description de l'Afrique*, 2 vols. translated by A. Epaulard (Paris: Adrien-Maisonneuve, 1956); as-Sadi, *Tarikh es-Soudan*, translated by O. Houdas (Paris: Adrien-Maisonneuve, 1964); R. Caillié, *Journal d'un voyage à Timbouctou et à Jenné*, 3 vols. (Paris: Editions Anthropos, 1965); J. Barbot, *A Description of the Coasts of North and South Guinea* (London, 1746); W. Bosman, *A New and Accurate Description of the Coast of Guinea* (London: Frank Cass, 1967); V. Fernandes, *Description de la côte occidentale d'Afrique*, translated by T. Monod, A. Teixeira da Mota, and R. Mauny (Bissau, 1951), along with V. Fernandes, *Description de la côte d'Afrique de Ceuta au Sénégal*, translated by P. de Denival and T. Monod (Paris: Larose, 1938); D. Pacheco Pereira, *Esmeraldo de Situ Orbis*, translated and edited by G. H. T. Kimble (London: Hakluyt Society, 1936); and H. Barth, *Travels and Discoveries in North and Central Africa*, 3 vols. (London: Frank Cass, 1965).

Secondary works to supplement these sources should include E. W. Bovill, *The Golden Trade of the Moors* (London: Oxford University Press, 1958), particularly the new 1968 edition with revisions and additional materials by Robin Hallett; A. G. B. and H. J. Fisher, *Slavery and Muslim Society in Africa* (London: C. Hurst, 1970; New York: Doubleday, 1971); J. S. Trimingham, *A History of Islam in West Africa*, 2nd ed. (London: Oxford University Press, 1962); J. Rouch, *Contribution à l'histoire des Songhay* (Dakar: Institut Français d'Afrique Noire, 1953); M. Delafosse, *Haut-Sénégal-Niger*, 3 vols. (Paris: Larose, 1912); Y. Urvoy, *Histoire de l'empire du Bornu* (Paris: Larose, 1949); and R. Mauny's splendid and encyclopedic *Tableau géographique de l'ouest Africain au moyen âge* (Dakar: Institut Français d'Afrique Noire, 1961; Amsterdam: Swets and Zeitlinger, 1967). See also the trenchant analysis of West African trade in A. G. Hopkins, *An Economic History of West Africa* (London: Longmans; New York: Columbia University Press, 1973), and T. Hodgkin's series on the Sudanic cities in *West Africa*, nos. 1883, 1884, 1890, 1891, 1896, 1897, 1903, 1904, and 1905 (1953).

9

〜〜

TRADING SOCIETIES IN EASTERN AFRICA

The East African Coast

Commerce and travel in East African waters are ancient activities, though their exact origins are lost in time. It is known that as far back as the third millennium before Christ, Egyptian galleys visited Punt on the northern Somali littoral to begin a long-lived and active traffic in ivory, gold, cattle, pelts, slaves, and aromatic myrrh for temple incense. At what point shipping first cleared Cape Guardafui is uncertain. Herodotus speaks of a Phoenician expedition that circumnavigated the continent by way of East Africa early in the sixth century B.C., and Greek ships are thought to have reached the Somali shores below the Cape by the third century. With the rise of Rome, trade throughout and beyond the Mediterranean greatly increased, and Roman captains began visiting ports in southern Arabia, Persia, and India, some probably venturing into East African waters as well.

About the time of Christ, Rome's entrance into the Indian Ocean commerce was greatly accelerated when Greco-Roman navigators discovered the cycle of monsoon winds. The monsoon, blowing from the southwest during the summer months and reversing to the northeast in the winter, made possible a rapid open-sea passage across the Indian Ocean between India and East Africa, thereby stimulating mercantile interest not only in India but in the East African coast as well. Without doubt this meteorological phenomenon had been known to Arab, Persian, and Indian mariners for long centuries, and surely as a result they must have visited East Africa in their travels. Nevertheless, it remained for a native of Alexandria, writing in the first century after Christ, to set down the earliest surviving account of the East African trade.

The author, possibly an agent of the Roman imperial government, had himself visited the Indian Ocean ports, making notes that were gathered together in the form of an official report covering the entrepôts of the Erythraean Sea, as the Indian Ocean was known to the Greeks. This *Periplus of the Erythraean Sea* contained navigational advice, geographic descriptions, and occasional observations concerning the habits of local populations, but its main concern was commercial exchange. From its pages comes an image of East African coastal communities, which even in those ancient times reveals them essentially as mercantile centers belonging to the larger market complex of the Indian Ocean commerce.

According to the *Periplus*, the circuit began in one of the Egyptian towns on the Red Sea, an early stop at the Axumite port of Adulis preceding a number of calls along the Somali coast on both sides of Cape Guardafui. Opone was the last of the Somali emporiums to be visited, after which there followed a long voyage south to the East African shore of modern Kenya and Tanzania, a stretch that the Greeks named Azania. Somewhere along the Tanzanian coast above Cape Delgado, the traders turned eastward, catching the monsoon to India, leaving the southern coastline to the mysteries of the unknown where "the ocean curves westwards . . . stretching out from the south and mingling with the western sea."

There was a distinct pattern to the commodities exchanged. Ships from the Red Sea brought processed goods—cloth, copper, brass and iron, axes and swords, goblets, olive oil, and a little wine, along with gold and silver plate destined for the kings of Axum. At Adulis these items were traded for natural products such as ivory, rhinoceros horn, and tortoise shell; similarly, in Somalia they obtained myrrh and frankincense, cinnamon and slaves, in exchange. On the Azanian coast the chief exports, again, were animal by-products such as ivory, tortoise shell, and rhinoceros horn, along with some palm oil, these goods bartered for shipments of lances, hatchets, swords, awls, and small glass vessels, to which were added token quantities of wine and wheat to sweeten the bargain.

It is clear that this commerce had existed before the era of the *Periplus*, sustained over the years by shipping from southern Arabia. While the Azanian ports were self-governing, they were considered at the time to be subordinate to the Himyarite kingdom in southwest Arabia, a power that granted control of the East African coast to mariners from the Yemeni port of Mouza. These seamen not only traded along the Azanian shore, many also married and settled in the market towns, thereby establishing an early beginning to the Afro-Arabian population that came to be known as Swahili.

The *Periplus* gave no clue to the identity of the indigenous people, but by the fifth century, the much edited *Geography* of Claudius Ptolemy had declared that Azania was then inhabited by "Ethiopians," presumably adding to a growing population engaged in expanding the size and importance of its ocean trade. Thereafter, for several centuries, the condition of East African commerce may only be surmised. The Mediterranean world found itself shut off from the Azanian coast by the powerful kingdom of Axum, while the first reports from Arabic sources did not appear until the tenth century. That trade within the Indian Ocean complex continued, however, may be inferred by the seventh-century account of considerable numbers of black warrior-slaves in Mesopotamia, presumably brought there from East African markets.

The great expansion of peoples out of Arabia following the era of Muhammad did not bypass the coast of East Africa—Zanj, as the Arabs called it, the land of the blacks. Coastal tradition claims a conversion to Islam dating from the era of the Prophet, but in fact the market towns, which by the tenth century extended to Sofala south of the Zambezi River, were inhabited by pagan Africans, interspersed with small communities of Muslim Arab traders. Muslim colonies, dating probably from the ninth and tenth centuries, were established as far south as Zanzibar; most, however, were concentrated along the Somali coast, while such southerly communities as Kilwa and Sofala appear to have been almost exclusively African.

In time the merchant settlers were followed by other immigrants, Arabs and Persians from Shiraz on the eastern side of the Persian Gulf. By the twelfth century, these Shirazi had settled in Mogadishu and other Somali towns, whence they moved farther south to a number of sites, most notably Kilwa, establishing ruling dynasties and introducing the elements of Islamic civilization. The bulk of the population was indigenous—pure-blood Africans comprising for the most part peasant farmers, unskilled laborers, and slaves. The Shirazi and other northern immigrants, always small in number, quickly intermarried with local Africans; hence, the governing castes—merchants, craftsmen, Muslim scholars, and landowners, along with princes and their courts—came to be a mixture of Arab and African strains, both genetically and culturally.

Here, then, was the basis for a new society peculiar to the East African coast. Neither African nor Asian, it evolved from the transplant of Islam to new soil, gradually developing the idiomatic characteristics of Swahili civilization. Called Swahili after a regional tribal grouping, it eventually produced its own language of the same name, a tongue with poetic forms linked to Arabic, a grammatic structure of Bantu origin, and literary inspirations and vocabulary derived from both.

The Swahili language emerged slowly, more slowly than the population mix, following upon the introduction of Arabic which had arrived on the coast with the northern immigrants. In the sixteenth century Arabic was still the official written language in the city-states, although its construction and diction suggest that an early form of Swahili was already the common speech in Kilwa and possibly at Pate and other points as well. As for the Islamic religion, it had become established in a number of centers by the close of the thirteenth century. The Kizimkazi mosque on Zanzibar Island, for example, dates from 1107; in the tenth century the ruling family of Kanbalu (Pemba Island) was already Muslim; the great mosque at Kilwa was begun as early as the thirteenth century; while the ubiquitous Ibn Battuta, visiting the Zanj coast in 1331, could report a devoutly Muslim population at both Mogadishu and Mombasa.

Indeed, from Ibn Battuta and other early observers comes a picture of

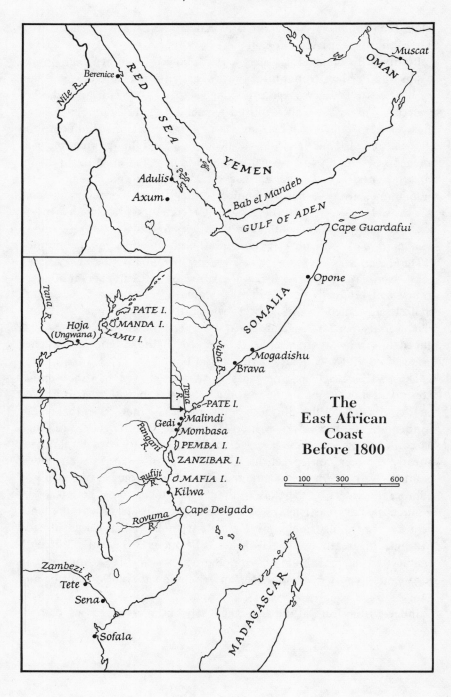

The
East African
Coast
Before 1800

coastal society prospering on the profits of its commerce, planted in Africa but facing outward toward the markets of the north and east, its quality of life a provincial version of the urban sophistication to the north, its effect on the African interior negligible. To begin with, most market towns were located on large offshore islands like Zanzibar or on smaller coastal isles such as Kilwa or Mombasa, separated from the mainland by tidal waters. In this way they could be defended from landside attack, yet the immediate mainland contained fields and orchards in which the islanders raised such local staples as rice, millet, and citrus fruits, along with farmyard poultry, sheep, and cattle. All this made for a sumptuous, if not elegant, cuisine. Ibn Battuta noted that the people of Mogadishu were exeedingly fat and went on to explain why—enormous meals consisting of rice prepared with ghee, supported by side dishes of stewed meat, fish, fowl, and vegetables. Along with this came unripe bananas cooked in fresh milk, curdled milk seasoned with peppercorns, pickled lemons, vinegar, salted green ginger, and mangoes. The mangoes were served both ripe and green, the latter pickled and eaten with rice.

Such feasts were repeated three times each day, implying a prosperity that was reflected as well in dress and domestic arrangements. At Mogadishu, Ibn Battuta and his companions were outfitted as guests in robes of heavy silk supplemented by imported materials from Egypt and Jerusalem, all topped with decorated Egyptian turbans. During the early sixteenth century, Portuguese travelers remarked on the rich gold, silk, and cotton garments of Kilwa, the women of the city bedecked with gold and silver chains, bracelets, and earrings. When Mombasa was sacked by the Portuguese in 1505, the city yielded great quantities of gold, silver, and copper jewelry, an indication of affluence that the Portuguese also noted at Mafia, Zanzibar, Pemba, and other coastal centers.

On arrival at Mogadishu, Ibn Battuta was impressed with the size of the town, the lavish hospitality of the sheikh effectively carried out in his richly appointed palace. Traveling on to Kilwa, he found the city large and elegant, its buildings, as was typical along the coast, constructed of stone and coral rag. Houses were generally single storied, consisting of a number of small rooms separated by thick walls supporting heavy stone roofing slabs laid across mangrove poles. Some of the more formidable structures contained second or third stories, and many were embellished with cut stone decorative borders framing the entranceways. Tapestries and ornamental niches covered the walls and the floors were carpeted. Of course, such appointments were only for the wealthy; the poorer classes occupied the timeless mud and straw huts of Africa, their robes a simple loincloth, their dinner a millet porridge supplemented by wild fruits gathered in the nearby forest.

As always, prosperity on the East African coast was linked to commerce, a commerce in which natural products continued as before to be exchanged for processed goods from abroad. There was indeed some local manufacturing—Mogadishu produced a cloth that was favored in Egypt, both Mombasa and nearby Malindi controlled profitable exports of worked iron, and Sofala processed imported Cambay cottons for the interior trade. Primarily, however, the demand centered upon animal products such as tortoise shell, wax, ambergris, leopard skins, and, particularly, ivory. From the tenth century onward, gold exports grew steadily in importance; slaves, on the contrary, were rarely mentioned, the era of the slave trade coming much later in the eighteenth and nineteenth centuries.

The skins went to Arabia to be converted into saddles, the tortoise shell into combs, the ambergris for perfume manufacture. Ivory in large quantities was shipped off to India and thence to China. The tusks of the African elephant were larger and less brittle than those of its Indian cousin; thus, the African ivory was much favored for decorative carved objects, for sword and dagger handles, and for the ceremonial bangles that were of great ritual importance in Hindu marriage ceremonies. The Chinese provided an additional utility—ivory employed in fashioning the carrying chairs of the nobility.

In return for these goods, the traders brought south some foodstuffs, but mostly they carried craft products, particularly simple pottery, glassware and beads, and a great variety of cloth. Many stops and transshipments were made. A shipload of cloth, for example, might be disposed of in part at Mombasa or Kilwa for ivory destined for the kingdom of Cambay in India, the ivory gathered either in the hinterland of these towns or perhaps farther south at Sofala, Mozambique, or Cuama at the mouth of the Zambezi River. Some of the cloth would then proceed down the coast to Sofala, taken there by its original shippers or by local coastal traders. In either event, heavy duties, in kind and in currency, were paid to the king at Mombasa or Kilwa, and in Sofala the cloth was again taxed, the total of all duties exceeding 80 percent of the original value. Such confiscatory taxation left the merchants unfazed, for huge profits were still to be realized by exchanging the fabrics, as well as the highly popular glass beads, for gold brought down to the coast from the interior. Colored fabrics from Cambay, unraveled and rewoven with local white cottons, were in such demand up-country that the gold, it was said, was exchanged for them unweighed.

Thus did the coastal cities prosper, their merchants and their kings living comfortably in the substantial houses and palaces that marked their growing affluence. Unfortunately, the absence of statistics makes difficult any estimate of the value of the coastal trade, the few available figures, Portuguese in origin, showing major discrepancies. Between 1512 and 1515, the Portuguese reported taking approximately two thousand ounces of gold from Sofala each year; yet they estimated the value of Sofala exports less than ten years earlier at one hundred times that figure. Such a dramatic falloff may represent the decline in trade so often attributed to the Portuguese occupation of the East African costal towns; more likely, however, it is the result of error based perhaps on exaggerated Portuguese expectations or on inflated Arab claims. No doubt, before the arrival of the Portuguese the Sofala commerce exceeded a two-thousand-ounce annual production, but it need not have approached anything like two hundred thousand ounces to account for the prosperity of the coastal trade.

The Interior Trade

The vagaries of Portuguese economic reporting reflect an enigma. The thriving character of the Swahili city-states has been repeatedly affirmed by traveler account and archaeological record; yet, gold aside, there is little indication of any substantial trade with the interior much before the late eighteenth century, a trade, that is, sufficient to sustain the prosperity of the coastal emporiums. Most exports, it would seem, must have been gathered and produced locally on the coast and within its hinterland. Large-scale systematized contact between the Swahili ports and the African heartland in effect awaited the era of the ivory hunt and the slave caravan which directly preceded the introduction of colonial control late in the nineteenth century.

Nevertheless, a modest commerce between coast and interior surely existed for centuries, accounting for the exchange in small quantities of natural products, chiefly ivory, for manufactured imports. As such the trade operated not via long-distance caravan routes, but through a network of small-scale, short-range stages involving numerous repurchases and transshipments between the point of origin and their final destination. Although the interior was peopled primarily with communities of subsistence farmers and pastoralists, such a trading network seems long to have existed as a means whereby local staple shortages might be relieved while regional craft specialties were made to satisfy market demands beyond their immediate vicinity. If this flux of domestic trade also had coastal outlets, such external markets were but by-products incidental to the needs of the interior commerce. If overseas markets came in time to intrude upon and subvert the inland commercial structure, this was a development not generally apparent before the beginning of the nineteenth century.

The earliest trading contacts very likely arose with the settlement of Bantu farmers in subequatorial Africa. However simple, agricultural communities were more complex and less self-sufficient than the hunting societies that preceded them. They needed skins, foodstuffs, building materials, and other products in short supply; more particularly, there was always a demand for salt, iron, and copper, which were scarce in certain areas, difficult to extract in others, and everywhere much valued. Ironstone outcrops of good quality were often inaccessible and refining methods ill understood by many societies which nonetheless relied upon arrow- and spearheads, axes, hoes, knives, and other implements to sustain their living standards. Salt was also difficult to obtain; hence those who controlled deposits such as the Ivuna salt pans at Lake Rukwa developed salt-refining industries and an attendant commerce through which this precious commodity gained extensive distribution. Copper, too, was widely favored, particularly for jewelry, moving along from hamlet to hamlet over considerable distances, the object of intervillage barter which was at first the essential means of exchange.

It is not difficult to envision the process of dispersion. Along river courses dwelt cultivators who also fished, while the dry plains encouraged cattlemen and perhaps farmer-hunters. Some peoples had a knack for making pots of exceptional utility and design; others lived near workable iron sources, developing clans of smiths adept at crafting hoe blades and other implements. The wooded areas encouraged beekeeping, with its production of wax and honey, or bark and palm cloth manufacture. Some farmers grew root crops, others leaned to cereals; all were engaged in subsistence production but none was so self-sufficient as to be totally indifferent to the output of others.

In particular areas the location of a brine spring or salt pan would have attracted strangers coming to distill their own salt supply for use at home. Others, however, might have found it convenient to obtain their salt from those native to the region, the latter perhaps carrying their product to neighboring villages where they could exchange it for foodstuffs or other goods. If all the salt thus obtained were not consumed locally, some might have been moved on to still more distant points, perhaps to be bartered for beeswax, copper wire, or much desired iron hoe blades. Pots associated with salt manufacture could also have become a trade item in their own right, while smiths, guarding their knowledge of metallurgy, were able to double as sometime traders, taking to the road to peddle their supply of tools or weapons, returning home perhaps with grain or that precious livestock which occupied such a central position among the peoples of Bantu Africa.

In this way, the more durable and less bulky goods might have moved over substantial distances as part of a vast trading flux, itself a composite of limited, localized transactions. Indeed, recent excavations of ancient sites in the Katanga, the Zambezi River valley, and elsewhere tend to confirm just such a development. At Sanga near Lake Kisale, at Ingombe Ilede on the middle Zambezi, and at a scattering of other locations, there is abundant affirmation not only of an extensive interior trade flourishing as long ago as the first millennium after Christ, but also of early commercial links with the East African coast and beyond. The burial grounds at the village of Sanga, which have been dated back to the seventh century A.D., show evidence of highly developed copper mining and crafting industries which produced a range of elaborate ornaments as well as standardized bars possibly utilized as an incipient form of currency. Present also were small quantities of coastal seashells and glass beads indicating the existence even at that remote time of commercial activities connecting the eastern coast with the deepest sections of the upper Congo watershed, a thousand miles removed in the interior.

Ingombe Ilede, situated on the Zambezi floodplain, was a farming community, but its convenient location encouraged trading activity which brought a variety of imports to the region. By the fourteenth and fifteenth centuries, the population had access to iron artifacts such as bells, long-bladed hoes, and wire drawing devices, to ornaments, utensils, wire, and cross-shaped ingots of copper, and to gold beads, all clearly introduced into an area deficient in these products. Further, seashell necklaces and a variety of glass beads, along with traces of imported cloth, indicate that traffic with the Indian Ocean ports had reached substantial and systematic dimension.

In exchange for these goods, the inhabitants of Ingombe Ilede provided salt and possibly ivory, for elephants were abundant in the district. Copper appears to have served many purposes from trade item and local ornament to unit of commercial exchange, but ivory must have had a clearly recognized export value, stimulated by the continuing demand for that commodity on the East African coast. In like fashion gold was transshipped downstream from mining sites located on the plateau to the south, although a portion was retained for ornamental purposes, supplementing the copper, bead, and shell imports.

For the long-distance commerce, then, it was ivory and gold that were the principal merchandise, the gold in particular first establishing the prosperity of Kilwa and her outpost at Sofala, then capturing the fascinated attention of the Portuguese from the time of their arrival on the coast early in the sixteenth century. The mines were scattered across rolling country south of the Zambezi, long populated by Bantu farmers who, by the early fourteenth century, had begun to construct stone monuments at Zimbabwe and other sites, thus marking the emergence of a powerful state which the Portuguese called Monomotapa after Mwene Mutapa, the praise name of the ruling *mambo*, or king.

Beginning with the Mwene Mutapa period, if not earlier, the gold trade was organized as a royal monopoly. Within the state internal exchange took place in the form of tribute whereby the *mambo* received copper, iron, ivory, foodstuffs, and gold from his subjects as annual requisitions, in return making gifts of such foreign trade goods as cloth,

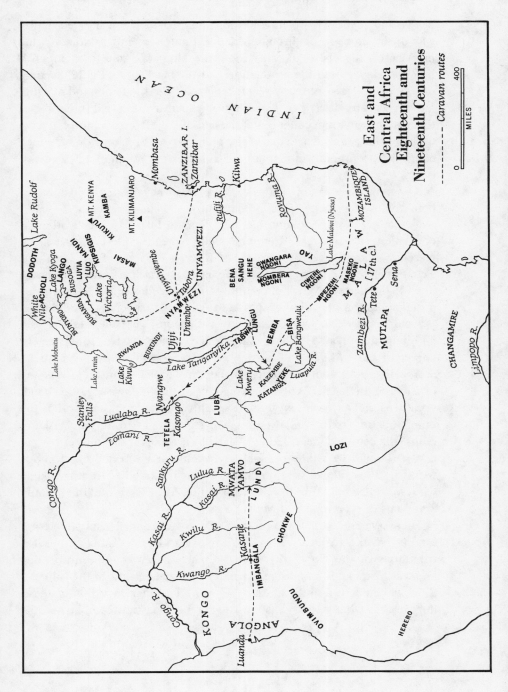

East and
Central Africa
Eighteenth and
Nineteenth Centuries

----- Caravan routes

0   400
MILES

beads, and shells. The royal gold thus obtained was then shipped out by way of the Zambezi or through Manica country, eventually to reach the markets on the coast. In this fasion, the king was able to maintain a monopoly over both the production and the marketing of gold, keeping outsiders, African or otherwise, far removed from the mines and denying his subjects any direct participation in the lucrative external trade. When the Mutapa kingdom collapsed at the end of the fifteenth century, it gave way to other states, particularly the rising power of Changamire, which continued to practice monopoly control over the mining and export of gold.

Apparently the mining states of the plateau never attempted to carry their gold directly to the Swahili markets on the coast. Probably at first it was moved through many hands in small lots, later collecting at convenient centers like Ingombe Ilede whence interior or coastal merchants could have brought it downriver to the sea. Both Sena and Tete, far up the Zambezi, started life as Arab trading posts; but as the inland commerce developed, certain African peoples began to emerge as professional shippers, similar in role to the Dyula traders in West Africa.

Among the earliest of these merchant groups were the Malawi who had migrated eastward from the Congo region to the southwestern corner of Lake Malawi during the early fourteenth century, eventually establishing an important state, its economy based upon the marketing of ivory on the coast. When the kingdom of the Malawi began to break up, it was the Yao who, by the late seventeenth century, emerged as the dominant traders to coastal points like Kilwa and Mozambique Island. Although centered near Lake Malawi, Yao mercantile interests were related to the deep interior, for they maintained working connections with the Bisa situated east of Lake Bangweulu, another trading people who were the chief Indian Ocean outlet for the formidable Lunda kingdoms of Kazembe and Mwata Yamvo.

These two states were the product of Lunda expansionism which first established the realm of Mwata Yamvo astride the Kasai and Lulua tributaries of the Congo River in the early seventeenth century, one hundred years later founding the tributary Kazembe state in the valley of the Luapula River south of Lake Mweru. Together they dominated a huge area in what is today eastern Angola, northeastern Zambia, and the

southern Katanga, maintaining close communication and mutual cooperation. Each was engaged in long-distance trade through African
middlemen, Mwata Yamvo with the Angolan coast and Kazembe with
the Swahili ports of East Africa. Mwata Yamvo sent slaves west to
Angola in caravans provided by Imbangala traders, while copper, ivory,
and slaves went eastward to Tete, Sena, and the coast in the hands of
Bisa merchants who sometimes made the full journey and sometimes
transshipped through the Yao. In return the two Congo states received a
variety of merchandise including mirrors, china, silver flatware, beads,
wool and silk fabrics, and various currencies, including cowries.

It was the Portuguese who first challenged these indigenous trading
networks. In the west, their activities brought collapse during the
sixteenth century to the kingdom of Kongo, previously a thriving
confederation lying south of the Congo River. Though apparently
powerful both politically and economically, Kongo soon proved vulnerable to the newcomers whose preoccupation with slaving decimated the
population, corrupted the rulers, and divided the country to the point of
civil breakdown. Moving southward into Angola, the Portuguese applied
the same tactics of militant slaving where they also quickly produced a
state of widespread chronic unrest. Such depredations were halted short
of the inland center of Cassanje, the stronghold of the trading Imbangala
who controlled the routes beyond to the realm of Mwata Yamvo;
nevertheless, the Portuguese did persuade the Imbangala to bring forth a
plentiful supply of slaves from the interior to fill the ships headed from
the Angolan ports of Luanda and Benguela.

In East Africa the record was vastly different. In the first place, the
Portuguese found the coast occupied by established, experienced traders
who, though they were unable to deal with Portugal's military superiority, generally succeeded in diverting the interior commerce away from
the eager grasp of the intruders. To capture the gold trade the Portuguese
occupied Sofala, only to find the precious traffic had slipped away to the
Zambezi route. When they subsequently took Sena and Tete and
reduced the Mutapa kingdom to vassal status, they learned that the
former great state had shrunk to insignificance and the gold had come
under the control of Changamire, where it lay still beyond their reach.
North of the Zambezi, the ivory and copper traffic remained in the hands

of Malawi, Bisa, and Yao traders, while east and west, the inland kingdoms of Mwata Yamvo and Kazembe were screened by distance and the exertions of African middlemen.

At the end of the eighteenth century, the Portuguese authorities determined to open a trade route between the east coast and Angola by way of Kazembe and Mwata Yamvo, thereby spanning the continent while gaining direct access to these important interior markets. Between 1798 and 1831 three expeditions were sent forth, including one by two *pombeiros,* or mulatto traders, who succeeded in making the full crossing from west to east and back. Nevertheless, the overall results were discouraging and the Portuguese eventually were unable to establish their transcontinental connection, largely because of Kazembe's hostility toward the prospect of European-dominated trade routes.

Although penetration of the interior was soon to come, it did in fact arrive from a different quarter. The early nineteenth century witnessed a buildup of traffic to the east coast, initially through the activities of Nyamwezi traders from the plateau country east of Lake Tanganyika who inaugurated long-distance caravans devoted chiefly to providing increasing supplies of African ivory for the hungry markets of Asia and Europe. Nyamwezi success appears to have encouraged coastal traders who quickly organized caravans in their own right, pressing farther and farther inland in a search first for ivory and then for slaves. By the middle of the nineteenth century, trade in the interior had been transformed, now dominated by the armed caravan, hundreds and even thousands strong, preying heavily on the animal and human populations of the interior and contributing in substantial measure to the political and social upheavals that characterized the East African interior during these years.

Economic Exchange in Traditional Africa

It has often been noted that modern Western economies are propelled by the principle of the marketplace. In this case, the term *market* suggests process rather than location since its essence rests with the exchange of goods and services responding to the imperatives of supply and demand. The market can, and often does, have a physical location, but it may function anywhere, and wherever it exists, it becomes the engine that generates momentum in the economy, creating and expanding wealth through profit seeking in the buying and selling of capital and labor—the so-called factors of production. A healthy market thus becomes central to a healthy society; it cannot be damaged without chaotic consequences everywhere.

In early African societies the basic economy was the subsistence economy. The economic unit was the family, its function food production for survival, its prevailing economic characteristic self-sufficiency. By contrast with the dynamism of Western market economies, traditional Africa appeared static, conservative rather than acquisitive. The marketplace was an accepted but not intrinsic feature, as a very substantial movement of goods and services took place through the medium of social or political institutions. The market process, therefore, stood on the edge of the traditional economy, in no sense essential to social stability.

Nevertheless, subsistence economies rarely achieved true self-sufficiency, thus compelling reliance upon the exchange of material goods related to everyday needs. Such merchandise was usually traded at local marketplaces, usually by barter. Unlike the profit-oriented economies of the West, equity rather than gain seems to have been the prevailing objective, and commodity supply and demand had little or no effect on future production and market transactions. The classic market was that held periodically in a particular village, dealing mostly in local produce and patronized mainly by farm women from surrounding areas.

Subsistence economies in traditional Africa were marked by other characteristic features, not the least of which was the parallel existence of multiple avenues of traffic in goods and services, each with its own commodities, media of exchange, and rules of procedure and each largely unaffected by the transactions taking place in the others. Where cattle were so highly valued, a continual exchange of livestock took place quite independently of any extant commodity markets. Negotiations involving bridewealth constituted another specialized exchange relationship, employing specialized currencies such as cattle, spearheads, or metal rods with valuation applicable only to this type of transaction.

The institution of bridewealth has its counterpart in the dowry and arranged marriage of the West; in similar fashion, both the modernizing societies of the West and African traditional economies have employed government for wealth redistribution, the West through taxation and African communities by means of gift giving. In their concept of land and labor, however, the two societies show little similarity. While Western economies have distinguished both as full-fledged market commodities, traditional Africa offered neither for sale in any present-day sense of the term. Land, being plentiful, simply had no marketable value. Labor, exclusive of that provided through slavery, was available under largely social circumstances. Each farming family supplied its own work force, but gang labor could be recruited by all who needed it, its essential economic function screened by the recreational and sportive aspect of its utilization.

Early Traders and the
Market Principle

Despite the basic adherence to subsistence agriculture supported by subsistence exchange, tropical Africa early experienced market-oriented, long-distance trade complete with profit motive, capital accumulation, production specialization, currency and credit devices, and the emergence of full-time professional traders. The vast commercial network of West Africa that connected with the trans-Saharan trade dates at least as far back as the glory days of ancient Ghana and was instrumental in breaching the physical isolation of the African heartland, introducing the products and the cultures of other continents. The transactions were complex and sophisticated, often involving a series of intermediate moves—for instance, European arms purchased on the coast and exchanged in the interior for textiles, textiles converted to salt, and salt used to buy slaves who were marched back to the coast for sale to the European shippers. All this presumed an appreciation of such complications as varying price structures, multiple currencies, and shifting market conditions. The successful merchant developed a businessman's experience and judgment which enabled him to extract a good profit from his labors.

Within subequatorial Africa, long-distance commerce showed itself through the exertions of Malawi, Bisa, Yao, and other professionals; yet even before the appearance of these entrepreneurs, the kingdoms of Kongo and Loango bracketing the Congo River entrance had organized complex commercial systems complete with specialized craft production, recognized currencies, and an active market exchange. In Kongo the crown dominated the economy through taxation and its monopoly of the currency, a small shell called *nzimbu* which was collected on the coast, chiefly at the island of Luanda. Trade goods consisted of salt, ivory, iron and copper, pottery, palm cloth and mats, as well as foodstuffs, a range of items that reflected the merchandise typically available at the Loango markets farther up the coast. In Loango a flourishing palm cloth industry provided both clothing and currency, its quality giving it a popularity that extended to Kongo and other territories where it was accepted as a medium of exchange. Among various mercantile activities, Loango conducted a copper industry that involved slave mining, transport of the ore to crafting sites, and final sale at coastal markets—all in all a well-articulated industrial-commercial enterprise.

Impressive in its achievements, the professional trading network within precolonial Africa nonetheless was unable to produce either a general conversion from subsistence exchange to a market economy or a movement of sustained economic growth based upon systematic capital accumulation and reinvestment. Various suggestions have been put forward in explanation.

To begin with, the external commerce, for all its dimension, failed to provide sufficient impetus for genuine economic metamorphosis. It has been argued that in West Africa the international trade demanded nonrenewable, wasting, mineral assets and productive labor in return for finished consumer goods, an inequitable exchange that drew off potential resources for local development, offering in place merchandise of diminishing utility. More serious, however, may have been the fact that expensive imports, such as horses for savanna armies and muskets to arm forest kingdoms, were available primarily to powerful ruling groups and exerted a minimal influence upon the workings of the essential subsistence economy. Horses and guns employed in military adventures or slave raids at best redistributed, and more often destroyed, existing economic assets; in any event, they were scarcely involved in stimulating the basic economy to greater productivity.

In other regions the international commerce was directly destructive to enhanced economic activity. Portugal's disastrous intrusion into the Kongo kingdom, for example, or the massive ivory and slave hunts that afflicted eastern and central Africa during the nineteenth century played havoc with traditional societies and indigenous trade. Consumer demand may have been expanded somewhat through the introduction of new trading articles, but payment came, as in West Africa, through export of productive manpower and wasting assets; more than that, the system was predatory, producing political chaos rather than an accelerating economy, depressing the African standard of living closer to the limits of its meager resources.

Beyond the difficulties of warfare and brigandage lay other, more serious, impediments to economic growth. While it is true that centralized states and well-organized caravans were able to establish stable conditions over wide areas, the important problem of transport was never satisfactorily resolved. The desert passage yielded to the camel's special talents, particularly in the case of high-value cargo like gold, but elsewhere long distances, rigorous climate, and disease combined with technological limitations to complicate the easy movement of goods. River systems like the Niger were put to good use, but many streams were encumbered by rapids as well as seasonal flooding and drought. Pack animals were utilized effectively in parts of the West African savanna; however, in much of tropical Africa, sleeping sickness barred the use of animal transport, while roads were everywhere difficult to construct and maintain. Such complications placed the main burden in the passage of goods on human carriers, but head porters could not be employed economically in moving bulky commodities of low unit value, for the cost of maintaining the porters in long journeys would have soon come to exceed the value of their burden.

Finally, and more generally, it is possible that the African farmer or cattleman, his economic ideas keyed to self-sufficiency, looked upon trade essentially as a way to obtain goods for his own use, not as a means for capital accumulation. The early nineteenth-century British traveler

T. E. Bowdich lamented the fact that the Ashanti appeared indifferent to the potentialities of plantation development, content to exchange their gold and gather their kola nuts for what consumer goods they required. Such an attitude, widely apparent among traditional African societies, limited the range of trading items to natural products like gold and palm oil, to modest amounts of craft goods, and eventually to slaves, these last encouraging unproductive predatory societies that fed upon warfare and violence.

Perhaps, in the final analysis, the resistance of the African villager to a market-oriented economy grew from the same source as his skepticism of innovation in farming techniques. Long trial and error had brought him to the limits of what his technology could achieve, operating within his particular environment. In such a context self-sufficiency was the rational man's goal, and an exchange that built up a network of mutual obligations was his means. Well-established systems of gift exchange and tribute were known to deal effectively with such matters. At best, trade could be expected to add but a small measure of insurance against the inevitable next season of scarcity.

SUGGESTIONS FOR FURTHER READING

There is considerable general literature dealing with the East African coast. See, for example, the work of G. S. P. Freeman-Grenville, *The East African Coast* (Oxford: Clarendon Press, 1962), which provides substantial excerpts of original documents dealing with the subject; *The Medieval History of the Coast of Tanganyika* (London: Oxford University Press, 1962); his chapter and that by Gervais Mathew in R. Oliver and G. Mathew, eds., *History of East Africa*, vol. I (Oxford: Clarendon Press, 1963), and the article "East African Coin Finds and Their Historical Significance," *Journal of African History*, vol. I, no. I (1960). Also valuable are the chapters by N. Chittick and F. J. Berg in B. A. Ogot and J. Kieran, eds., *Zamani* (Nairobi: East African Publishing House; New York: Humanities Press, 1968), as well as articles by Chittick in the *Journal of African History*, "Kilwa and the Arab Settlement of the East African Coast," vol. 4, no. 2 (1963), and "The 'Shirazi' Colonization of East Africa," vol. 6, no. 3 (1965). Other sources include J. Kirkman, *Men and Monuments on the East African Coast* (London: Lutterworth Press, 1964); John Gray, *History of Zanzibar* (London:

Oxford University Press, 1962); and J. Strandes, *The Portuguese Period in East Africa* (Nairobi: East African Literature Bureau, 1961). For Ibn Battuta in East Africa, see H. A. R. Gibb, ed., *The Travels of Ibn Battuta*, vol. 2 (Cambridge: Cambridge University Press, 1962).

Material dealing with the subequatorial continental interior is scattered. To be consulted are Oliver and Mathew, cited above; B. Fagan, *Southern Africa* (New York: Praeger, 1966); G. Balandier, *Daily Life in the Kingdom of the Kongo* (New York: Pantheon Books, 1968); Jan Vansina, *Kingdoms of the Savanna* (Madison: University of Wisconsin Press, 1966); and P. L. Shinnie, ed., *The African Iron Age* (Oxford: Clarendon Press, 1971). Even more interesting than these is R. Gray and D. Birmingham, eds., *Pre-Colonial African Trade* (London: Oxford University Press, 1970).

For discussions of markets and exchange in traditional Africa, see Gray and Birmingham, cited above; Claude Meillassoux, ed., *The Development of Indigenous Trade and Markets in West Africa* (London: Oxford University Press, 1971); P. Bohannan and G. Dalton, eds., *Markets in Africa* (Evanston, Ill.: Northwestern University Press, 1962); and R. Firth, ed., *Themes in Economic Anthropology* (London: Tavistock Publications, 1967).

10

THE SLAVE TRADE

African Origins

In Africa, as elsewhere, slavery was an ancient institution. The pharaonic dynasties of Egypt, their wealth secured by the labor of peasant serfs, had scant need for bondsmen; yet war booty and tribute flowing in from Nubia and the kingdoms of the Middle East included slaves employed by the crown as soldiers, palace servants, or plantation workers. By the early Christian era others were coming in small numbers from Opone on the Somali coast, which the *Periplus of the Erythraean Sea* regarded as a source of "the better sort of slaves." Very likely, Somalia supplied the Tigris-Euphrates region as well, for late in the seventh century A.D., an uprising in Mesopotamia of black soldier-slaves implied a commerce in chattels reaching Middle East markets from the East African coast. Although the Somali "horn" may have been the initial source, as the trade continued over the centuries it probably extended southward to tap the flourishing emporiums along the Tanganyika coast.

The volume of this trade seems never to have been large; in like fashion, slaving across the Sahara, though dating back at least to Roman times, was a minor segment of a long-lived but unpretentious commerce. Limited Carthaginian contacts to the south were expanded somewhat by

Rome, her merchants in the second, third, and fourth centuries A.D. exchanging glassware and other products with the Garamantes of Fezzan for ivory and some black slaves. These latter the Garamantes obtained from the south, presumably from the Sudan where the intruders may have gained a degree of ascendancy over the local people as the basis for their slaving activities. In any event, it was not a memorable traffic. When the Arabs overran the Fezzan in the middle of the seventh century, they pushed south past Tibesti to Kawar, but there they could learn nothing of what lay beyond in the region of Lake Chad, a country now forgotten that once the Garamantes had known.

The Muslim Factor

If some trans-Saharan slaving existed in ancient times, this need not imply that the blacks themselves had then known and practiced the institution of slavery. Nevertheless, by the time the Arabic-speaking community had begun to take note of the West African Sudan, both bondage and the slave trade had become fixtures in that part of the world. The earliest reports, dating from at least the tenth century, speak of slaving in the Sudan wherein war prisoners were sold off to northern dealers while other chattels were provided through raids especially organized for the purpose. The chronicles are silent as to whether these activities had predated the arrival of the Arabs or simply arose in response to demands originating in the markets of the Maghrib, or North Africa.

A likely possibility is that certain analogous traditional customs mutated when confronted with the new external demand. Indigenous societies in more recent times have variously made use of such institutions as clientship, pawning, and sale of individuals for debt to obtain food in times of famine. There is, moreover, the process of assimilation whereby defeated peoples have become absorbed into the conquering society, serving at first as lowly members of the master group, their status allowing few rights and privileges. Such customs and institutions might readily have shifted to accommodate slavery with its principle of ownership both of person and of labor, particularly if the bondsman, assimilated into his new surroundings, soon began to gain prerogatives and status which tended to blur the distinction between slave and free.

Whatever the origins of slavery in West Africa, Sudanic rulers found ample sanction for the practice in the tenets of Islam which they had come to embrace as personal and state religion. Under Islam slavery was recognized as an established, long-lived institution. Following the Quranic precepts, Islamic law enjoined adherents to treat their slaves with kindness and to avoid overworking them, but there were no moral or theological reservations concerning the institution itself—only the injunction that bondage was to be imposed exclusively upon unbelievers. Conquering Muslim armies, therefore, frequently gave freedom to Muslim prisoners while enslaving all others, but there were also instances where status as a Muslim was uncertain or disputed, others where it was ignored, and still others where Islamic injunctions regarding servitude were set aside for personal gain. *Sunni* Ali, the great conqueror from Songhai, for example, an indifferent Muslim at best, was known on occasion to have enslaved true Muslims for distribution as gifts among other true believers. His successor, *Askia* Muhammad, while noted for liberating all slaves who could prove their right to freedom, also caused other good Muslims to be sold into slavery.

In times of war, moreover, definitions of orthodoxy leaned toward ambiguity, and a *jihad,* or holy war, originally conducted to spread the true faith, could degenerate into a slave raid for booty. In one recorded instance, Muslim Timbuktu obtained surrender from a pagan village by offering the Islamic alternatives of conversion or taxation, but such an arrangement necessarily precluded the possibility of spoils. Through the machinations of a dissatisfied commander, an attack was subsequently ordered in violation of the agreed-upon truce; there followed destruction of the village, death for its male inhabitants, and slavery for the children and many of the women. Such outrages were visited on high as well as low—witness the complaint of the *mai* of Bornu that Arabs from Egypt were indiscriminately raiding his people, enslaving them and selling them off in the eastern markets despite their status as true Muslims.

Islamic sanction thus combined with a demand for slaves in Mediterranean centers to develop a substantial and persistent movement of chattels across the desert. While many societies employed servitude to punish such criminal or civil offenses as theft, adultery, debt, or witchcraft, the great majority of slaves were recruited through force—kidnapping, armed raids, and warfare. Broadly speaking, the larger states of the savanna preyed upon the decentralized peoples living south in or near the forest, but eventually no region was safe. In many areas princes were known to victimize even their own subjects; Muslim markets, wherever they existed, were notoriously dangerous places for nonbelievers, while pagans in all quarters seem to have suffered the disability of their religious convictions. The animist Bambara, though situated near the great commercial center of Jenne, were frequently unable to trade outside their own country for fear of enslavement; elsewhere most village chiefs cultivated the favor of Muslim traders, resident and itinerant, mainly in an attempt to divert potential slave raids away from their own people.

Among the numerous accounts of slave procurement, the description by Leo Africanus of sixteenth-century Bornu combines vividness of detail with an insight into the economics of slaving. At the time Leo visited the kingdom, the *mai* was a powerful monarch commanding a host of infantry supported by fully three thousand horsemen. This potent force was employed primarily in campaigns against neighbors, the purpose booty to replenish the national treasury, much coming in the form of slaves offered to Maghrib merchants in exchange for horses used to sustain the raids of royal cavalry. Such cyclical economic activity was repeated in the adjacent Bulala kingdom of Gaoga, where Leo reported the adventures of an enterprising slave who murdered his master, a successful merchant, utilizing the fortune thus acquired to build a flourishing state in its own right. Once again, slaving was an important prop for national wealth. A series of campaigns brought in substantial numbers of captives, which, when exchanged for horses, gave rise to a formidable army and eventually to a stable and prosperous state.

Clearly, these predatory campaigns, widely practiced, nourished the long-standing commerce in slaves. Numerous accounts by travelers, spaced over centuries, attest to the continuing presence of caravans in the desert making their way northward, typically with hundreds of slaves under guard. In the fourteenth century, Ibn Battuta accompanied a Saharan caravan with 600 slaves, while *Mansa* Musa brought a similar number with him to Egypt and the Holy Land, in part to help finance the expenses of his journey. Five hundred years later, the explorer Heinrich Barth remarked a caravan leaving Bornu for the Fezzan with 750 slaves in its ranks.

In the sixteenth century, the son of *Askia* Daud of Songhai boasted that a single night's raid would result in at least ten thousand prisoners, while in mid-nineteenth century a raid against the Musgu of the Lake Chad region reportedly netted some four thousand captives. These numbers were traded for horses and other goods at various rates of exchange depending on supplies and the locality. In Bornu, according to Leo Africanus, a horse cost between fifteen and twenty slaves; in fifteenth-century Senegal the price ranged between seven and fifteen; whereas the great nineteenth-century conqueror Samori paid four to twelve slaves per horse, giving two, three or four captives for a musket. In time there was a decline in the price of horses exchanged against slaves, possibly because of the growing popularity of firearms, which placed more emphasis on infantry, and minimized cavalry mounts, which were expensive and subject to the ravages of sleeping sickness and other diseases.

The exchange value of individual captives varied according to sex, age, and skills. Small children and older adults brought less, attractive girls and eunuchs commanded the highest prices, and females generally were valued above males because of the steady demand for harem or household service. Those who survived the trip across the desert brought three or four times what they had cost in the Sudan, thereby ensuring a handsome profit even when travel losses were severe.

It is nonetheless difficult to assess the overall value of the trade, for, despite the numerous witnesses of caravan treks and market transactions, there are no statistics available to indicate the total numbers involved in the Saharan traffic. Rough guesses vary between ten and twenty thousand a year, but such tallies presumably apply only to peak periods and cannot be used as annual averages century after century. One recent attempt at a composite estimate has suggested fourteen million slaves crossing the desert between the seventh and the twentieth century. This must be regarded as a questionable reckoning since it generalizes broadly from a very few discrete estimates of limited utility—for example, the statement of Gustav Nachtigal, the nineteenth-century German traveler, that fifteen thousand captives were exported from Wadai each year; the calculation that Heinrich Barth made in 1851 of five thousand slaves leaving Kano annually; or the mid-nineteenth-century report that two to three thousand slaves were deposited yearly in the Fezzan market at Murzuq.

Whatever the validity of these figures, there are indications that, in addition, a large number of captives did not survive the raid, the confinement, or the desert march. Those not killed during a raid were subjected to the chains and shackles, the disease and inadequate food, of the staging area, the debilitated survivors then forced into the long Saharan trek during which laggards were beaten and, if unresponsive, put to death by their disappointed masters. Many accounts speak of the fearful losses to epidemic, mountain cold, brigandage, hunger, and thirst. Desert travel was difficult for all who attempted it, but slaves normally were the chief sufferers. Some observers witnessed fever-ridden slave children driven on toward the next oasis by threat of the whip, others reported slaves frozen dead from winter cold or burned to death in village fires. Nachtigal at one time accompanied four slaves from Bagirmi to Bornu but only one survived the march; during the same trip, his guide lost five of six captives. One estimate concluded that it took five fatalities to bring a single slave successfully to journey's end. Another reckoned the fatality ratio in the still higher order of ten to one.

Although Sudanic princes sent their captives in large numbers across the Sahara, many slaves remained—doubtless the greater part, for slave power was an essential component of the domestic labor supply. This was especially true for the larger kingdoms where the state required armies of retainers and workers, but it applied generally to all Muslim areas, where a premium was placed upon large contingents of slaves as servingwomen and concubines. The law forbade the pious Muslim an excess of wives beyond the fourfold sanction of Islam, but the size of the seraglio was without limit, and wealthy merchants and officials competed with one another in the numbers of their servants and concubines and the lavishness of their domestic arrangements. Indicative, if unusual, was the policy of Bashir, chief minister of Bornu in the middle of the nineteenth century, who systematically recruited into his harem of three or four hundred, perfect specimens of the many different peoples of Africa, so it was said, to enable him to recall the distinguishing features of each tribal group.

Nevertheless, the bulk of the slave population worked in the fields. Dyula merchants typically utilized slaves to cultivate their farms while they occupied themselves with commercial matters. Within the eighteenth-century Fulani state of Futa Jalon, the ruling groups of a hierarchical society relegated agricultural labor to slave villages, and a similar arrangement appeared within the vast empire of Sokoto which emerged from the holy wars of the early nineteenth century. In the region of Adamawa, for instance, the governor commanded huge slave gangs who worked his lands and were available for other duties as well. The usual arrangement established specific hours during each day in which the slave labored on his master's farmland, the remaining time being free for work on his own plot. At harvest he received a small amount of the general yield in addition to what he and his family were able to produce from their own exertions.

Slaves were liable to requisition for a variety of activities. Some were employed in crafts, but more usual was heavy manual labor in building and repairing houses or city walls, in quarrying and mining, or in the many tasks that accompanied the long-distance caravan traffic. It was slaves who worked the salt mines at Taghaza and served as porters in the caravans threading their way through the rough and disease-ridden country where animal transport could not function. In Hausaland Leo Africanus saw slave porters on the march to the mines of Ashanti, each supporting one hundred pounds of supplies in a calabash tray on his head, some loaded with trade goods and some with provisions for the journey. They made a good ten miles each day in ranks that were guarded by other slaves armed for the purpose.

Indeed, armed slaves were widely employed, their lowly status no deterrent to assigning them important military functions, although their arms were sometimes a temptation to disloyalty, revolt, and usurpation of power. In Egypt Mamluk slaves dominated the government from the middle of the thirteenth century until the early years of the nineteenth, while in the Cayor of Senegal royal *tyeddo*, or slave-soldiers, long abused their position to terrorize the peasantry of their own countryside. The Kanem-Bornu leader al-Kanemi pursued his wars with Sokoto aided by slave contingents, and the rulers of the medieval Funj and Darfur sultanates, among others, maintained troops of slave bodyguards. In Songhai, the *Askia* Daud converted his freeman army into slaves by decree; within the Sokoto empire slaves very likely performed military functions, Barth reporting that Adamawa officials used their slaves by the thousands in expeditions. When Muhammad Ali of Egypt conquered the Sudan in 1821 he recruited many of its people into his army as *jihadiyya*, slave-soldiers who became proficient riflemen and eventually formed an important component of the forces that brought Ahmad, the expected Mahdi, to power along the Sudanese Nile during the 1880s.

Soldiers or bodyguards were but part of the service required by kings and nobility. Harems were protected and presided over by slave eunuchs, those serving kings sometimes rising to become important counselors of state and even on occasion gaining the throne themselves. Beyond the harem, there were myriad tasks to be performed in the household of a wealthy man, and that much more in the king's palace. Furthermore, there were those individuals who enjoyed the authority that wealth and power placed in their hands; large retinues of slaves therefore became a mark of status, the more so if they could be decked out in rich costumes while passing their time in evident idleness. Finally, slaves were a means by which obligations could be met or favors solicited—payment for services rendered, gifts offered in friendship or from hope of gain, contributions prompted by religious or political considerations, dowry settlements, liquidation of debts, or simple generosity.

The Atlantic Commerce

It was at one time widely maintained that the Atlantic slave trade exerted a major influence upon the peoples and civilizations of Africa. To begin with, there were the apologists of the trade and their abolitionist opponents. The former insisted that slavery was intrinsic in backward African societies; thus the trade alleviated the lot of many by drawing off large numbers of blacks. The latter supported Western colonialism because it put an end to slavery and the slave trade, for in this way began the process of redeeming a previously barbarous continent. Defenders of African culture argued the exact reverse—that

African civilization, extending back to the glories of ancient Egypt, was in fact deformed and barbarized by the effects of the Atlantic trade. Recent research has only begun to reexamine the consequences of the Atlantic trade; even so, it has already passed beyond the old debate to provide new perspectives, a growing body of information, and increasingly dispassionate analysis.

Essentially, the new view assigns a much less profound impact to the Atlantic slave trade—in no way superficial, but well removed from the shattering effect once ascribed to it, more subtle as additional data come to light, clearer in detail but more resistant to easy generalization. First of all, the quantitative dimension of the trade, long a matter of conjecture and wide divergence of opinion, has now been subjected to analysis based upon a careful scrutiny of the available published data. The more serious older estimates offered a range of five to twenty-five million slaves crossing the Atlantic during the four hundred years ending with the middle of the nineteenth century. Further, it was suggested that for every slave who reached American shores, one other perished from shipboard disease, warfare, or accident; hence, the total loss to African societies was doubled—perhaps as many as fifty million individuals, not including, of course, the incalculable hosts who had been marched away across the vast wastes of the Sahara.

Recently, analysis of such statistical evidence as port and shipping records, population censuses, export-import totals, and personal tallies of traders have scaled down the older estimates of slave arrivals in the Americas, a carefully calculated overall figure of 9.56 million now given for the period 1451–1870. Beyond this, there is the attrition of the Atlantic passage, computed as varying between 10 and 20 percent of each cargo, for a total of 1.5 million, with losses declining during the later centuries but generally occurring in direct proportion to the length of voyage.

Such figures, substantially lower than earlier estimates, require still further qualification. For one thing, the traffic in slaves was unevenly distributed over time. During the first century and one-half ending in 1600, only 275,000 crossed the Atlantic, less than 3 percent of the total. Gradually the trade expanded, then peaked in the eighteenth century when approximately 6 million slaves were transported, fully three-fifths of the overall estimate. Though the rates declined during the nineteenth century, it too recorded heavy traffic, upwards of 2 million, or 20 percent, until the trade tailed off at mid-century.

Furthermore, as the Atlantic traffic became heavier, it also began to shift in its areas of procurement. During the earlier centuries the main sources appear to have been located along the western reaches of the Windward Coast in Senegambia, but with the eighteenth century, this preeminence had moved to the lower Guinea coast. Toward the end of the seventeenth century, the British Royal Africa Company had found the Ivory Coast its most profitable area of activity, while the Portuguese drew their main supplies from Angola; one hundred years later, four-fifths of all slaves taken from West Africa and close to half the total exports of the continent came from the stretch between the Gold Coast and the Cameroons. In the nineteenth century this concentration along the eastern Guinea coast continued, major supplies coming through Dahomey, the Yoruba ports of Lagos and Badagry, and the Niger Delta emporiums, these last long supported by a heavy flow of captives from Iboland.

Some of these preferences were occasioned primarily by external factors such as transatlantic wind patterns or, during the nineteenth century, the activities of anti-slavery patrols. Generally speaking, it was most expeditious to take slaves from an African port near the latitude of their intended destination in the Americas; thus, Angola sent most of her cargoes to Brazil while the Windward Coast passage made directly for the Caribbean. Later, when naval patrols tightened their hold on the West African coast, those regions like the Niger Delta which featured labyrinthine inland waterways were much favored for the cover they provided against detection and capture.

Basically, however, the slavers congregated where they could obtain cargoes; hence the growing focus upon the eastern stretch of the Guinea coast. At one time it was thought to be the trade that forced the political upheavals marking this section of West Africa—the rise of Ashanti, for example, or the breakup of the Oyo empire—but it now appears that these crises were independent phenomena, one unanticipated result of which was the availability of large numbers of war captives to help feed the growing appetite of the slave trade. In this event the trade was more effect than cause of the unrest that characterized the times. Yoruba historians have insisted that the demise of Oyo and the subsequent Yoruba civil wars were the consequence of internal factors, just as the fortunes of Ashanti or the nineteenth-century Fulani conquests evolved from parochial stresses. "I cannot make war to catch slaves in the bush like a thief." Such was the scornful judgment of the Ashanti king, who added, "But if I fight a king, and kill him when he is insolent, then certainly I must have his gold, and his slaves, and the people are mine too." The slave trade therefore thrived upon the political upheavals of West Africa but seems little to have contributed to their origins.

Yet wars for empire and honor could at times mutate into something quite different. David Livingstone testified that Mwata Yamvo paid for trade goods by descending upon a hapless village, dispatching its headman, and selling off the inhabitants, while both the kingdom of Dahomey and the Aro Chuku oracle in Iboland underwent basic changes in form and purpose in response to the demands of the slave trade. The latter, representing the voice of the supreme god Chuku, utilized its hold on the Ibo population, imposing fines and penalties in the form of slaves ultimately sent off to the Atlantic trade by way of the Niger Delta ports. For its part, Dahomey reluctantly but firmly entered the slave trade early in the eighteenth century, turning it into a royal monopoly and establishing itself as one of the major West African procurers during the eighteenth and nineteenth centuries. The kingdom of Kongo, moreover, collapsed as a direct result of Portuguese slaving activities, while along the upper Guinea coast the institution of slavery, virtually unknown before the arrival of the Europeans, became in time an established feature of indigenous society.

The evidence is therefore contradictory, dependent, it would seem, upon the particularities of local circumstance. In Kongo and Angola, the determined slaving of the Portuguese not only brought political chaos, it also decimated and scattered the population. Across eastern and central Africa the slave trade was one of the major factors causing serious ecological imbalances, while Dahomean predatory raids are said to have virtually denuded a number of adjacent territories during the eighteenth century. Against such dismal results must be balanced the evidence from Yoruba country where the heavy exports of captives during the civil wars apparently had little permanent effect. Much the same can be said concerning the long-lived drain of manpower from Iboland where a high birthrate kept pace with the inroads of the slave trade, leaving population and the national vitality unimpaired.

Beyond the testimony of specific example, analysis becomes diffused in generalizations, frequently unsustained or mutually contradictory. The trade, it is said, strengthened indigenous societies for it rid them of criminals and other undesirables while sparing lives that otherwise might have been lost in war. On the contrary, comes the rebuttal, slaving brought inordinate injury to African communities, for it siphoned off the youthful vigorous elements, their ranks often including princes and war leaders, their energies still before them. Again, slaving was essentially a matter of economic choice, some societies preferring to sell the excess labor of war captives, others retaining their productivity or exchanging just enough to secure firearms and manufactured goods not available within Africa. Possibly so, is the rejoinder, but the slave trade also brutalized, predator no less than prey—the former corrupted in his creative energies and finer sensibilities, converting his orderly community into a slave-catching enterprise and his economy from peasant self-sufficiency to a traffic in human cargo quite dependent upon the vagaries of European fancy.

That most African societies emerged from the era of the slave trade with population and vigor essentially intact would seem to argue that the overall effects of the trade were minimal or at least temporary. Perhaps the only certainty was the misery and heartache of those individuals who were caught up in its imperatives. Not many survived the agony of capture and enslavement to record the events and emotions of their ordeal, as did the celebrated Yoruba patriot and clergyman Samuel Ajayi Crowther: "[We] were overtaken and caught by the enemies with a noose of rope thrown over the neck of every individual, to be led in the manner of goats tied together . . . . Farewell, place of my birth, the play-ground of my childhood, and the place which I thought would be the repository of my mortal body in its old age . . . . Whose heart would not bleed to have seen this?"

Slave Caravans in
Eastern Africa

In eastern and central Africa the slave trade arrived late, and, though it sorely tried many people, its overall dimensions never matched the massive exploitations in the west. To be sure, a modest traffic had existed over long centuries, its principal source the populations lying directly back of the Indian Ocean emporiums, shipped off to India and the Middle East as plantation workers, soldiers, and concubines. Later came faint echoes of the Atlantic traffic when the Dutch capture of Portuguese outlets in Angola and the Gold Coast brought Brazilian slavers temporarily to Mozambique ports. Nevertheless, the main stimulus did not arrive until the middle decades of the eighteenth century, urged on through the need for plantation labor, not by the Americas but by the French Indian Ocean plantation islands of Ile de France (Mauritius) and Bourbon (Réunion).

Though trifling by the standards of contemporary Atlantic commerce, the numbers were substantial—over forty-six thousand taken from Mozambique between 1781 and 1794, toward the end of the century an average of fourteen hundred leaving Kilwa each year, while additional numbers were also obtained at Zanzibar. For a few decades after 1800 these exports rose sharply in response to growing Brazilian demands upon Portuguese Mozambique, but in fact the main expansion during the nineteenth century took place under quite other auspices. It was the Arabs of Oman, asserting long-standing claims over the Swahili coast, who came to dominate the East African slave traffic, eventually pushing into the deep interior, their influence felt with disastrous consequences as far off as the shores of Lake Malawi and the upper Congo region west of Lake Tanganyika.

The impulse was imperial. Sayyid Said, seizing the throne of Oman in 1806, saw political and commercial possibilities in the Swahili ports which induced him to reassert Omani suzerainty over these ancient trading centers. Having survived Portuguese incursions in the sixteenth and seventeenth centuries, the Swahili littoral had later fallen under the nominal influence of Oman, but now Said secured direct control of the coast and eventually moved his seat of government to the island of

Zanzibar. There followed a quick mercantile penetration of the interior, Said dispatching caravans of Arabs up-country where they established entrepôts supported by Indian capital from the coast, their objective the merchandise, chiefly ivory, that had already begun to find its way to the Indian Ocean commerce through Nyamwezi and other African traders.

Among his enterprises, Said introduced the cultivation of cloves to Zanzibar and neighboring Pemba, an undertaking so successful that Arab immigrants from Oman were soon directing large and profitable plantations manned by slave contingents brought down from the interior for that purpose. Slaves had already begun to appear on the coast in Nyamwezi caravans, eventually reaching Arabia, the Persian Gulf area, and India where they joined African slaves originating in Ethiopia and the Sudan. By 1811 an estimated six to ten thousand slaves passed each year through the Zanzibar market, but, encouraged by domestic and foreign demands, that figure reportedly had doubled by the 1860s. At this later date, Kilwa accounted for twenty thousand slaves annually, a large portion of these sent on to Zanzibar where they contributed to the exports of that island. Those who remained in Zanzibar helped to build up the great and growing slave population of African plantation workers; in any event, as the nineteenth century unfolded, the traffic contributed increasingly to waves of brigandage and warfare which spread across vast areas of the interior.

To be sure, the slave trade was responsible only in part, for this was the era of the Ngoni whose long odyssey of conquest took them a thousand miles and more from their origins in Zululand to spread death and destruction through central and eastern Africa almost to the edge of Lake Victoria's shores. Nevertheless, the demands of Arab slavers and ivory hunters, translated into the activities of Yao agents, Nyamwezi competitors, or the exertions of their own hunting parties, set in motion the infamous raids and the dismal caravan marches described in such shocking detail by Doctor Livingstone and other observers of the age. With shrewd design, the slavers encouraged African villagers to make war on one another, while others were supplied with firearms that they might engage in predatory hunts against their neighbors. The result was villages burned out, their fields overgrown, their people butchered, the survivors added to the caravan which moved on to the coast leaving behind the sun-bleached bones and the silence.

By all accounts the treatment of slaves on the march was senseless in its calloused cruelty—the heavy bonds and burdens, the long marches, the inadequate food and rest, and the ultimate slaughter of those who could not maintain the pace, dispatched lest they recover and add to the wealth of another. Most of those who survived were obliged to endure the ocean passage, but many others in fact never left the African interior, relatively fortunate to become the household servants or field workers of Arab, Yao, Nyamwezi, and other masters. Ironically, the treatment of captured slaves deteriorated as a direct result of abolition when the Arab trade was outlawed by treaty between Britain and the sultan at Zanzibar in 1873. The agreement quickly caused an oversupply up-country where life, already cheap, became cheaper still. It was during these years that occurred the most persistent atrocities and the greatest loss of life, and although slavery itself was finally abolished in Zanzibar in 1897, its presence in East Africa persisted well into the twentieth century.

Commerce and the State

Whatever the impact of the slave trade on African societies, it remained part of a larger phenomenon—the interaction between commerce and political organization. In precolonial Africa long-distance trade and interregional markets demanded political structures of a dimension and conception far beyond the horizons of the farming village. That large-scale states did appear is the historical fact; what remains to be examined is the nature and extent of their relation to the trading component.

Indeed, traditional Africa offers many examples of the influence of commerce in the development of states and the evolution of their political institutions. The great savanna kingdoms of West Africa appeared coincidentally with the emergence of the trans-Saharan traffic, their governing classes eager to cultivate that traffic from which they obtained much profit. The preoccupation of the rulers of Mali and Ghana with the gold trade, the diplomatic and military contest that Songhai and the kingdom of Morocco conducted during the sixteenth century over control of the Taghaza salt mines, the slaving expeditions of

Kanem-Bornu organized in order to purchase Barbary horses, the royal receptivity throughout the savanna to both Islam and the advice of Muslim scholars, the emphasis everywhere on the policing of markets and caravan routes—all are impressive evidence of the responsiveness in these early states to the exigencies of international merchandising.

The element of protection doubtless bulked large, peaceful security being essential to the continued success of commercial enterprise. Nevertheless, it is clear that African states were concerned with much more than the assurance of safe passage; the wealth amassed by savanna monarchs or the rise of powerful, centralized governments within the West African forest suggests a deeper involvement. In Ashanti, for example, the state appeared initially during the late seventeenth century as an early confederation of village principalities linked together by membership in the royal Oyoko lineage. As Ashanti subsequently grew through conquest, there came a great expansion of territory involving peoples and spheres of activity beyond the experience of a traditional administration based in hereditary chieftaincies. A new type of state emerged, much more highly centralized in the authority of the king and much less responsive to political organization governed by kinship ties. However Ashanti expansionism developed, commerce surely was a consequential factor. Military thrusts north and south were mixed in motivation, mercantile as well as strategic, as the organization of the new imperial government clearly indicates. The *asantehene* maintained close surveillance over trade, either directly through state enterprises or by a strict scrutiny of private ventures. Gold mining, ivory hunting, and harvesting kola nuts became virtual state monopolies; taxation in the form of poll levies, tribute, tolls, and death duties kept the royal treasury filled; and moves were made to regularize, and thereby to control, financial administration through records keeping, first by traditional methods of reckoning in cowries and eventually through permanent accounts in Arabic.

The impact of the slave trade on eighteenth-century Dahomey is well known. The political machinery of the state, already highly centralized, became even more closely integrated under royal control and increasingly focused upon acquisition of captives until the national economy had fallen hostage to the imperatives of the Atlantic traffic. Far across the continent, the powerful kingdom of Buganda simultaneously marshaled its energies to prey upon neighbors for slaves and ivory exchanged against goods that had begun to make their way inland from the Indian Ocean ports. Both of these formidable nations employed a previously developed state organization to respond to the attractions or the demands of the international market, but there were other African communities, the genesis of which was even more directly linked to the emergence of large-scale international commerce.

As with Ashanti, the seventeenth-century expansion of such Akan principalities as Akwamu and Denkyira came in response to trade, particularly that arriving from the coast, but it was along the Atlantic shore itself that a new type of state emerged as a result of the expanding maritime commerce. On the Gold Coast, European trading forts converted quiet fishing hamlets to bustling market towns, urban centers of cosmopolitan character in which political organization, once administered through clan loyalties, gave way to quite novel, nontraditional forms of government. Traders from up-country mixed with a floating population of laborers and middlemen, drifters and soldiers of fortune. While Europeans for the most part remained aloof within the confines of their forts, the undisciplined, polyglot nature of these burgeoning communities required a new style of vigorous leadership in a rough-and-ready world far removed from the formalized constraints of traditional village life.

At Cape Three Points, to take one notable but characteristic example, an African named John Conny took charge of the unproductive trading stations of the Brandenburg African Company, initially on behalf of the Prussian flag but eventually as an independent, *de facto* ruler in his own right. Reestablishing the effectiveness of these posts, Conny kept Dutch and English competitors at bay while building a cheaper and safer commerce with the interior. During the early eighteenth century his coastal fort became the major terminal for the trade route that led inland to Ashanti, his competition becoming such an embarrassment to the Dutch that they were obliged eventually to conduct a protracted military campaign that finally eliminated the rivalry of this resourceful African merchant prince.

In similar fashion, the Atlantic trade brought substantial changes in political organization to the Niger Delta. The indigenous states in this region of growing mercantile activity had begun life as fishing communities settled among the placid creeks and mangrove-bordered lagoons behind the open sea, their people living in loosely organized wards under the nominal control of a village head. With the onset of the European trade and its increasing preoccupation with slaving, the traditional fishing ward transformed itself into a closely knit trading house, its purpose to develop a growing slave traffic with the interior, its means the war canoe bristling with armed raiders, its original lineage-related population greatly enlarged by infusions of slaves, and its leadership vested in a democratically elected but autocratic trading chief who, with other house heads, formed the oligarchy that directed the affairs of state. In this competitive world, ability was valued above tradition and even slaves could rise to govern a canoe house; nevertheless, it should be stressed that many of the ancient values remained despite the economic revolution and its political ramifications—man's relationship to the universe of spirits and ancestors, for example, or belief in the eternal character of the sea whence all gifts came.

In fact, it is possible to overemphasize the interrelation of trade and politics in traditional Africa, for it is apparent that political development often took place undisturbed by economic stimulation, while commerce prospered even where no state emerged to assist and protect. For all their vaunted reputation as keepers of the peace, the savanna kingdoms exercised little effective police power within the desert, yet the caravans made their way across the Sahara century after century, sustained by their own capacity for self-protection, both diplomatic and military. When Songhai fell to the Moroccan troops of Judar Pasha in 1591, the great Sudanic empire fragmented, but the Saharan commerce proceeded much as before, while trade throughout the savanna and forest areas appears to have been undisturbed, its fortunes secure in the hands of Dyula entrepreneurs.

Much the same may be said for other areas in Africa. Trade between the East African interior and the Indian Ocean ports covered an enormous terrain where centralized, large-scale states were a rarity, yet the pace of commerce slowly accelerated across this vast expanse, its progress encouraged by local merchant or long-distance trader, its development rarely encumbered by any want of extensive political organization. The professionals, moreover—Malawi, Yao, Nyamwezi, and others—pursued their vocation effectively, unembarrassed by the fact that their own people lacked cohesive, centralized governments. In Iboland, the predominantly stateless character of society failed utterly to discourage the traffic in slaves. There, the Aro section of the Ibo people employed the prestige of their oracle to organize the trade along truly heroic proportions, giving rise to what possibly came to be the most intensive traffic in slaves in all of West Africa.

Value, Profit, and Trading Currencies

Africa before the colonial era knew many media of exchange. Salt and gold, rods or rings of iron, copper, and brass, shells and beads, slaves, cloth, skins, agricultural products, domestic animals, or manufactured articles—all were utilized many times over. If, as seems likely, exchange originated with barter, it would follow that certain common items of trade might have acquired utility as standards of valuation—lengths of cloth for assessing quantities of salt, slaves to mark the price of horses or ivory, iron hoes to rate poultry and weights of gold to value slaves, pieces of salt and cowrie shells for the retailing of foodstuffs. Even the worth of wealthy men was most readily assessed in terms of livestock holdings.

The convenience that trading currencies offered in establishing valuations was perhaps even more useful than their service in effecting actual exchange. In one particular community, a cloth might have been valued at two brass bars, a bull at five cloths, and a cow at twenty bars. Thus, the bull was worth ten brass bars at the prevailing exchange, or half as much as the cow. In a market transaction, one cow at twenty bars would have brought two bulls at ten bars each, but no bars would have been needed to effect the transaction; only their equivalency value was required in what was essentially a form of barter.

The concept of equivalency valuation played an important role in the early Atlantic commerce which brought together European merchants accustomed to profit transactions and monetary dealings with African traders whose activities were guided essentially by the desire for equity in barter exchange. The two systems were reconciled through the sorting and the trade ounce whereby combinations of European goods changed

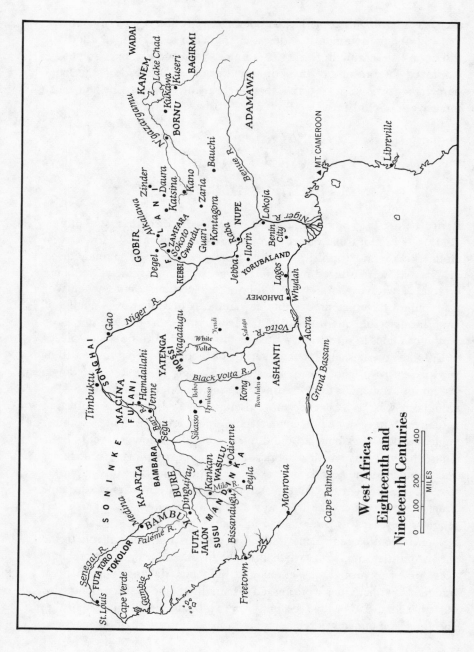

West Africa,
Eighteenth and
Nineteenth Centuries

hands against quantities of African commodities on a direct parity. Thus, one slave valued at eight gold ounces was exchanged for one sorting, a variety of items such as cloth, guns, powder, hardware, and tobacco also valued at eight ounces. The European trader gained his profit by marking up the price of his goods in terms of gold ounces, while the African achieved his equivalency by the quantities and type of goods he required in each sorting. Eventually the so-called trade ounce emerged, a hypothetical valuation worth half the gold ounce and used as an equivalency in making up sortings, chiefly for the slave trade. In either event, it was the principle of equivalency that guided the transactions.

The European shippers engaged in the Atlantic trade computed their profit by determining production costs at home then adding a markup of 100 percent. Within Africa, valuation was also related to production costs, although pricing seems to have been somewhat less responsive to the effects of market supply and demand. If unattractive European trade items were brought to Africa, exchange could not be effected simply by lowering the price, for the African buyer was concerned with acquisition of certain products he lacked, not with the idea of a bargain. At the same time, in a local African market the African merchant who was unable to find a willing buyer would frequently leave his merchandise unsold, production expenses usually outweighing the factor of a quick turnover.

It is difficult, however, to generalize about systems of pricing and valuation in traditional African societies; some relied upon criteria familiar in the West, others did not. While many peoples apparently took no account of time and distance as elements of cost, others consistently included the expense of labor and of transport in bringing a product to market. Although a more recent example, Nupe marketing practices a half-century ago are illustrative. Agricultural products in Nupe normally showed seasonal cost variations reflecting fluctuations in supply and demand, while valuation of craft goods took into account working time and individual skill. Highly refined work was not necessarily more valued than a coarser product, however, at least not when the latter was a necessity and the former a luxury. Prices generally rose directly with distance from the source of production, but since market conditions were common knowledge, bargaining was minimal although there was no system of established prices. Quite a contrary situation prevailed in Dahomey where many trade and production associations established fixed prices, enforcing them with illegal but effective coercion, a monopoly control that virtually eliminated bargaining and a free market.

Though barter in Africa was a basic form of exchange extending well into the recent past, and though the use of money often involved valuation with little actual currency circulation, the concept of credit was widely understood and early practiced. It is well known that Europeans trading along the West African coast advanced credit in the form of goods against the ensuing season's harvest of slaves or palm oil. Similarly, savanna princes were often slow in payment to Maghrib merchants, thus in effect introducing a form of forced loan. Less well known, however, was the offer of credit to visiting English shippers made by one sixteenth-century *oba* of Benin, an overture scarcely surprising in light of the degree to which the institution of credit was embedded in traditional African society. Pawning was a form of money lending, while the whole system of gift exchange grew from the notion that present payment would yield future dividend. Barter frequently involved deferred deliveries, food lending was a standard procedure during periods of famine, seeds were often loaned for repayment after harvest, while artisans not infrequently were expected to await remuneration until after the harvest or successful hunt. The Hausa, among others, engaged in a form of merchandising akin to a credit device—selling goods for an immediate loss in order to obtain capital to cover purchases that, when later sold, yielded profits more than sufficient to make up the original forfeiture.

The wide assortment of exchange media employed in Africa suggests that accessibility and familiarity were necessary qualities, but so too were durability and intrinsic value, this last characteristic measured by capacity for conversion to practical use. Most items met the test admirably. Salt and iron were obviously utilitarian, while beads and shells served much more commonly as ornaments than as currency. Pack animals such as donkeys and camels were frequently obtained for their carrying capabilities during a particular journey, at the end of which they were sold as a form of ambulating merchandise, a fate that was also shared by slaves. The resourceful merchant, needful of porterage for his goods and sometimes lacking easily converted currency to cover his trip, might purchase slaves to carry the freight, disposing of them as he sold off his stock, thereby making double utility from his bondsmen whose sale helped defray expenses once they were no longer needed as labor.

Beyond these qualities, currencies were required to be reasonably stable and acceptable over extensive areas and, if possible, free from counterfeit. Despite the best efforts of monarchs, fraud was widely practiced, not only in currencies but in the adulteration of merchandise, and nowhere was this more common than in the Atlantic trade. Both Africans and Europeans were culpable. The former became most adept at debasing gold dust with ground coral or brass filings, covering copper molds with gold plating, or combining gold with silver or copper in plausible but inferior alloys. Thus many a ship returned to Europe with a cargo of false gold, but the traders were only being paid back for what they themselves practiced. Gunpowder was regularly cut with charcoal and rum with water, while short weights and short counts were standard procedure. Africans and Europeans preyed on their own people with equal impartiality, the latter encouraging fraud in order to injure rival merchants, the former conspiring for unfair advantage—take, for example, the Fanti policy of selling overpriced muskets in Ashanti, exploiting local unfamiliarity with market conditions.

Of Africa's many trading currencies, the cowrie stands out as a major engine of commerce, serving the market transactions of West Africa over a period of at least six hundred years down to the end of the nineteenth century. Other exchange media—salt cakes, iron hoes, brass or copper manilla bracelets, for example—were also extensively circulated and predominated in particular areas of the continent, but the cowrie eventually overshadowed them all, its utility based upon common acceptability, resistance to counterfeit, and strength in withstanding wear or damage, perhaps most of all upon its almost limitless capacity for subdivision into the smaller denominations that characterized most African market transactions.

Cowries appeared early in West Africa's commercial history. They were known by the people of Kumbi Saleh and, as early as the eleventh century, had become a major import in the western savanna, although there is no evidence that they were used as money during the supremacy of ancient Ghana. By the middle of the fourteenth century, they were established as a leading currency within the Mali empire with an accepted exchange against the gold dinar and mitkal. Gradually their circulation extended throughout the Niger watershed, moving as well along north-south trade routes, and eventually, during the eighteenth and nineteenth centuries, they found their way eastward into Hausaland and Bornu.

The cowrie came a great distance to participate in the savanna trade. The shells originated in the shoal waters of the Maldive Island archipelago, the species *Cypraea moneta*—the most widely used cowrie— first shipped from its Indian Ocean source to Bengal, where it was also popular, and then on to the western Sudan by way of Cairo and Sijilmasa. Bean sized and oval shaped with characteristic crenulated mouth and milky polished surface, the *moneta* cowrie was also introduced to the Guinea coast by the Portuguese in the sixteenth century, becoming a favorite from Benin to Whydah and slowly pushing into the interior until it encountered the expanding savanna zone in Yorubaland and the lower Niger valley.

In time *Cypraea moneta* was joined by *Cypraea annulus,* a heavier, larger gastropod from Zanzibar, better than twice the size of the Maldive cowrie but never as popular and more expensive than the smaller species. *Cypraea moneta* averaged about four hundred to the pound, its low cost and convenient utility as ship ballast giving rise to a heavy traffic by European merchantmen once the Western powers had begun to penetrate the Indian Ocean trading area. Returning to home waters, the Europeans either introduced their cowries into the West African coastal traffic or dispatched them across the desert to the Niger country from North Africa's Mediterranean ports. Enormous quantities were involved, with annual estimates early in the eighteenth century rising to five hundred tons, a weight that, converted into quantity, amounts to four hundred million shells.

The cowries made their way to the interior by classic means—desert camel, savanna donkey, and forest porter with canoe transport where possible. Internal transport costs were high, and overland passage of a bulky product of low unit value forced the price close to uneconomical levels. A distance of three hundred miles north of the Guinea coast caused a doubling in price, while cowries moving south from Morocco also doubled, a markup that barely covered expenses and normal profits for the desert crossing.

It has been suggested that cowries were seized upon by West African rulers as an aid to political centralization, helping to create a market economy through an exchange medium that could be controlled and used in taxation. The early traveler chronicles, however, indicate royal preoccupation with the gold trade that dominated the trans-Saharan traffic; hence, it seems more plausible that cowrie currency was introduced informally along the trade routes, its popularity based upon utility in petty trade. Whatever the official influence, cowries maintained a value of approximately eight thousand to the gold ounce from the middle of the fourteenth century until the sixteenth century when, urged presumably by massive European imports, the shells depreciated to twenty thousand when valued against gold. On the coast the ratio was sixteen thousand to one during most of the eighteenth century, but toward the close of the eighteenth and into the nineteenth century, the rate doubled to thirty-two thousand to one while maintaining its twenty-thousand-to-one ratio along the Niger.

In the long run, therefore, the cowrie depreciated substantially when measured against gold, but there were extended periods of stability indicating a viable currency at work in a healthy market, and depreciation was not excessive considering the heavy imports of cowries that took place century after century. Assessment of valuation is difficult because of local idiosyncrasies in counting—for example, the Bambara "hundred" by convention contained only eighty cowries—but it appears that both the geographic extension of the cowrie zone and the economic expansion of the West African internal market succeeded in absorbing cowrie imports without greatly injuring their real purchasing power in terms of consumer goods. At the beginning of the nineteenth century, a man could live comfortably on the coast on a per diem allowance of two strings of forty cowries each. In the savanna, one hundred cowries a day was sufficient to feed a man and his horse.

During the second half of the nineteenth century, the imports of cowries continued, their ever-increasing numbers eventually forced to compete with newly introduced colonial currencies capable both of circulating internally and of paying for new, expanding commodity imports from Europe. Under these circumstances the cowrie market finally broke, unit values eventually falling to that inflationary point where the sheer bulk of the currency made its transport more costly even than its total worth. By this time, however, the internal market economy of West Africa, so long served by the ubiquitous cowrie, had begun to turn to that much larger international commercial exchange of which it was to become an integral part.

SUGGESTIONS FOR FURTHER READING

Although there is substantial literature dealing with the slave trade, relatively little is concerned with the effects within Africa, least of all with reference to regions under Muslim influence. In this respect, however, see A. G. B. and H. J. Fisher, *Slavery and Muslim Society in Africa* (New York: Doubleday-Anchor, 1972; London: Hurst, 1970), wherein the authors have compiled and summarized comments and references from traveler accounts, ancient and recent. See also R. Mauny's two volumes, *Les siècles obscurs de l'Afrique noire* (Paris: Fayard, 1970) and *Tableau géographique de l'ouest Africain au moyen âge* (Dakar: Institut Français d'Afrique Noire, 1961; Amsterdam: Swets and Zeitlinger, 1967); N. Levtzion, *Ancient Ghana and Mali* (London: Methuen; New York: Harper, 1973); E. W. Bovill, *The Golden Trade of the Moors*, 2nd ed. (London: Oxford University Press, 1968); and whatever eyewitness accounts from Ibn Battuta to Heinrich Barth the reader is moved to consult.

For the impact of the Atlantic trade on West Africa, a wealth of traveler commentary may be supplemented by modern works, especially those of Philip Curtin. See his *Atlantic Slave Trade* (Madison: University of Wisconsin Press, 1969); his edited series of slave accounts, *Africa Remembered* (Madison: University of Wisconsin Press, 1968); and, with Jan Vansina, his "Sources of the Nineteenth Century Atlantic Slave Trade," *Journal of African History*, vol. 2, no. 2 (1964). Also useful is J. D. Fage, "Slavery and the Slave Trade in the Context of West African History," *Journal of African History*, vol. 10, no. 3 (1969), and sections of A. G. Hopkins, *An Economic History of West Africa* (London: Longmans; New York: Columbia University Press, 1973).

The slave trade in East Africa also had its share of firsthand observations such as Livingstone's reports in his *Last Journals*, but there are a number of modern studies as well. For example, see the pamphlet by E. A. Alpers, *The East African Slave Trade* (Nairobi: East African Publishing House, 1967); J. Duffy, *A Question of Slavery* (Oxford: Clarendon, 1967); the two works by Reginald Coupland, *East Africa and Its Invaders* (Oxford: Clarendon, 1938) and *The Exploitation of East Africa*, 2nd ed. (London: Faber and Faber, 1968); J. E. Harris, *The African Presence in Asia* (Evanston, Ill.: Northwestern University Press, 1971); and relevant sections of R. Oliver and G. Mathew, eds., *History of*

East Africa, vol. 1 (Oxford: Clarendon, 1963), and of R. Gray and D. Birmingham, eds., *Pre-Colonial African Trade* (London: Oxford University Press, 1970).

For the economic aspects of slaving and related trade matters, including discussion of pricing and currencies, the reader should consult anthropological studies such as M. J. Herskovits, *Dahomey* (Evanston, Ill.: Northwestern University Press, 1967); economic analyses like Karl Polanyi, *Dahomey and the Slave Trade* (Seattle: University of Washington Press, 1966); or particular historical works including I. A. Akinjogbin, *Dahomey and Its Neighbours* (Cambridge: Cambridge University Press, 1967), and Alan Ryder, *Benin and the Europeans* (New York: Humanities Press, 1969). For the cowrie, see two articles by Marion Johnson in the *Journal of African History*, vol. 11, no. 1 and no. 3 (1970).

Part Five

THE CRAFTSMEN

Brass figure, Ashanti.
The Museum of Primitive Art.
Photo by Charles Uht.

11

❧❧

TRADITIONAL INDUSTRIES

The Early Technology

Technological advance normally appears in response to clearly felt need. The inventor applies existing knowledge in new forms to solve specific problems that will save labor, reduce cost, increase facility, or eliminate some identifiable insufficiency. Since the process involves satisfaction of a practical unmet want rather than the urge of intellectual curiosity or the thirst for knowledge, invention does not come from men whose time is already profitably occupied or who do not readily perceive the necessity for improvement of existing techniques. Neither does it originate in communities where the essential prerequisite knowledge is lacking.

In Africa, early technological development seems to have evolved according to these principles. Fifty or sixty millennia past, at a time when *Homo sapiens* was beginning to populate the continent, man in Africa became a regular user of fire, this late adoption presumably in response to the appearance of moister, cooler climatic conditions. At about the same time toolmaking began to show basic adaptations to

255

environment, implements among forest dwellers tending toward larger, heavier chisels and adzes designed for woodworking or rooting, while the savanna tools became smaller and lighter, featuring thin blades and points appropriate for hunting.

Environment could limit as well as stimulate. The intense desiccation that had descended upon the Sahara by the middle of the third millennium before Christ tended to discourage subsequent communication between the peoples of tropical Africa and the burgeoning civilizations of the Middle East. This was an unfortunate isolation for it came at a time when important advances in agriculture, writing, and metallurgy were contributing to the remarkable flowering of pharaonic Egypt and contemporary Mesopotamia, technological refinements that were slow to make their way across the desert barrier to the south. Isolation thus combined with the exigencies of environment to restrain the development of technology in Africa. While the former minimized the importation of novel techniques through the process of cultural borrowing, the latter imposed a conservative technology in two ways. First, limitations of climate and soil dictated reliance upon experience over experiment, for unsuccessful novelty could easily lead to disaster. Secondly, at least insofar as food production was concerned, early technology, though rudimentary, became established with comparative ease; hence, once installed, it tended to remain fixed, unresponsive to the adaptation and inventiveness of change that characterized agricultural techniques in other parts of the world.

The Mine and the Forge

Unlike Egypt, tropical Africa produced no age of copper and bronze, but ironworking found ready acceptance among its peoples. They employed it for the spear blade and arrowhead of the hunters and warriors, for the farmer's hoes, axes, and knives, for trade currency and trade merchandise; they adorned themselves with its bangles and made music with its gongs; they exchanged it for cattle and accumulated it to obtain a wife; they even made it a badge of state, the double bell in Kongo and elsewhere utilized to announce the royal presence, to open official gatherings, to mark the solemnities of death, and to assert the omnipresent power of the ancestors.

Such manifold utility and popularity was not always matched by accessibility, for the ore, though widely available throughout precolonial Africa, did not necessarily present itself in uniform abundance or quality. West Africa was best endowed, the massive deposits in the hills of modern Liberia and Guinea supplemented by many sites throughout the savanna and forest where quarries brought forth yields of workable standard. The highlands of Ethiopia also possessed ample supplies; but in the subequatorial latitudes of Bantu Africa the ore was present only in certain areas, its overall scarcity ensuring the continued existence of a major trade in iron artifacts.

The sites were various. Surface outcrops, bogs, or riverbeds yielded grades of ore, sometimes excellent, sometimes hardly worth refining, but where a satisfactory purity was discovered, important mine fields developed, at times covering wide areas with an underground latticework of shafts and galleries. In southern and central Africa, open pits and trenches predominated, and Livingstone reported a fine-quality ore in the district of Tete where the local people dug ferrous lumps from the river mud with pointed sticks. Ironworking in West Africa, dating back before the time of Christ, was widely practiced by 500 A.D. Where possible the ore was removed directly from hillside surfaces or dug from shallow pits. If the rich veins pitched below ground, however, the miners followed by putting down vertical shafts, which in extensive fields were connected by lateral tunnels, sometimes extending over hundreds of meters.

Once collected, the ore was crushed between stones to remove the grosser impurities, the residue washed and placed in a kiln for smelting. Furnaces varied in design, ranging from open holes dug in the ground to elaborate clay structures six or eight feet high. The simpler versions allowed for alternate layers of ore and charcoal filling an excavation fanned with bellows or on occasion by natural draft. The more elaborate furnaces were generally enclosed to control the supply of oxygen, which was introduced by blower systems capable in the most efficient designs of reducing the ore to fully molten form. The air blast typically was directed into the base of the furnace through small clay pipes attached to a bellows consisting of two animal skins alternately pumped by means of long, thin sticks attached vertically to the top of each bag. Most furnaces were constructed of heavy clay walls surrounding a shallow pit and capped by a domed summit in which was located a narrow ventilator slot. This opening provided draft while permitting the introduction of additional supplies of ore and charcoal fuel. While one worker operated the bellows, stokers fed the furnace, occasionally removing the accumulation of slag. The process lasted several hours and sometimes as much as two days, but a normally efficient furnace could produce a yam-sized ball of refined iron after a good day's work.

In many communities, mining and smithing were the preserve of particular families and clans, their monopoly making others completely dependent upon their work. Certain nations, the Bakongo for example, exalted their ironworkers. The king owned the mines and the blacksmith —master of iron, fire, and water—ranked with the nobility and the priests. Others, like the Wolof or Masai, relegated smithing to an inferior caste or regarded its practitioners as ritually unclean. Whatever his status, however, the blacksmith was the source of essential implements and weapons, a craftsman who combined the traditional strength of arm with the skills of centuries to create the artifacts of Iron Age technology.

The smith worked with the most elementary of tools. His forge was a slightly domed iron plate or a simple stone slab, his hammer a heavy iron rod with both flat and rounded surfaces. In a small, charcoal-fired furnace driven with characteristic goatskin bellows, he melted his ingots, then proceeded to hammer them into the desired hoe blade, ax head, machete, ring, hook, hinge, nail, or other required form. Slowly the crude lump took shape, moving back and forth from hearth to forge until completed; then the glowing metal was plunged into a bowl of water for tempering and finally set aside on a bed of fine ashes to be cooled.

Aside from the celebrated slag heaps of Meroe, many other extensive sites have survived, some with thousands of tons of accumulated debris attesting to the antiquity and importance of the iron industry for the traditional societies of Africa. In like fashion, the mining and processing of gold preoccupied many peoples, although in this instance the main driving force seems to have been the long-lived and voracious demand of other continents. Like iron, gold was widely scattered throughout Africa, but its fields were more concentrated within certain limited areas—Lobi,

Bure, Bambuk, and the Ashanti deposits in West Africa or the Shona plateau of the Mutapa kingdom south of the Zambezi River.

Ultimately, the gold lay in ancient Precambrian strata holding quartz pebbles in which were embedded the precious particles. Over time these formations had been eroded, their material loosened and carried away by upland streams that slowly formed river valley beds of soft alluvial deposits, many of them buried under several feet of hard lateritic crust. Technologies that were unequal to the task of separating tiny golden flecks from a tough metamorphic matrix had no difficulty with alluvial mining. In West Africa, shaft and tunnel excavations predominated, whereas the mines on the Shona plateau were more usually worked by means of open trenches.

The trenches were dug alongside a reef, following it down as far as air supplies and water table would allow, sometimes reaching a depth of 150 feet. The soil was loosened with hammers and wedges, some stone and some iron, the extracted ore then crushed in stone mortars preparatory to separating out the gold dust through a panning process. In West Africa, shafts were cut through the laterite to reach the alluvial beds which were worked along galleries extending out in all directions from the central pit. The floors of the narrow passages were awash with seepage, the ceilings propped at intervals with beams to forestall collapse. Miners, both slave and free, most of them children or young girls because of their small stature, floated the soil back to the minehead in baskets woven from tree branches. At the surface it was laboriously washed in calabashes until the heavy gold particles had settled and separated from the gravel. This procedure, widely practiced throughout Africa, necessarily recovered only the clearly visible grains; hence a good deal of microscopic ore was lost in the tailings.

Mining in West Africa was a seasonal occupation reserved for the dry months when little labor was required in the fields. In the Bure region, however, the miners reportedly pursued their occupation full-time, importing all foodstuffs except some cattle and poultry despite the exceptional fertility of their soils. In districts such as these where the alluvium ran rich, the density of the workings often demanded massive gangs of workers. Even today the Siguiri fields in Bure attract as many as ten thousand prospectors each season, while early in the nineteenth century a similar number of slaves were employed in Gyaman, northwest of Ashanti, washing the gold that had accumulated in the stream beds during the annual rains. At one West African site, an area scarcely more than a half-mile square, there survive the remnants of over fifteen hundred mineshafts interconnected by a vast labyrinth of underground galleries, testimony to the importance of a once thriving mining community.

Domestic Crafts

The salt supplies of Taghaza and other mines did not begin to meet the constant demand; hence, salt making in various forms was a feature of domestic economy throughout the continent. On the coast, seawater was evaporated, either by boiling or simply by trapping a tidal overflow and allowing it to evaporate in the sun. Inland, likely vegetable matter such as leaves, roots, or other parts of salt-retaining plants were burned, their ashes mixed with water and sieved through close-woven grass, the water then boiled until a salty residue was obtained. This did not always make for a palatable condiment; nevertheless, in some regions distillation was not considered necessary and housewives mixed the ashes directly with the ingredients of the daily fare.

The extraction of salt from plants underlines the basic reliance of traditional society on its organic resources. Baskets, roofing, and sometimes the walls of buildings were woven from reeds, branches, or straw, while mats of palm fronds or grass were part of every household interior. Gourds, many with highly decorated surfaces, were used for storage and dishware; bark was processed into clothing fabrics, as were hides of both wild and domestic animals. Trees met every conceivable need. Stools and bedsteads were made of wood, the former carved of a piece from soft species; logs were hollowed to make canoes or the ageless mortar of the African housewife; all manner of tools and weapons were provided with wooden handles or shafts; while wood was standard for many musical instruments and dancing masks. Most of these materials were simply gathered in their wild state, but with the arrival of cotton, a cultivated plant of great consequence came into play which ultimately introduced sub-Saharan Africa to fundamental changes in clothing design and manufacture along with the important craft of textile weaving.

The earliest areas of concentration were the East African coast, where cotton culture was imported by way of the Indian Ocean, and the western savanna and forest, its textile industry of uncertain origin, possibly inaugurated through the agency of the Saharan trade. The earliest mention of cotton clothing in the western Sudan dates from the eleventh century at which time it was a luxury reserved for the wealthy, but cotton was raised extensively in Mali and subsequent savanna states, its cloth manufactured and widely used from Senegal to Chad and beyond, and from the Gulf of Guinea to the desert homeland of the Berber nomads.

The world's earliest surviving textiles are Egyptian linens, woven on a horizontal ground loom about six thousand years ago. In West Africa, by contrast, the standard loom came to be a vertical machine of narrow gauge producing a cloth that rarely exceeded a width of four inches. The longitudinal threads of the warp were anchored by a massive boulder some fifty feet away and drawn steadily toward the loom as the work proceeded. Seated before the loom, the craftsman alternated the odd and even strands through a mechanism controlled by his toes, a band of cloth slowly taking form at the rate of five or six feet a day. These cloths varied in quality and design from some of the simple unadorned Hausa fabrics to those elegant colored patterns of Ashanti *kente* cloth which delighted the nineteenty-century English traveler, T. E. Bowdich with its "fineness, variety, brilliance, and size."

These narrow strips were sewn into cloths of varying dimension depending upon need and function, and in some areas like Dahomey, raffia palm was substituted for cotton. It was in Kongo, however, that raffia cloth reached the ultimate heights of sophistication. The palm leaves were specially cultivated and prepared to produce long, fine threads that were woven on vertical looms into patterned damasks and brocades as well as materials with a velvet finish on both sides. These fabrics ranged up to three or four feet in width, lightweight yet remarkably impervious, so much so that visiting Portuguese employed them as tenting because of their resistance to wind and rain. Threads for fabrics were dyed variously, indigo being a favorite; so too were the fibers used in baskets and mats.

Vegetable materials also figured in the tanning of hides, an ancient industry, and in the colored decoration of clay pots, the potter's craft predating even the beginnings of cultivation in Africa. Pots were almost everywhere the work of women, possibly because of their association with the kitchen. All African pots were hand shaped, for the potter's wheel was nowhere employed. In some regions, Ashanti, for example, the pot was constructed from a solid conical mass of clay which was scooped out and gradually molded until the desired form had been achieved. Stacked upside down on a bed of cut wood that also enveloped them, the pots were fired, then smoked to permeate the heated clay with carbon and tar.

A more typical method of construction involved the use of clay strips coiled about the circumference as the walls of the pot were shaped and developed. The essential process varied only to account for differences in size and function for each pot. First, the worker molded the top few inches, finishing off the mouth before turning the opening over, bottom side up. The walls were then constructed from successive coils of clay, the potter smoothing and kneading them into place manually as she maintained symmetry solely by experience and sureness of eye. Gradually, as she reached the bottom, each additional coil slowly narrowed the opening until only her arm, then her hand, then fingers, were fitted into the shrinking hole. When the pot was finally rounded off and sealed, it was stippled, fired, and decorated, eventually to find its way into a village household, utilized in cooking, storage, or the many other purposes this ancient vessel has served so well.

Time, Distance, and Number

Early astronomical computations in ancient Egypt exemplify man's inventive response to economic necessity. Once cultivation had become established in the fertile Nile valley, calculation of the annual inundation assumed crucial importance, particularly when it became apparent that the initial rise of the waters at the southern apex of the Delta occurred over the years with remarkable regularity. The average annual interval came to be recognized as 365 days, recorded first through observation, then with some system of notation, and finally by the Egyptian calendar, essentially the same calendar now used throughout the modern world.

Twelve months of thirty days each were created with an additional five-day period rounding out the year which was established to begin on the midsummer morning that Sirius first appeared at sunrise, a moment marking the initial rise of the Nile waters at the site of Memphis. Although the Egyptian calendar contained an error of one-quarter day a year, this margin, though recognized, went uncorrected since it was imperceptible during the average life-span. The calendar year gradually wandered from the true astronomical cycle, eventually moving through all the seasons until it returned to its initial point over a period of 1,460 years.

In tropical Africa the anticipation of seasonal fluctuations was also an essential element of successful agricultural production. In view of the vagaries of the climate, however, the numerical precision practiced in the Nile valley was superfluous, the seasons normally marked by natural phenomena—the first rains, the winter wind, the appearance of a particular flower or insect significant in the rhythm of seedtime and harvest. Months were reckoned by the moon, the year punctuated by those lunar intervals related to food production. The months, therefore, had no uniform number of days, nor was the exact length of the year calculated with precision. Of more consequence was the count of moons from a key moment like the onset of the rains so that the proper time for weeding, harvesting, and clearing could be correctly computed. Once the important seasonal milestones had passed, the remainder of the year was allowed to run out unnoticed until the time for a new cycle arrived. Longer cycles were similarly treated. When a piece of land was put out of production or its crops rotated, the time lapse was computed not in calendar years but in stages of rejuvenation as marked by the successive appearance of certain forms of animal and vegetable life in the soil.

In similar fashion, weekly periods were keyed to the sequence of markets, which operated on four-, five-, six-day, or other established intervals. Each day of the week took the name of its particular market, the name thus denoting both a place and a date. In some societies, each locality had its own collection of markets and consequently named its weekdays differently from those of an adjacent district which, however, might share one or two market days with its neighbors. Markets held at longer intervals, a ten-day market cycle, for instance, were simply inserted as they came due, substituting for the more usual market of the four-, five-, or six-day week, the name of the day appropriately altered. Similarly, in one neighborhood a particular market name might begin each weekly cycle, while for an adjacent set of villages it would appear at a different point in the week. Such shifting of names was avoided by some communities which simply named each day after the first market that had been established on that day.

Spatial measurements also grew out of pragmatic considerations. Linear distance was based on parts of the human body—measuring cloth by arm length, for instance—a system that yielded a rough and manageable accuracy. More difficult was the problem of volume which did not lend itself to simple forms of standardization. For measuring agricultural produce gourds were employed, but their varying sizes called for constant vigilance; in any event, equality of value was sought above equality of weight or volume, and a measure of poor-quality millet would necessarily be larger than one of higher grade. In Ashanti with its system of gold weights, considerable variations existed between weights of ostensibly common standard. Such inaccuracies were calculated, and each purchaser was expected to make sure for himself that he received his full stated weight. In some cases, the differences were sanctioned by custom. The chief's weight, for example, was always heavier for any given standard, a privilege that went unchallenged, for, as the saying went, "a man does not rub bottoms with a porcupine."

Numeration in traditional African societies also appears to have originated with concrete transactions before proceeding to the abstract. Systems of counting were based upon utility; hence, among San hunters who required little arithmetic, numbers progressed from 1 and 2, or sometimes 3, to a word denoting "many," whereas agricultural and trading peoples evolved precise numerical systems capable of recording any desired total. In most cases, these latter were formed on a base number of 5 in combination with a secondary base of 10 or 20, indicating a probable use of fingers and other body parts in the early evolutionary stages of their computation systems.

Some of the resultant variations appear complex in Western eyes. Among Bantu peoples who employed a 5 and 10 base, numbers like 6 or 9 were often formed either by adding to the base of 5 or subtracting from 10, but sometimes they developed directly from sums, in this case, 3 + 3 or 5 + 4. Similarly, numeration based upon 5 and 20 constructed a number like 17 from (5 × 3) + 2, or 50 as (20 × 3) − 10 in some cases, and (20 × 2) + 10 in others. Such an arrangement holds no oddities for those familiar with the French *quatre-vingt-dix* or *soixante-quinze,* but other combinations became considerably more complex. The Yoruba, whose system was based upon 20, formed many calculations through subtraction. For example, 45 became (20 × 3) − 10 − 5, and 106 was (20 × 6) − 10 − 4.

Such involved manipulations seem very likely to have arisen from rapid counts of cowries, pebbles, or other monetary units. Indeed, the higher sums frequently were identified by words related to specific currencies. In Nupe, the term, twenty thousand, is even today the name of the grass bags in which cowries were formerly packed, while the Hausa word, hundred, also doubles as a currency denomination. Typically, cowries were counted in units of five which were assembled in hundreds, thousands, ten thousands, and so on. In some areas, the word hundred was conventional rather than descriptive, as with the so-called Bambara "hundred" of eighty cowries. Various explanations for this particular discrepancy have been offered, but it was not due to faulty arithmetic. Possibly it enabled a merchant to buy in bulk at the discounted Bambara rate and to sell retail at the full denomination, his profit thus ensured without the necessity of a markup.

Of course, counting was not all commercial, and calculations made mentally were sometimes recorded by marks on a wall, by beans or sticks in a jar, or in the celebrated case of the Dahomey census, by bags of pebbles. For Dahomey the purpose was military—to determine the potential size of each year's armed forces through a population count, village by village. Each local chief was obliged to provide a tally in pebbles for all adults and children under his jurisdiction, including registration by age and sex of the numbers of births and deaths each year. From these collections of pebbles, all identified by appropriate symbols marking each village, it was possible for the king to know the precise population of his realm, broken down into districts and classified by age and sex. On the basis of such estimates, the military potential could be calculated before actual mobilization, the accuracy of the count assured by an elaborate system of internal accounting and comparison against the data supplied from previous years.

The Weapons of War

Like other tools, arms in Africa followed the exigencies of circumstance and environment; technological improvements, therefore, were adopted only when they demonstrated a clear advantage in utility. Their ancient beginnings in the hunt, weapons were not designed primarily for combat, while military tactics were generally keyed to defense. Warfare certainly existed to mark the eternal imperfection of human society, but its ravages were limited to considerable extent by its objectives. Raiding was common, particularly among cattle people, while feuds contributed everywhere to chronic, if small-scale, combat. Only occasionally did major warfare erupt, the result of unusual developments—a conquering genius, perhaps, or the white heat of religious conviction. Usually, the conditions for total war were absent, for land was plentiful and, if contested in one location, could easily be compensated by remove to another. Only occasionally did pressures of population accelerate to convert casual skirmishing to massive slaughter.

The classic armament of Africa comprised beating and thrusting instruments, along with missiles. Clubs ranged from the handy tree branch, shaped and trimmed for use, to well-forged axes. The thrust was contained in spear, sword, and dagger, while the bow took its place alongside the throwing lance as the essential missile. The arrival of iron greatly increased efficiency in these weapons but did not seriously alter their design. The barbs of ancient stone arrowheads reappeared in iron, while the transfer to metal made spear tips lighter and more effective without any great change in appearance.

In the heavily forested areas of West Africa and the Congo River watershed, the foot soldier predominated, for not only were horses less maneuverable over closed terrain, they also fell frequent victim to the sleeping sickness infection, trypanosomiasis. Some form of battle order was usual, although surviving accounts differ considerably concerning the efficacy of tactics, a variation that may reflect local distinctions in military prowess. The Fanti in the seventeenth century, to take one example, grouped their forces so that spearmen went into action first, followed by archers and then by forces in general hand-to-hand combat, usually a desultory affair because field commanders had no devices for massing their men and coordinating their movements. In the Congo, by contrast, the maneuvers were well articulated, the troops divided into companies, each distinguished by its particular emblem, their movements governed by signals from drums, bells, and horns made of elephant tusks. The initial attack usually came with skirmishing by scattered groups who began with volleys of arrows, then followed with close combat. When these forces had tired, they fell back on command, as fresh contingents were moved into place. In this fashion, the front line was consistently engaged and the army's total strength brought into play.

Among the cattle people of the high plains in eastern Africa, armed raids carried out in stealth were the chief form of warfare. Groups of warriors, each carrying his cowhide shield and a handful of slender throwing spears, would scout the herds of neighboring peoples, searching out an isolated or ill-defended victim, then swooping suddenly upon their prey, driving away all defenders and making off with the stock. Pursuit and counterattack usually followed swiftly, with luck, speed, and daring to determine the victor, but livestock losses aside, there were few serious casualties to mark the affair. Similar raids were conducted by camel-riding Tuareg and other desert nomads, but it was in the great states of the western and central Sudan that African cavalry warfare reached its highest development.

There was infantry as well to garrison strong points and fill the ranks of field armies, but the mounted forces, like the knights of medieval Europe, were the true military aristocracy of the savanna. Their mobility and striking power was reserved for the attack, for those swift and terrifying raids that swept whole villages into slavery or the rapid envelopments that surrounded and engulfed enemy contingents. Nevertheless, mobility was relative and similarity to the European chevalier more than metaphoric, for the savanna horse soldier relied heavily on protective armor that sacrificed maneuver and speed for defensive strength.

Among the Fulani-Hausa armies of Sokoto, both horse and rider were shielded, the mount wearing kapok-stuffed cotton quilting that covered chest, shoulders, and flanks while his master rode to battle in finely wrought chain mail or quilted coat. The chain armor was frequently of Mamluk design, but the quilting was a local invention that combined practical protection with theological invocation—tight paper rolls inscribed with Quranic verses intended to turn aside spear thrust or sword stroke. Whatever their spiritual powers, these wads, encased in leather and sewn between layers of cloth, could blunt slashing blows, though they were less effective against arrows. For helmet the knight wore a round or conical straw hat over his turban, its surface reinforced with leather. A heavy shield of elephant or hippopotamus hide added further protection, as did the large saddle and stirrups, these last also effective in offense, for the sharpened front and rear edges could disembowel an unprotected enemy mount or turn with equal destructiveness on opposing foot soldiers.

The Sudanic cavalry fought with sword, battle-ax, and broad-bladed spear, while bowmen in African armies normally campaigned on foot. Less spectacular than the horse soldiers, the archers were nevertheless an essential military component, for theirs was a weapon that could punish at a distance, be it the frail instrument of the San hunter conveying poison to its quarry or the powerful five-foot bows of the Fulani. Others, like the Yoruba and Mossi weapons, were somewhat smaller, but with a full draw in excess of forty pounds they could send an arrow one hundred paces, although the effective range was between half and two-thirds that distance. Arrows cut from reeds and grasses were short, their barbed iron tips often carrying poison, in West Africa a plant named *Strophantus hispidus* which induced paralysis of the heart. Though frequently unfeathered, the arrows could be delivered with remarkable accuracy; more impressive, however, was the rapidity of fire of experienced archers who could keep several shafts in the air simultaneously, sometimes firing two arrows at a time.

Though archers were prominent in attack, their effectiveness was even more pronounced in defense, especially if they were stationed upon the battlements of walled towns where their fire bore heavily upon massed charges by cavalry or infantry. The Yoruba reportedly employed crossbows, probably as defensive weapons, but the full ingenuity of

African defensive technology was contained in the design of fortifications and prepared positions, each solution admirably suited to local conditions. Among the cattlemen of eastern and southern Africa, the thorny barrier of the kraal held off predators, both human and animal. In the depths of the Congo forests, the natural density of the growth was supplemented by concealed ditches and barriers of sharpened stakes set along narrow labyrinthine paths leading to each fortified village. Once the enclosed settlement had been reached, surprise attack was further discouraged by a complex of heavily guarded interior yards and passages, a defensive system of entrapment that also characterized the great stone enclosure of Zimbabwe where dwelt the royal Rozwi *mambo*.

Defensive positions in West Africa also reflected the necessities of terrain. Forest citadels like Benin and the Yoruba towns supplemented the tangle of undergrowth with walls and earthworks, while encampment sites were chosen to take advantage of natural strongpoints like the hills of Ibadan or the rocky heights of Abeokuta. The Yoruba frequently fenced their towns with two or more barriers, but in the savanna the fortress cities were more typically surrounded with a single towering wall built upon ramparts that fronted on a system of ditches. The battlements were crenellated or slotted for maximum firepower from archers who patroled a ledge along the inside top of the walls. At Kano these fortifications achieved massive proportions. By the nineteenth century they enclosed almost ten square miles of territory with walls forty feet thick at the base and fifty feet in height, overlooking a double ditch planted with layered rows of live thorn trees. Such strongholds were able to withstand all but the artillery and machine guns employed by European armies in their late nineteenth-century conquest of African states.

Firearms had been known and utilized by Africans almost from the earliest European contacts, but the importance of guns in revolutionizing warfare in Africa has probably been exaggerated. In the first place, the early muskets were inefficient and inaccurate; hence, they were at a serious disadvantage when facing rapid-firing bowmen or the charge of cavalry. Further, African technology could not consistently manufacture guns and ammunition, while shortages of powder, shot, or spare parts severely limited essential indoctrination and drill. Guns were popular and much sought after, but their military effect may have been primarily psychological, at best a temporary advantage soon neutralized as continuing imports over the years introduced them to widening numbers of users. Against European forces, moreover, firearms were not likely to be effective, for the invaders were normally equipped with the latest models—rapid-fire, breech-loading rifles, for example, combined with rockets or powerful cannon. Against these arms, smooth-bore, muzzle-loaded flintlocks made but an indifferent showing.

If firearms failed to precipitate a thoroughgoing military revolution across the African continent, this need imply no indifference to innovation. During the upheavals that accompanied the career of the Zulu king Shaka, a broad spectrum of peoples throughout southern Africa quickly absorbed basic changes in weapon design and military tactics, altering their whole way of life and transforming the pattern of African nations through large sections of the subequatorial continent. To begin with, the system of large standing armies based upon age grade regiments had been instituted by the Mthethwa ruler Dingiswayo, and to this Shaka added fundamental reforms in equipment; more than that, he transformed the quality of warfare from the quasi-sportive cattle raid to a deadly struggle for survival. Striking power replaced defensive tactics and annihilation of the enemy became the all-consuming objective. Thus the heavy stabbing assegai replaced the light throwing lance; the great cowhide shield was used offensively to maneuver an opposing soldier into position for the fatal thrust; sandals were forbidden in order to enhance speed and footing; while coordinated tactics carried out under iron discipline were employed to envelop and crush the enemy. Such innovations were the product of a genuinely original military thinker and, once demonstrated on the battlefield, became the enforced standard, with variations, for all who followed.

Traditional Medicine

Prescientific in its world view, traditional Africa attributed all illness to supernatural causes. Treatment, therefore, involved, first of all, exorcism of the invading spirit, then a direct medical attack on the malady, usually by means of herbs. Many diseases were readily recognized and identified; but since their appearance was always ascribed to a spiritual force, malign or offended, no cure could be effected until this contamination had been removed. The afflicted individual, therefore, consulted an oracle or witch doctor, essentially for assistance in identifying and expelling the intruding force, usually found to be the agent of a witch's spell, although sometimes it was brought on by the activities of a displeased ancestor.

Normally, a process of transfer was introduced, sometimes withdrawing the disease by means of incantation and transposing it to an animal provided for the purpose, in other cases cupping or sucking the affected area, performing the rite often at a crossroads so that the patient could proceed along one path while his malady departed by another route. This stage accomplished, the victim might then be provided with special charms or amulets to prevent reinfection while the witch doctor moved on to the business of curing the disease itself.

Since medical practice was preoccupied with supernatural causation, anatomy was overlooked and only symptoms treated, to be dealt with in symbolic or sympathetic fashion. Thus, elephantiasis was ministered by rubbing the afflicted region with the ashes of an incinerated elephant foot. To gain strength, a patient imbibed a brew containing an extract of lion heart; to improve an ailing limb, the potion was made of rabbit sinew; for durability, prescription might call for medication of tortoise shell. Among some peoples, epilepsy was cured by warming the patient before a fire since it had long been observed that monkeys similarly stricken recovered when exposed to the warmth of the sun. Frequently, patients responded to directions received in dreams, conveyed perhaps by a deceased parent still actively concerned with a child's welfare. Because of the emphasis upon ritualistic and mystical qualities, many of the drugs employed had little medical value, yet the African witch doctor, through long practice, had developed an enormous pharmacopoeia, and doubtless numerous herbs or procedures were retained because they had been observed to possess genuine curative powers.

Nevertheless, the strongest asset of traditional African medicine was its psychological potency. The witch doctor was a thoroughly impressive figure, bedecked in the elaborate costume of his office, his exotic drugs on display, his supernatural strengths pitted in a battle for good against the evil machinations of the witch. This elemental struggle of occult forces vying for possession of the victim was well understood and appreciated by the victim himself, and his own total commitment added the considerable thrust of psychic persuasion to the effectiveness of the cure. Disease in Africa contained many maladies beyond the skills of the traditional practitioner, but in the realm of psychosomatic trauma, he likely knew few peers in his own or any other age.

SUGGESTIONS FOR FURTHER READING

Information dealing with technology in traditional Africa is copious but widely scattered throughout the many accounts of early travelers. There have been recent attempts, however, to collect such evidence in more convenient form. See, for example, R. Mauny, *Tableau géographique de l'ouest Africain au moyen âge* (Dakar: Institut Français d'Afrique Noire, 1961; Amsterdam: Swets and Zeitlinger, 1967); R. Gray and D. Birmingham, eds., *Pre-Colonial African Trade* (London: Oxford University Press, 1970); B. Fagan, *Southern Africa during the Iron Age* (New York: Praeger, 1966); G. Balandier, *Daily Life in the Kingdom of the Kongo* (New York: Pantheon, 1968); and T. R. De Gregori, *Technology and the Economic Development of the Tropical African Frontier* (Cleveland: Case Western Reserve University Press, 1969). Furthermore, modern anthropological studies often contain useful analyses of African technologies; in this connection the reader might consult such works as M. J. Herskovits, *Dahomey*, 2 vols. (Evanston, Ill.: Northwestern University Press, 1967); S. F. Nadel, *A Black Byzantium* (London: Oxford University Press, 1942); or R. S. Rattray, *Ashanti* (Oxford: Clarendon Press, 1923).

African mathematics is a virgin field with information to be found in discrete bits throughout the reports and memoirs of early travelers, but with virtually nothing available in the way of modern systematic study. For a beginning, see Claudia Zaslavsky, *Africa Counts* (Boston: Prindle, Weber, and Schmidt, 1973). The situation is much better with reference to military technology and strategy. Works like D. R. Morris, *The Washing of the Spears* (New York: Simon and Schuster, 1965), and J. F. A. Ajayi and R. Smith, *Yoruba Warfare in the Nineteenth Century* (Cambridge: Cambridge University Press, 1964), contain information on particular traditional societies, and these may be supplemented by appropriate periodical literature. *The Journal of African History* has published a series of articles on firearms (vol. 12, no. 2 and no. 4, 1971, and vol. 13, no. 4, 1972) which touch upon traditional armament, as does the piece by R. Smith,

"Yoruba Armament," appearing in the same journal, vol. 8, no. 1 (1967). See also M. Crowder, ed., *West African Resistance* (London: Hutchinson, 1971), and the interesting ideas offered by J. Goody in his *Technology, Tradition, and the State in Africa* (London: Oxford University Press, 1971).

Amidst a wealth of material dealing with disease in Africa, there is little to note concerning traditional medical practices and drugs. Witchcraft has been the subject of study—see, for example, E. E. Evans-Pritchard, *Witchcraft, Oracles and Magic among the Azánde* (Oxford: Clarendon Press, 1937), and Michael Gelfand, *The African Witch* (Edinburgh and London: E. and S. Livingstone, 1967)—and Professor Gelfand has alluded to earlier practices in his writings on the recent medical scene in Africa, but as yet no systematic study of traditional medicine has appeared. Note should be taken, however, of the psychiatric work of Dr. T. A. Lambo of Nigeria which has looked toward the reconciliation of modern and traditional medicine. See, for example, T. A. Lambo, ed., *First Pan-African Psychiatric Conference* (Ibadan: Government Printer, n.d. [1961]).

12

✤✤

TECHNOLOGY
AND ART

The Function of
Traditional Arts

In traditional Africa art lacked self-awareness. This is not to say that
there was no effort to embellish utility with design, no standards of
beauty to inspire the creative spirit, no awareness of the elusive gift that
converts good craftsmanship to great art. What it does suggest is that
traditional societies saw no distinction save ability between craftsman
and artist and viewed all artistic production essentially as a function of
daily life. The subtle arc of the Zulu dwelling delighted the eye as it
sheltered each family within its encircling unity; the power of the
well-carved Senufo mask lent the forcefulness of its aesthetic expression
to the ceremony of the ancestors; the rhythmic complexities of the
Ashanti drums announced both the joys of music and the majesty of the
royal house. For some, the plaintive note of the shepherd's reed was
enough to fill the lonely heart with contentment; for others there were
the architectural prodigies of Zimbabwe or the rich bronze plaques of the
Benin palace to teach respect for law and order. It was art for art's sake
that held no concurrent meaning.

The Builders

The functionalism of the arts was at once apparent in building design. Architecture suggests shelter, but in a parlous world it was not only the elements that had to be turned aside; livestock had need of refuge from human and animal marauders, while each community banded together in mutual defense against the recurrent threat of attack. Hence, most habitations were designed in part for protection, their variety reflecting both the exigencies of environment and the range of human ingenuity. In East Africa, Dodoth compounds, surrounded by heavy brush thickets, contained doorways made of forked poles, the prongs jammed into the ground in such a way that entry was possible only by single individuals squeezing through the narrow opening on hands and knees, their exposed and defenseless heads first to appear on the inside. Zulu houses, constructed with the dense texture of basketwork, were tough enough to turn aside the thrust of an assegai, while among the Kikuyu and other peoples defense also included the option of flight, engineered by means of an unobtrusive rear door.

In Ashanti, the towns were laid out without attention to defense, for, it is said, the military success of the kingdom minimized the likelihood of attack by outsiders. Others in West Africa were apparently less confident, for the pattern in many areas tended toward large settlements for mutual protection, their populations drawn together behind stout barriers enclosing houses that stressed fortification. In Nupe all villages were protected by walls which also encircled each individual compound. The Hausa states were celebrated for their imposing town walls, but equally characteristic were the Hausa residences—slab-sided structures with heavy, blank exteriors pierced by occasional window slits and narrow doorways, the line of their roofs giving the appearance of battlements. Like the rugged exteriors of Italy's quattrocento palaces, the Hausa facades were a shield against the outside world. It was inside the compound that the life of the family and of the community blossomed.

The design of Hausa architecture was highly idiomatic, not only in the generally angular aspect of the compounds, but also in such features as the horn-shaped spires that topped the parapets at intervals or the graceful and complex arabesques molded into the mud facing of the entranceways. The walls were made of mud, their core ellipsoid, sun-dried bricks set in a mortar of mud, manure, and grass. The roofs varied. Some were constructed of thatch on a conical bamboo or raffia palm frame, others were of mud laid flat across palm tree beams. If the interior dimensions exceeded ten or twelve feet across, the roof was domed. Reinforced palm beams were raised from the four corners to curve inward and upward toward the apex, then the open bays were covered with smaller boards split from palm trunks. To this was added a layer of mats and finally an application of mud three or four inches thick. All walls and roofing were faced with waterproof plaster, wooden spouts set along the roof at intervals to drain off the rainwater.

Such a structure was snug and dry. Thick, windowless walls retained interior coolness during the long, hot, rainless months, while the mud construction was quite equal to the rigors of tropical storms. It was necessary, however, that all work be kept in continuing good repair. Indeed, the earthen building materials that characterized so much of traditional architecture in Africa were subject to rapid deterioration unless properly maintained, a process that cost a great deal in labor and time for every village community. Heavy tropical storms quickly eroded even the popular, widely used laterite, and the problem was especially severe where runoff undercut foundations or uneven terrain complicated the stability of walls. Roofing, too, was in constant need of repair. Thatch added the complication of fire to chronic leakage, while the dry grass became a refuge for varieties of insect life. Vermin control was an endless struggle for most African householders who combated insect pests, sometimes with smoke, sometimes through special deterrents like the mixture of cow dung and earth with which the Kololo plastered their floors.

For all its lack of durability and regular need of repair, traditional African housing was a successful solution to the problem of habitation in a varying tropical setting. Demanding in labor and time, it took what the African villager could best afford, while its modest requirements in material meant a minimal cost to peoples living in a subsistence economy. Impermanence, moreover, was often more advantage than liability. Among the Baqqara nomads of the eastern Sudan, housing was a compromise between privacy and the need for open breezeway; more than that, shelter suggested light tenting material, easy to transport and quick to assemble. In like fashion, the insubstantial animal skin domes of the Khoikhoi cattle keepers, if not the most commodious of habitations, were cheap to build and simple to move—important qualifications to a peripatetic people. Even among sedentary town dwellers, there was advantage in the design of impermanence, as compounds constantly expanded or contracted to accommodate their ever-changing populations. Many societies followed the custom of burial beneath the floor of the house, the mud walls soon collapsing to mark the grave of the former resident. At the same time, as families multiplied, new houses were quickly and cheaply erected or additional rooms grafted to the basic structure of the compound.

Environment dictated house design, both through its pattern of climate and rainfall and through the materials it offered. Along the inland waterways of the West African coast, fisherfolk designed characteristic aquatic dwellings—mangrove stilts driven into the lagoon bed, supporting a slight platform structure of palm fronds, bamboo, and grass that provided maximum comfort in a region of consistent heat and humidity. The overhanging eaves of thatch roofs screened out both rain and sun, slatted walls provided for air circulation while offering privacy and a darkened interior, communal platforms furnished outdoor social and working areas, while the marine location of each community guaranteed protection against unwelcome visitors.

Far to the north in savanna flatlands, subsistence farmers built family compounds of laterite, enclosures that made slight but subtle distinction between public and private apartments for a simple folk who shared their modest quarters with their livestock and whose granary was their most important building—economic support, symbol of family unity, and architectural hub for the community. In the forests of the Congo watershed, where the arts of weaving and basketry flourished, the people applied their skills to the variety and plenitude of vegetable material, constructing their small, box-shaped houses of well-fitted branches and fronds.

Among the Nguni-speaking Bantu of southern Africa, a different form of weaving made good use of prairie grasses to create the characteristic beehive architecture of Zulu and neighboring homesteads. Though farmers, the Nguni regarded their livestock with a passion worthy of the most devoted Nilote pastoralist; hence, each homestead centered on a kraal contained within a defensive stockade. The houses were set in a ring around the stockade and were in turn protected by another palisade, both barriers made of heavy stakes driven vertically into the ground. Dwellings were of lighter construction, possibly reflecting the comparative value placed on human life, but doubtless also a measure of available building materials combined with the survival of long-lived nomadic traditions.

In its Zulu version, the Nguni house consisted of a domed frame of flexible saplings sunk in the ground along the circumference of the circular floor plan then curved and bound together to form a latticework of lateral arches that were finally bent toward the central apex where their cests were fastened together. Over this frame, resembling an inverted basket, went a blanket of thatch, kept in place with grass ropes fastened to the thatch and arranged horizontally and vertically like global longitude and latitude markings. These basic patterns were frequently enriched with ornamental work woven into the exterior in attractive geometric designs. What resulted was a dwelling of sound construction, snug yet well ventilated and reasonably secure against attack, compelling in the simple perfection of its domed profile, and elegant in the harmony of its decorative embellishments and basic architectural design.

With the emergence of Shaka during the early nineteenth century, these technical and artistic achievements mutated dramatically to create a form of urban planning unusual if not unique among the traditional societies of tropical Africa. To be sure, many urban conglomerates had come before. The cemeteries and slag heaps of Meroe, the ruins of Kilwa, Gedi, and other Azanian towns, the savanna emporiums from Timbuktu to Kano, bespeak great cities ages old, while the architectural complexities of Zimbabwe and its related sites suggest a long line of sophisticated builders at work. Like most cities the world over, however, these earlier centers seem to have expanded and declined in response to natural population pressures, old ramparts periodically replaced by new walls, neighborhoods burgeoning or dying off without plan, palaces and mosques located according to the desires and needs of the moment. By contrast, the royal kraal of Zululand was conceived as a unit, a functional and aesthetic entity, from which a whole metropolis emerged.

The need was military, for Shaka's dream of conquest demanded total mobilization and a professional fighting force sequestered in Spartan seclusion at the headquarters of the king himself. In time a substantial number of these military camps developed, but initially Shaka established three centers under his aegis to house all able-bodied men under forty, dividing his charges into age grades with many of the young women enrolled in parallel organizations. The traditional Zulu kraal had been a modest affair, suited largely to the activities of individual families. Now Shaka stretched the basic pattern to a new dimension, converting it from domestic compound to planned city.

Each royal kraal extended out to cover an enormous expanse, the diameter of its inner area almost a mile across, the space between the inside and outside stockades filled with beehive barracks—a three-mile circumference of residences stacked in tiers four and five deep. At one encampment fourteen hundred dwellings were counted, and population estimates for these towns ranged into the thousands, mostly fighting men with additional complements of women and herd boys, these last acting as squires for the warriors. At the top of the kraal opposite the main entrance was the king's own compound with its buildings exactly in the classic Zulu design but of such royal dimension that the interior roofing required a series of special supporting columns set in rows and carrying crossbeams to hold the vault. The enormous interior enclosure was meant to hold the royal cattle, but its main function came to be military and political. There, essential maneuvers were drilled to fine perfection; there, the monarch reviewed his troops, held council, and conducted audiences.

Thus the Zulu homestead was expanded to contain a whole city, a flexibility of design that nonetheless placed considerable strain on routine domestic requirements. The logistics must have been formidable for such matters as daily meals and waste disposal; moreover, most soldiers were unmarried and obliged to remain so until they had been mustered out of service. With women's quarters segregated, the normal impulses of love were expected to feed martial passion; yet despite an iron discipline and the preoccupation of military objectives, an enforced celibacy must have been as difficult to endure as the formidable problems of supply and services in these massive urban conglomerates.

Artists and Artisans

Early rock drawings aside, the visual arts in traditional, sub-Saharan Africa seem always to have favored the medium of sculpture over painting. While this preference may imply circumstantial restraints—a limited range of pigments, for example, or a scarcity of permanent wall surfaces—it much more likely describes the free choice of societies preoccupied with the utility of their arts. Finely sculpted objects might please the eye, but they also performed necessary functions, whether as modest domestic utensils in any normal household, or as the more exalted symbols of religious expression and royal authority.

The plastic arts were rendered primarily in wood, metal, and clay. Ancient carvings in stone have survived, their dating uncertain, their appearance indicating ability to shape quartz and other hard materials; but their relative paucity betrays the greater attraction of other media. No doubt wood carving early achieved the popularity of more recent centuries; nevertheless, the finest surviving examples of earliest African sculpture are the Nok terra-cottas unearthed south and west of the Jos plateau of central Nigeria. These figurines, named after the village where the first example was discovered, have an established antiquity of two thousand years, created at a time when the use of iron was first entering West Africa. The sensitive modeling and delicate attention to detail are impressive artistic achievements, but these are matched by a technology able to control the firing of full-scale clay heads and torsos of human figures two-thirds life-size.

The terra-cottas of Nok were followed in time by the splendid pottery sculptures of Ife, renditions of human and animal subjects varying in style from fantasy to portraiture but predominantly naturalistic in treatment. Dating from the eleventh century A.D. and quite possibly earlier, the human figures in particular tended toward life-size models, shaped in sections that were later assembled while the clay was drying, supported at weak points by internal iron armatures, and baked with great skill in huge open fires, for there is no evidence that kilns were used.

Terra-cotta was not the only medium employed by the Yoruba artists of Ife. A traditional center of religious activity, Ife contained numerous shrines and forest groves where stone carvings, including granite monoliths, had served along with the pottery figures as objects of worship; yet it was a series of bronze heads, presumably representing the divine rulers of this sacred city, that came to be the most notable examples of a remarkable artistic production. Many of the pottery sculptures had been royal portraits embodying a subtle blend of realism and idealism and fashioned with a technical facility that indicated thorough mastery of the medium. The bronzes were patterned after the terra-cottas, which they closely resembled in style and technique, the art of metal casting introduced because of the durability it offered.

The casting process closely followed the method known as "lost wax," a procedure developed in the Middle East as early as the fourth millennium before Christ and utilized in Egypt during ancient times. Very probably, knowledge of this skill came across the Sahara in connection with the gold trade, for the refining and working of gold was practiced in savanna cities such as Awdaghost by the eleventh century, and the southward movement of technology would have been a normal consequence of the desert commerce. In any event, a tradition of brass and gold casting emerged throughout the forest belt of West Africa, from Baule country in the Ivory Coast to the Cameroun highlands, including the civilizations of Ife, Benin, and Ashanti and represented in its earliest-known manifestation by the ninth-century bronzes of Igbo-Ukwu in eastern Nigeria.

As practiced in West Africa, the lost-wax method displayed only minor local variations on a well-established technique. First of all, the sculpture was modeled in clay until a rough likeness emerged, then the surface was coated with a layer of wax that received the final details of the artist's intentions. Next, an interconnected network of wax rods was added, radiating outward from the sculpture as the basis for a series of ducts that would eventually convey the molten metal to the cast area while permitting the escape of gasses generated by the great heat. The wax surface was then carefully painted with a fine clay, layer added upon layer until all of the wax mold had been covered. This thin coat, in turn, was invested in a coarser envelope of clay, care being taken to fix the outer investment to the inner clay core to prevent slippage. When the clay had hardened, the wax was melted out in an oven, clearing the ducts and leaving an exact impression of the wax image on the fine clay facing of the mold. Finally the molten metal was introduced, reaching all parts of the cast by means of the ducts, cooling and hardening into an exact replica of the final wax sculpture. When the investment was opened and the inner core removed, there remained only the need to cut away the ducts, now filled with bronze, and to buff and polish the joinings.

At Ife the casts were thin, while those of the Benin bronzes were much heavier; but in most cases the metal employed was more brass than bronze for it was zinc rather than tin that was added to the copper base. Indeed, many of the pieces were almost pure copper, and considerable speculation has developed as to the source of the metal. Perhaps it was imported as part of the Saharan trade or, alternatively, gathered from many small deposits in West Africa. In any event a sufficient supply sustained a bronze-casting industry of great aesthetic power and utilitarian value—the shrine figures of Ife, the commemorative plaques of Benin kings, or the ubiquitous gold weights of Ashanti.

With African sculpture, however, metalwork was always the lesser part. Carving was the essential craft and wood the primary material from which came the artifacts of traditional societies. There were spoons, stools, combs, plates, or door panels in the household. There were staves of office and drums to signal the authority of kings. There were knife handles for the warrior, shuttles for the weaver, *wari* boards for the gamester, and canoes for the fisherman. The great festivals required the masks of spirits and ancestors and the shrines their votive figures. Even the secret societies relied upon the carver for some measure of their dread illusion.

The African wood-carver needed only a modest battery of tools to achieve his results. Chisels, awls, and knives were standard equipment, but his main instrument was the adze, utilized for cutting and splitting but mostly for chipping. Each object was fashioned from a single log, for piecing was unusual, the block rotated by hand with no vise to hold it in place. As the sculpture gradually took shape, the adze was sometimes used as a knife to cut details into the surface; then, as the piece neared completion, it was buffed with stones or special woods to give a smooth finish and, in some cases, a characteristic color. Carving from a solid block accounts for the enclosed aspect of African wood statuettes, but it also placed an additional burden on the talents of the craftsman—for example, when he was obliged to produce an animal mask with extended horns, all cut from a single solid piece. Working with simple tools, the best carvers were extremely skillful; witness the intricacies of ornamental openwork in wood and ivory or the subtle multidimensional arcs traced by the horns of antelope masks. Small wonder that such craftsmanship transmuted to high art, especially in communities where the artist's place was honored and secure.

The carver sometimes lent his talents to the creation of music, producing and embellishing a variety of instruments, although African villagers, ever pragmatic, more usually focused their musical technology on aural objectives. Instruments were rarely elegant in appearance, but their rough exterior was deceptive, for it often obscured skillful construction, its effectiveness realized in the beauty of sound reproduction. Well-designed instruments, moreover, went hand in hand with great variety, for every African was a potential musician; hence, often an actual designer of instruments. For every complex marimba orchestra of East Africa's renowned Chopi musicians, there were the legions of improvised pit xylophones that any child could build by laying slats across a hole dug in the ground. Again, the subtleties of the Yoruba talking drum were but the end result of a long progression begun with the simple beating of two sticks in accompaniment to an improvised village dance.

The range was formidable. There were the stringed instruments—bowed and plucked, fiddle-designed or harp-shaped, single- or multi-corded. There were the winds, some of them flutes shaped from natural material like reeds, grasses, or bones, others of a trumpet design, usually side-blown antelope horns or elephant tusks. There were the famed African drums ranging in sound from the majestic voice of the great royal tympani to the nervous staccato of the hand instrument. There were the ubiquitous idiophones, Africa's most common music maker—the great slit-log signal drums, rattles made of gourds and rattles made of baobab-seed shells, gongs with clappers and gongs without, castanets and clangers, calabashes that were scraped and others that were struck, hand pianos, and the many forms of xylophone.

For all its instrumentation, much of African music was vocal, a condition arising from the essentially social and communal character of musical performance. Weddings, funerals, puberty rites, the enthrone-ment of princes, communal labor, the solemnities of cult groups and other associations, religious festivals, or spontaneous leisure-time cele-brations involved much singing and dancing, mostly in public places by large segments of the population. A general ebullience accompanied the drumming, singing, blowing of pipes and horns, shouting, and dancing of these occasions; yet, enthusiasm was tempered by aesthetic considera-tions that, in the vocal line, called for matching melodic development with the tonal structure of the language.

In the many areas where tonal languages prevailed, melody, therefore, was conditioned, not only by song verse but by the relatively limited pitch of the speaking voice. Such a restriction could have had a deadening effect on vocal composition, relegating it to little more than the coincidence of word and tune that characterized the widely used talking drums. In fact, the African musician made a virtue of necessity by introducing a subtle interplay of conflict and harmony between lyrics and their supporting melody. Thus a musical line might begin by underscoring the speech tones of the text only to seize upon an expression in the lyrics to begin a musical life of its own, at times following the speech curve, then sometimes ignoring or combating it. This duality of competition and accommodation, unpredictable yet logical, encouraged double meaning and the humor of the unexpected while heightening musical interest through the tensions that developed between the speech tone and its musical accompaniment.

Despite the harmonics and dissonances of tonal composition, how-ever, the main line of African musical expression was uncontestably rhythmic—polymetric as opposed to polyphonic—a phenomenon amply illustrated by instrumental design and practical composition. While most of the winds and a few stringed instruments were capable of sustained notes, the bulk of African musical expression came from the percussive groups, producing notes of great intensity but short duration. The consequent necessity to create large numbers of short-lived notes tended to emphasize rhythmic patterns at the expense of overarching melodies, and preoccupation with rhythm brought metric complexities far beyond the simple meters found, for example, in the tone-oriented music of the West. Composition therefore focused upon the counterpoint of rhythmic voices—the balance of several complex percussive patterns joining or clashing within a phrase, the improvisation of drumming variations set against each other and against the basic beat, the utilization of offbeat phrasing, or a rhythm containing an absent or implied beat to be filled by a dance step or simply by expectancy in the mind of the listener. Such intricacies demanded a firm understanding of basic principles by both composer and performer, particularly in view of the lack of notation in a preliterate society.

The African Technology

It was at one time fashionable to describe what was regarded as congenital backwardness in African societies by citing their ignorance of basic technological devices or scientific knowledge commonly found elsewhere in the world. The African never learned to use the plow, it was said. He had no sail for his boats, no irrigation for his fields, no fertilizer for his crops. His iron tools were primitive in design, brittle or soft in quality. For medical understanding he substituted superstition and magic, and when at last his clothing graduated from animal skins to woven fabrics, he fashioned his poor textiles on looms that produced scraps of cloth scarcely three or four inches in width. Knowledge of writing eluded him until he was finally taught by others; indeed, he had never even thought to invent that ancient instrument, the wheel.

Here was a wide-ranging indictment that suggested civilizations of deficient capabilities and substandard performance, yet more searching analysis reveals this assessment as simplistic in its conception and ignorant of those prerequisite conditions that have always undergirded past human achievement. To begin with, the charge contained many errors of fact. Broad-weft looms, for example, were standard equipment in many parts of Africa; if the narrow cloths were more common, their use was a matter of choice, not ignorance. Woven mat sails, moreover, had long been employed along both the eastern and western continental coasts, while irrigation was an ancient adjunct to cultivation, both for Saharan oases and in the gardens of the great savanna caravan cities. As for the plow, its early appearance and continued use in Egypt, Ethiopia, and the Maghrib makes plausible the hypothesis that it failed to appear in sub-Saharan Africa not because the tropical farmer was unaware of its existence but because he felt he possessed more effective alternatives.

Alternatives imply differing degrees of suitability; surely, herein lies a deeper reason for the absence within tropical Africa of certain types of technology that were established firmly in other lands. Sails were unknown along inland African rivers, but this was scarcely surprising, considering their restricted utility on narrow waterways marked by strong currents, stretches of rapids, and sharp seasonal changes in water level. Plows, too, had limited utility for the sub-Saharan farmer. In Africa, soil fertility tended to rest thinly on the surface, while characteristically heavy showers greatly increased the possibility of erosion through runoff. Deep plowing was antagonistic to these conditions which instead called for shallow cultivation of a variety of crops planted concurrently on plots where their growth offered mutual protection against wind, rain, and sun. Furthermore, plowing required draft animals, an additional disqualification in forest and bush country where lurked the trypanosome-carrying tsetse fly.

Much the same might be said concerning the wheel. Although the principle of rotary motion for such techniques as drilling or fire making was an ancient practice in Africa, the wheel did not make its way southward from Egypt because the camel in the desert and the donkey in the savanna proved to be more efficient, each in his own area, than the oxcart. Within the forest, moreover, beasts of burden fell easy victim to the fly-borne pestilence; hence, human portage, though expensive, came to be the most economical means of transport until the era of the railroad and motor vehicle.

Nevertheless, if some machines were absent by choice, often it was choice misplaced for it limited African societies at crucial moments and in fateful fashion, stifling efforts that might otherwise have brought them into closer and more adaptive harmony with their surroundings. Surely, the failure of tropical Africa to embrace the concept of writing as it had developed to the north introduced serious complications in the retention of knowledge and the cumulative impact of technological and other experience. Though the wheel, making its way across prehistoric Saharan chariot tracks, may have been rejected in favor of more efficient forms of transport, its absence complicated a fuller exploitation of the rotary motion principle—the application of winches, pulleys, or screws, for example, to add mechanical advantage to various aspects of agricultural production. Iron manufacture, moreover, though an early development, experienced little progress in technique over the centuries; hence, when firearms appeared in Africa, local forges based upon low-temperature refining processes were ill prepared either to manufacture guns of local design or to maintain in working order those weapons imported from outside sources.

Why, then, the dark image of self-interest that encouraged some advances while ignoring others, that perceived the significance of certain technologies but failed subsequently to enhance their efficiency? Possibly the answer lies less in opportunities gained or lost in creating and adapting new tools than in the irreducible imperatives of the African environment, acting upon the human spirit and conditioning the response of man's ingenuity. In the first place, there was the almost limitless availability of land. Fertility remained low, to be sure, but the advantages of intensive cultivation through improved tools and tech-niques were more than offset by the accessibility of unworked acreage, easily put into production with only the modest expense of its clearing. Like the American frontiersman, the African farmer had no incentive to conservation. He cultivated his plots until they were worn, then moved on, drawn by the appeal of nearby virgin lands and unconcerned by soil exhaustion, his imagination unchallenged, his inventiveness unrespon-sive.

Secondly, while such wasteful practice discouraged sophisticated technology, it produced only enough food and other necessities to sustain village life at subsistence level, sometimes permitting an occa-sional margin of surplus for trade in the more productive seasons, sometimes depressing the population with the affliction of famine during the inevitable times of trouble. Hence, potential demand lay heavy but prostrate in the bellies of hungry villagers whose efforts at improved productivity were continually defeated by disease, flagging energies, or the assaults of a capricious climate. Food surpluses did not therefore develop as they had in pharaonic Egypt, surpluses to precipitate a population explosion and inaugurate another of the great cultural flowerings of world history.

Finally, there is the principle of marginal utility, which argues that man will not engage in economic activity that produces benefits of lower value than the effort expended in their behalf. Subsistence agriculture, its technology stabilized, its range of crops only occasionally augmented by new additions, eventually achieved that stage of efficiency wherein no further savings could be gained from current systems of land and labor utilization. The compulsion was strong, therefore, to hold with the old ways. They were not ideal, to be sure, but experience taught that an endurable equilibrium had been achieved. To venture beyond was to court disaster.

This was no unreasoned submission to custom. Despite their respect for the rule of tradition, the counsel of the elder, and the example of the ancestor, the peoples of Africa had repeatedly demonstrated their ability to change in the face of necessity. Their great population movements underscored the continuing urge toward a more effective balance of nature. Shifting forms of government and social organization searched out a better design for living. Throughout their history, Africans had repeatedly changed their languages, their religions, their abodes, their ways of life—indeed, their very identity—as they strove to improve their condition. The conservative impulse, therefore, was circumstantial, not pathological.

For traditional Africa, then, the balance point had been reached between the thrust of experimentation and the constraints of environment, working within the limitations and isolation of a preindustrial society. When change came to upset the balance, it came in the form of new methods of production and transport and new market demands from the wider world. During the nineteenth century, these forces began a transformation within Africa whereby her riches could be sent off with advantage to far distant points and her economies could look beyond subsistence to a newer and more profitable productivity.

SUGGESTIONS FOR FURTHER READING

Little study of traditional African architectural forms has been undertaken, and one must turn to accounts of travelers like Heinrich Barth or to various anthropological studies for occasional passing observations and information. See, however, one recent volume of interest dealing with the technology of traditional architecture—Paul Oliver, ed., *Shelter in Africa* (London: Barrie and Jenkins, 1971). Raymond Mauny has included much information on savanna cities in his *Tableau géographique de l'ouest Africain au moyen âge* (Dakar: Institut Français d'Afrique Noire, 1961; Amsterdam: Swets and Zeitlinger, 1967). See also P. S. Garlake, "Rhodesian Ruins—A Preliminary Assessment of Their Styles and Chronology," *Journal of African History*, vol. 11, no. 4 (1970), for discussion of the Zimbabwe and related building styles.

There are numerous works available on the subject of African art, but their preoccupation is aesthetic rather than technological. A good introduction may be had in Frank Willett, *African Art* (New York: Praeger, 1971), but see also the handsome and informative *Ife in the History of West African Sculpture* (New York: McGraw-Hill, 1967) by the same author. Once again, anthropological studies and traveler accounts will furnish much information for those with the patience to seek it out. See, for example, R. S. Rattray's informative *Religion and Art in Ashanti* (Oxford: Clarendon Press, 1927).

For African music, the two works to consult are A. M. Jones, *Studies in African Music* (London: Oxford University Press, 1959), and J. H. Kwabena Nketia, *Music of Africa* (New York: Norton, 1974). Also useful are Nketia's *African Music in Ghana* (Accra: Longmans, 1962), and the brief survey by A. P. Merriam contained in W. R. Bascom and M. J. Herskovits, eds., *Continuity and Change in African Cultures* (Chicago: Phoenix, 1962).

The important subject of the relationship between African technology and social-economic developments is touched upon in J. Goody's provocative *Technology, Tradition, and the State in Africa* (London: Oxford University Press, 1971). The most cogent statement dealing with technological and related factors as they touch problems of development in subsistence economies is contained in T. W. Schultz, *Transforming Traditional Agriculture* (New Haven: Yale University Press, 1964).

INDEX